Praise for
Bad Girls of the Bible

"The entertainment value of the book is obvious, but the take-home extra is the Bible study that follows each chapter. Who but Liz Curtis Higgs could so creatively reveal God's compassion, unconditional love, and mercy through such 'Bad Girls' in scripture?"

—CAROL KENT
speaker and author of *Becoming a Woman of Excellence*

"I loved it! A fresh perspective on those unique women. I loved the way Liz intersperses actual Bible text with her own writing."

—TERRY MEEUWSEN
co-host, *The 700 Club*

"A fresh concept—looking at what women have done wrong to figure out how we can live right. The conversational style and friendly, relational, upbeat tone (so true to Liz) are wonderful—sassy and yet challenging and inspirational. And the questions are top-notch!"

—RAMONA CRAMER TUCKER
editor, *Today's Christian Woman*

"This book could easily draw in a seeking unbeliever. When I got into the section on 'What Lessons Can We Learn?' I thought, Liz doesn't have to ask the Lord anymore, 'Why can't I be deep?' She *is* deep!"

—CANDY DAVISON
women's ministries coordinator, Sandy Cove Ministries

"Over the years we have wearied of the stories of the women of the Bible. Here we find them presented in fresh vibrant style. They leap to life not as the sinless saints of the past but as real women in want of the reforming touch of the Master."

—SIMONE MONROE
director of women's ministries,
First Baptist Church, Dallas, Texas

"*Bad Girls of the Bible* is not only a hoot to read, it is full of serious warnings about shaky choices and serious encouragement to take God's way for our own good."

—GLORIA GAITHER
author, speaker, and lyricist

"Excellent job! It's serious stuff we're talking about.... It also has her stamp of humor in it. Many women struggle with these same issues—*Bad Girls of the Bible* will give them a sense of hope."

—FRANCINE RIVERS
best-selling author

"This book will be great for personal or small-group studies. I love the way Liz can bring a tear to your eye—either by laughing so hard or reaching your heart!"

—MARGARET LEE
owner, The Harvest Bookstore,
San Francisco, California

"Liz Curtis Higgs looks deeply into the lives of ten women who failed miserably and extracts diamonds of delight and pearls of wisdom for all to enjoy."

—DIANA HAGEE
chief of staff, John Hagee Ministries

"Only Liz Curtis Higgs would take an otherwise taboo topic and bring it so close to where we live. As Liz beautifully blends a fictional story into the factual account, we are amazed at how much we actually resemble some of the "Bad Girls" and are reminded again of God's love and mercy toward us."

—JULIE BAKER
founder/executive producer,
Time Out... For Women Only!

"This work is God-breathed, the best ever to come from Liz Curtis Higgs. Absolutely life-changing! You'll alternately weep, sigh, gasp, rejoice—and yes, even giggle. And oh, is it filled with depth and grace."

—DIANE NOBLE
best-selling author

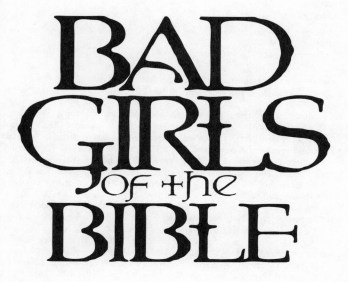

BAD GIRLS OF THE BIBLE

And What

We Can Learn

From Them

LIZ CURTIS HIGGS

WATERBROOK
PRESS

BAD GIRLS OF THE BIBLE
PUBLISHED BY WATERBROOK PRESS
2375 Telstar Drive, Suite 160
Colorado Springs, Colorado 80920
A division of Random House, Inc.

The contemporary story in each chapter is fiction. The characters and events
are fictional and are not intended to parallel exactly the biblical story.

ISBN 1-57856-125-6

Copyright © 1999 by Liz Curtis Higgs

Library of Congress Cataloging-in-Publication Data
Higgs, Liz Curtis.
        Bad girls of the Bible: and what we can learn from them / Liz
Curtis Higgs. — 1st ed.
            p.   cm.
        Includes bibliographical references.
        ISBN 1-57856-125-6 (pbk.)
        1. Women in the Bible.   2. Bible Commentaries.   3. Christian
women—Religious life.   I. Title.
        BS575.H54   1999
        220.9'2'082—dc21   99-21782
                                                            CIP

Printed in the United States of America
2005

25   24   23   22   21

ALWAYS AND FOREVER,

to my brilliant husband, Bill Higgs, Ph.D.—

who read every word (and changed several!),

who held my trembling hand through

the entire project, and who has extended

more grace to this former Bad Girl

than she ever imagined possible.

I love you with all my heart.

CONTENTS

ACKNOWLEDGMENTS

Heartfelt hugs to the following Good Girls who caught the vision for *Bad Girls of the Bible* from day one, read every chapter as it slithered out of their fax machines, and offered much-needed encouragement, loving guidance, and prayerful support...

Rebecca Price, *WaterBrook Wonder Woman*

Sara Fortenberry, *Amazing Literary Agent*

Carol Bartley and Laura Barker, *Editorial Empresses*

Lois Luckett, MSW, LCSW, *Therapeutic Princess*

Lisa Tawn Bergren, *Stellar Storyteller*

Cynde Pettit, *Queen of the Questions*

and especially Diane Noble—*my soul sister, e-mail encourager, best friend in fiction, and virtual midwife for this baby. I love and appreciate you more than 256 pages can say!*

Many thanks to those friends involved in women's ministry who read early chapters and gave me valuable feedback, wise direction, and a reason to keep writing...

Judy Russell

Rosanne Russell

Doris "Kentucky Mom" Foster

And to ten wonderful booksellers from the ten cities where our modern Bad Girls reside, bless you for reading the fictional portions and providing input and enthusiasm...

Joni Merchant, *Family Christian Stores, Savannah, Georgia*

Joyce Gronde, *Light & Life Bookshop, Indianapolis, Indiana*

Sandy Rowe, *The Mustard Seed, Ellensburg, Washington*

Brian Ehline and Angela Anthony, *Christian Supply, Portland, Oregon*

Sue Goodman, *Family Book Center, Dallas, Texas*

Linda Lewis and Rianne Rome, *Family Christian Stores, Pittsburgh, Pennsylvania*

Margaret Lee, *Harvest Bookstore, San Francisco, California*

Demetra Osirio, *Baptist Book Store, New Orleans, Louisiana*

Sue Cleveland, *Mardel Books, Oklahoma City, Oklahoma*

YoLonda Rivers, *Family Christian Stores, Charleston, South Carolina*

...One and all, you are the best!

Finally, I pray our collective efforts will bless *you,* dear reader, as you've certainly blessed me by choosing this book.

INTRODUCTION
TURN SIGNAL

And when she was good
She was very, very good,
But when she was bad she was horrid.

HENRY WADSWORTH LONGFELLOW

Ruthie never saw it coming. His fist flashed toward her so fast she couldn't duck or turn away in time.

"Nooo!" Her cry echoed off the windshield of the Pontiac but went no further. Who would hear her in this parking lot anyway? With trash cans and alley cats for neighbors, she could hardly expect some hero in a white Ford Mustang to drive by and rescue her, not at this late hour.

Hayden was leaning inside the open car window now, rubbing his knuckles as if to say, "There's more where that came from." As if she hadn't figured that out. As if she wasn't watching his every move.

Ruthie was nineteen, but she was nobody's fool.

Except Hayden's.

She stared at the dashboard, feeling her cheek swell as the pain inched around her eye, along her nose, toward her temple. In her whole life no one had ever deliberately hit her. Even as a child, she hadn't been spanked at home or paddled in school.

She was a *good* girl. National Honor Society. State chorus. Editor in chief of her small-town high-school newspaper.

Nobody ever needed to hit Ruthie, for any reason.

So much for that claim to fame. She'd been hit now, and hard. Slowly, hoping Hayden wouldn't notice, she moved her jaw back and forth, grateful it *could* move.

He snorted, obviously disgusted with her. "I didn't break anything. But I could have. Now slide over or get out."

Not much choice there.

The time for making choices was behind her—that was clear. Weeks ago she'd chosen to spend that Thursday night at the Village Nightclub, knowing the kind of men who went there. And the kind of women. *Women like me.* She'd chosen to drag Hayden home with her because he was the right size and the right age and in the right state of mind: drunk. Too drunk to care whether or not she had a pretty face.

Her face wasn't pretty now, of that Ruthie was certain.

And her choices were nil. If she got out of the car, he might hit her again. If she stayed in the car, he might drive like a maniac and wrap her new Pontiac around a telephone pole, with them in it.

Her new car. The one he routinely borrowed without asking. The one they'd been arguing about, right up until he parked his fist in her face.

She moved across the seat toward the passenger side, sliding her keys out of the ignition as she did so, feeling her head begin to throb. *Don't let me pass out! Please…Somebody. Anybody.* Resting her hand on the door handle, then carefully wrapping her fingers around it, she waited for her chance. As Hayden moved into the driver's seat and dug in his pockets for his keys, she took a deep breath, then shoved the door open, nearly falling out on the gravel-strewn pavement.

"Get in the car, Ruthie!" Hayden's bark was deadly.

She felt him grab for her and miss. "He-e-elp…" It was such a pitiful cry, like a kitten needing milk. Straightening awkwardly to her feet, Ruthie slammed the car door just as Hayden reached for her again. Judging by his curses, she'd unintentionally jammed his fingers in the process.

Maybe not so unintentionally.

She had one goal now: to locate her apartment key among the dozen on the ring she held in her trembling hands. Stumbling toward her security door as she heard the car door open, she found the key at last and forced it in the lock. *C'mon, c'mon!*

When the deadbolt turned, she fell through the entrance with a sob of relief, then turned to bolt the door behind her. But she was too late. He'd already wedged his leg in the doorway and was muscling his way inside.

Her heart sank through the linoleum floor, and the taste of dread filled her mouth.

Hayden was taller, wider, older, stronger. And meaner, so much meaner. Why hadn't she seen that? Tasted it in his kisses that first night, discovered it in his eyes that first morning?

His hatred for her was a living thing, rolling off him in waves.

"Don't you understand?" His chest was heaving, but not from the effort—from the anger. "That Pontiac is mine. You're mine. This apartment is mine. Nothing you do or say is gonna change that, Ruthie." With one hand he slammed the door with a noisy bang.

With the other hand he reached in his jacket and pulled out a gun.

Her heart thudded to a stop at the sight of it.

His cold smile told her all she needed to know.

"Upstairs." He waved the ugly black revolver at the staircase that led to her second-floor apartment. *Her* apartment. *Hers!* She'd scrimped and saved to have her own place. For what? So this…this…

It was no use. She started up the steps, doing her best not to trip, not to cry, not to let him see that he was tearing apart everything that made her Ruthie, step by awful step…

Define Bad . . .

Poor Ruthie.

Few of us made it our ambition in life to be a Bad Girl.

Still, for some of us, one day we looked in the mirror, and there she was.

Maybe we stumbled through a rebellious youth or wandered into an addictive habit or walked down the aisle with the wrong guy for all the wrong reasons. Perhaps our sense of self was so skewed we decided we weren't worthy of goodness or figured we'd gone too far to ever find the road home or concluded we enjoyed our favorite vice so much we weren't about to give it up—no way, no how.

There are some women who even wear badness like a badge of courage.

As Tallulah Bankhead put it, "If I had to live my life over again, I'd make the same mistakes, only sooner."

What labels a woman as "bad" hasn't changed since Eve. All the usual suspects are there: disobedience, lust, denial, greed, anger, lying, adultery, laziness, cruelty, selfishness, idolatry.

Badness—in other words, *sin*—doesn't have to be that dramatic. It can be something on the sidelines: an unkind word, a whisper of gossip, a neglected request, an unrepentant attitude, an intentionally forgotten event. *Ouch.*

It all boils down to a heart that's hardened against God—however temporary the condition, however isolated the tough spot.

To that extent, we've all been Bad Girls.

And to a woman, we long to be Good Girls.

I have trouble learning, though, from women who get it all right. I spend my energy comparing, falling short, and asking myself, *How do they do that?* It's discouraging, even maddening. It also doesn't get me one step closer to God.

So, for a season, I thought we'd look at women who got a lot wrong. I must admit I went into these stories with a bit of pride between my teeth and soon found my jaw hanging slack at the similarities in these women and me.

How is it possible, Lord? I love you, love your Word, love your people… How can I see so much of myself in these sleazy women?

Ah, sisters. Our sins may be a surprise to us, but they are no surprise to the Lord.

> For a man's ways are in full view of the LORD,
>> and he examines all his paths. *Proverbs 5:21*

Come, then, and meet our counterparts—for good and for bad.

My introduction to these ten Bad Girls of the Bible began a decade ago when I prepared a series of messages about famous women in Scripture for a national Christian convention here in Louisville. For a girl who loves to have fun, I found it the "meatiest" stuff I'd ever tackled. I savored every juicy minute of time spent studying the Bible and reading various commentaries. Not to mention examining my own life in juxtaposition with theirs.

Oops. Big mistake there.

Sarah was so faithful. Esther was so courageous. Mary was so innocent. I was so none-of-the-above.

Then I happened upon Jezebel, and something inside me clicked. I identified with her pushy personality, I understood her need for control, I empathized with her angry outbursts…and I was aghast when I got to her gruesome ending.

She was a Bad Girl, all right, but boy did she teach me what *not* to do in my marriage! It was then the seeds for this book were planted in my heart. These stories are in God's Word for his good purpose—and for ours.

> All Scripture is God-breathed and is useful for teaching, rebuking, correcting and training in righteousness. *2 Timothy 3:16*

Where to begin? With the *First Bad Girl:* Eve. Of course. Badness had to start somewhere.

Next, I found three women who were *Bad to the Bone:* Potiphar's Wife, Delilah, and Jezebel. These were women of whom not a single kind word was recorded. Women who had a pattern of sinning, with no evidence of remorse or a desire to change, who sinned with gusto from bad beginning to bitter end. Because they were made in the image of God, as we were, these Bad Girls weren't truly rotten to the core. They just behaved that way—and very convincingly!

Another three women were *Bad for a Moment.* Lot's Wife, Sapphira, and Michal were three good…uh…bad examples of women who made one colossal blooper—one big, life-changing mistake that was such a bell ringer it was recorded for posterity, chiming across the centuries. These three women were, by all appearances, believers in the one true God at the start, but when forced to make a choice, they each chose disastrously.

Finally, my favorite women—those who were *Bad for a Season, but Not Forever:* Rahab, the Woman at the Well, and the Sinful Woman who anointed Jesus' feet with her tears. Yes, they all had plenty of sin in their past, but they also were willing to change and be changed. What a joy to watch their encounters with God redeem them for eternity!

Because I love writing fiction, and because I wanted to make these women come alive for all of us, I've opened each chapter with a contemporary, fictional retelling of the biblical story that follows. The names have been changed to protect the guilty, but you'll spot their stories right away.

You might identify yourself in these narratives too…I certainly did. The same weaknesses, the same temptations, the same choices, and some of the same sorry results. Thanks to the tale of Lila from Dallas, Delilah will never again be a mere flannelboard cutout figure to me. And Lottie from Spirit Lake made me look at my beloved farmhouse in a whole new light, bless her misguided heart—and mine.

May these fictional stories speak to you as well.

Without missing a beat, we'll jump right into a verse-by-verse look at the real woman's story as it appears in the *New International Version* of the Bible, with plenty of "Lizzie style" commentary to keep you smiling as you learn what made that particular Bad Girl tick. Don't faint when you see footnotes—a research paper this isn't! But I believe in handling the Word of God with great care, so I studied more than fifty commentaries from the last two hundred years, along with ten different translations of the Scriptures.

Funny: The older scholars blamed the women for everything and painted the men as heroes. The newer writers blamed the men for everything and described the women as victims and the men as jerks. The truth lies somewhere in the middle, so that's what I aimed for: balance. And truth.

As writer Elisabeth Elliot phrased it, "The fact that I am a woman does not make me a different kind of Christian, but the fact that I am a Christian does make me a different kind of woman."[1]

Here's something you may not know about me, even if you've read any of my dozen books: My incredible husband, Bill, has a Ph.D. in Old Testament languages. The man not only reads the *Biblia Hebraica,* he understands it. Scary. He combed through my manuscript for errors—in translation, in interpretation, in application. You can breathe easier, girlfriend, knowing I'm not alone on this project!

You aren't alone either. That's the point of *Bad Girls of the Bible.* I want you to know, categorically and absolutely, that whatever your story is, you are not alone. There are lessons here for all of us. Each chapter ends with four of them, followed by eight questions worth asking ourselves and one another.

I had four kinds of readers in mind while I wrote: (1) Former Bad Girls who have given up their old lives for new ones in Christ and are struggling to figure out how and where they "fit" in God's family; (2) Temporary Bad Girls who grew up in the church, put aside their devotion to God at some point, and now fear they can't ever be truly forgiven; (3) Veteran Good Girls who want to grow in understanding and compassion for the women around them who weren't "cradle Christians"; and (4) Aspiring Good Girls who keep thinking there must be something *more* to life but aren't sure where to look.

This is the place, dear ones. Join in.

Find out what a twenty-first-century woman who loves God can learn from an ancient Egyptian temptress who did not: *plenty!*

> All share a common destiny—the righteous and the wicked, the
> good and the bad, the clean and the unclean…
>
> > As it is with the good man,
> >
> > > so with the sinner. *Ecclesiastes 9:2*

> For we must all appear before the judgment seat of Christ, that
> each one may receive what is due him for the things done while in
> the body, whether good or bad. *2 Corinthians 5:10*

In closing, a reminder that each chapter opens with fiction. Except this one. Ruthie is me. That's a small slice of my own early life as a Bad Girl, and, yes, it was very hard to write.

It got so much worse before it got better. Only a few trusted souls on this earth know how bad. Jesus knows. He knows every inch of my heart. He knows how bad I was, am now, and will be, before I leave behind this transient shell and go on to undeserved glory.

Here's the good news: He loves us anyway.

He loves us so much he will put people in our paths to lead us to him, just as he did for me—for Ruthie—nearly two decades ago. After years in the wilderness, I found myself at the end of my proverbial rope, so despondent I was willing to swing from that noose by my own stiff neck—anything to end the pain of disappointment and shame.

In my pursuit of earthly, fleshly pleasures—the whole sex, drugs, and rock-'n'-roll experience that many of us sampled—I discovered a sad truth: Fun and joy are not the same thing at all. Fun is temporary at best; it's risky, even dangerous, at worst. Joy, on the other hand, was a mystery I couldn't seem to decipher.

Oh, girlfriend! When I think of the shallow relationships, the misspent dollars, the wasted years, I can taste that bitter despair all over again. I was a woman without hope—a Bad Girl by choice and by circumstance—convinced that if I could just find the "right man," he would save me from my sorrows.

One wintry day in 1982 I met that "right man"—a man of sorrows—who willingly had given his life to set me free. *Me!* Sinful, disobedient, rebellious Ruth Elizabeth. My friends Tim and Evelyn, who'd shared their hearts, their hugs, and their lives with me, now shared the truth with me: I was a sinner in need of a Savior.

Finally I understood the depth of my badness and the breadth of God's goodness and so embraced his gift of grace with both hands. Yes, I was *Bad for a Season, but Not Forever.*

And my, oh my, have I found real joy!

With the courage of Rahab, the humility of the Sinful Woman, and the curiosity of the Woman at the Well, let's press on, my sisters, and see what good news our Lord might have waiting for us within these pages.

I promise I'll be with you every step of the way.

ALL ABOUT EVIE

*Man has his will—but woman has
her way.*

OLIVER WENDELL HOLMES

When she was young—and she seemed always to be young—Evelyn Whitebloom was convinced her father's garden covered the whole earth. If there were boundaries, she couldn't see them. Only endless garden plots carved into a thick carpet of fescue so green that on a wind-whipped day in Savannah, when the humidity lifted like a thick curtain, the intense hue of the lawn stung her pale blue eyes to the point of tears.

It was the only time she cried, and even then it wasn't truly weeping. Whatever for? Her life was too heavenly for anything but the brightest of smiles.

Her first memories were of walking with her father through row after row of mulberry trees covered with purplish black fruit. In no time she would be nose-to-chin purple, which delighted her father immensely. Although their home was one of the most venerable in the Historic District, where the wide expanse of Forsyth Park served as their front lawn, it was here in the garden, surrounded by her father's floral handiwork, that Evelyn spent most of her waking hours.

The Garden—he said it as if it were on the Register and needed capitalizing—was her father's pride and joy, eclipsed only by his love for his daughter. He demonstrated his love in infinite ways, not the least of which was his concern for her welfare.

"You may do this and this but not that," he often commanded. Evelyn teased her father that he treated her with such care one might deduce he'd made her by hand himself. If that were true, he'd assured her, then she was fashioned from pure ivory taken from the single finest animal in God's kingdom.

There were few things in life that mattered more to Evelyn than her father's love. In truth, she couldn't think of any others.

He'd designed his garden to please her, of that she was certain. Fragrant jasmine tickled her nose. Brilliant blue hydrangeas and saucy pink mandevillas tantalized her eyes. Trees heavy with pears and peaches, apricots and plums filled her mouth with their juicy, sweet fruit most months of the year. Stately ferns, taller than she, waved at her when the occasional soft breeze blew in from the Atlantic, eighteen miles to the east. Hosta skirted the borders of smaller garden squares, and wisteria spread its graceful tendrils along low brick walls, dividing the immense green space into manageable quarters, which converged at the centerpiece of the garden: the gazebo.

Not that she'd ever truly *seen* the gazebo. No one had. Ever. It was surrounded by a towering stand of live oaks, older than time and dripping with a heavy curtain of Spanish moss, smothering the whole gazebo in a gray-green shroud. Whatever the appeal had once been, the gazebo was to be avoided at all costs. Hadn't her father said so? Yes, indeed he had, numerous times. The only reason a young person would go there, he cautioned her, would be to look for trouble. The "trouble" was not described. He said only that she would be ruined. In fact, "dead to him" was how he'd phrased it, which made her shudder at the very thought.

"Because I've asked you not to" was the only explanation he ever offered. She loved him, adored him. Obeying him was effortless then. Only last week she'd overheard him making it clear to her beau, Adam Mann, that under no circumstances was he to step inside the gazebo—not alone, and especially not with his daughter, Evie.

Evie. Her father's favorite term of endearment for her.

Of late, Adam had tentatively begun to call her that too, which thrilled her. They were betrothed, were they not? Friends giggled at her old-fashioned name for it. "Where's the diamond?" they wanted to know. Not yet, not until they were officially engaged. That would come tonight at her debutante ball.

The ball! She jumped to her feet, startled. Here she'd sat, lollygagging on a stone bench in the garden, with her formal entrance into Savannah society mere hours away. *Move, child!* Hurrying across the spongy grass toward the enclosed porch that stretched the length of the house, she caught another glimpse of the moss-draped garden centerpiece, then quickly turned away.

Why would anyone want to venture inside the gazebo anyway? It had none of the lilting fragrances or eye-popping colors or luscious flavors that the rest of the garden offered in abundance. *Silly old gazebo.* If her father wanted her to keep her distance, she would do so. Adam, too.

Hours later, in her ivy-and-lilac-papered bedroom, her grass-stained chinos and sun-faded blouse had given way to the dress of her dreams. Not her wedding gown, not yet, but it might as well have been. Hooking the last tiny button at her neck, she held her breath and turned toward the full-length mirror.

Ohhh... The dress was breathtaking.

It was white moiré silk, the purest white her seamstress could find, to match Evelyn's pale, creamy skin and shoulder-length blond hair. Carefully tailored to her slender form, the simple gown would shimmer in the radiance of her father's chandeliers hanging like twin suns in the ballroom downstairs.

Other girls celebrated their debuts at museums and private clubs around the Historic District. Theirs were larger events with longer guest lists. Evelyn's would be a small but exclusive gathering. Savannah's finest in white tie and tails, gathered under the gabled roof of the wealthiest man for counties round—some said in all of Georgia. They'd dance properly and nibble divinely on low-country fare of exceeding good taste.

Absolutely none of that mattered one whit to Evelyn.

The man who was responsible for her very life would present her on his arm to the world at large and to one very special person in particular: Adam Mann. He was the brightest son Savannah had ever produced—an exceptional student, inundated with scholarships. Adam Mann, with his tall, athletic body and blond good looks, never failed to capture the eye of every woman in the room.

But he had eyes only for Evelyn Whitebloom. And she for him.

There was no one else and never had been since her very first glimpse of his manly face, bronzed from years spent in the sun producing prize-winning gardenias for the family nursery business. It was one of their shared interests that made them perfectly suited for each other.

Their mutual love for all things outdoors extended to the animal world as well. He was always naming her pets, which were legion. He knew all the best places to watch for creatures in their natural habitats, from woodland deer to box turtles. When they strolled hand in hand through the verdant squares of Savannah—Monterey and Liberty and Telfair and Oglethorpe—they both sensed a permanence about their relationship, mirrored in her father's approving eyes.

Adam was her best friend, the older brother she had never had, and her future husband—all rolled into one. In mere minutes she would see him in his white tails and fall in love with him all over again. He was everything good, everything pure, everything right.

And he was hers alone.

Smoothing her skirt for the umpteenth time, she stepped into a brand-new pair of silk dancing flats—white, again—grabbed a tiny purse that held nothing but her hopes for the future and one pink comb, and walked as serenely as she could down the long hall toward the staircase.

Her father waited at the top.

Adam waited at the bottom.

In the foyer the harpist waited for her father's signal that his daughter had arrived and the music could begin.

The chandeliers glowed. And she, Evelyn, glowed as well, inside and out. She could feel it, a sense of joy-bathed tranquillity, as she slipped her arm inside her father's. "Daddy," she whispered, not daring to say more. The look of love and pride shining in his eyes was too much to bear, it blessed her so.

They eased down the wide, curving steps in tandem, his large, black dress shoes next to her tiny white flats, while the harp music swirled around them and a roomful of friends and supporters lifted their sparkling glasses in her direction. The only thing she could take in, though, was Adam standing at the foot of the staircase, blue eyes locked with hers, straight white teeth in an ear-to-ear smile.

There was only one word for it all: *Paradise.*

Within moments her presentation to society was complete, their engagement was announced with a flourish from the harpist, and the evening's festivities had officially commenced.

Evelyn and Adam were ushered to the center of the ballroom floor, barely connecting at shoulder and waist as they whirled around the polished hardwood in graceful circles. Other couples were dancing as well, though they held each other more firmly and seemed to touch more, Evelyn noticed. Whatever that entailed, it was not for her, not for Adam.

She'd heard some of the words her friends called her when they thought she wasn't paying attention—"innocent" and "naive" and "virgin." Those words meant nothing to her.

In a very short time—because her father didn't believe in lengthy engagements—she was to be Adam's bride. She had in fact practiced writing her name that morning. *Mrs. Mann. Mrs. Mann.* How lovely it had looked in wispy letters drawn on heavy Crane stationery. *Mrs. Adam Mann.*

Her new name. It couldn't happen too quickly to suit her.

After several dances and many congratulations, what Evelyn needed—very quickly—was fresh air. The room had already grown stuffy with an abundance of guests and sterling silver warming trays filled with delicacies, not one of which she'd tasted.

Adam promised to join her momentarily, by way of the punch bowl. "May I bring you something to eat, Evie? Are you hungry?"

"Famished!" She flashed him a grateful smile, then wove her way through the crowded ballroom, carefully avoiding toes and elbows, her eyes trained on the tall French doors, her blessed means of escape.

Dear Adam. He'd bring her the perfect thing, knowing her appetite was as small as her waist. Fresh strawberries in light cream, no doubt. She opened both doors, then pulled them shut behind her, inhaling a deep breath of fragrant evening air as she surveyed the gardens yet again.

Twilight bathed the flowers with an ethereal glow, painting the sky with the same pale lavender as the impatiens clustered in the marble pots at her feet. Cautious to keep her pristine shoes safely on the flagstones and off the grass, now damp with evening dew, she tiptoed past a stretch of delicate white dogwood trees until she found her favorite stone bench, clean and dry, as if it had been readied just for her and her pure white gown.

She dropped onto it with a sigh of contentment.

"Psst!"

Evelyn whirled around at the low-pitched hiss. "Adam?" It was pointless to say his name. Her fiancé was too straightforward to play such games. And this *was* a game; she didn't spy a soul in the garden, even when her unseen visitor hissed again.

"Psst! Here, Evelyn."

At least he knew her name. She turned left, then right, then left again, only to find herself nose-to-boutonniere with a man dressed in the most elegant evening clothes imaginable. Not white tails though—black. A sleek black tuxedo with a silvery gray vest, cravat, and dress gloves, crowned with a black silk hat, silhouetted against the first twinkling stars of the evening.

She leaned back, either to get a better look at him or to put a bit of distance between them; she wasn't sure which. He sat down, rather too closely she thought, and let her have her look. It was hard to tell his age, though it appeared he'd been around for a season or two. Not young, but definitely not old. Thirty perhaps. His hair and eyes were as black as his attire, striking against the stark whiteness of his dress shirt and the pale hue of his complexion. Beneath the surface of his skin the shadowy hint of a beard accented his firm jaw line.

The only man she'd ever found handsome was Adam.

This man looked nothing like Adam.

Yet she could not deny he was arrestingly attractive.

"Who are you?" She blurted it out, without any evidence of her debutante manners, then dropped her chin, feeling her cheeks grow warm. "Sorry. This is…well…I live here, so—"

"So you thought you had a right to ask." He tipped her chin up with one long finger. "And you do." His smile reminded her of one she'd seen in a photograph of a quite large, quite ferocious Bengal tiger that had polished off its unsuspecting Indian trainer for dinner mere seconds earlier. Or so the caption had explained.

"So, your name is—"

"Devin." His voice was low and smooth, with no remnant of a hiss. "It's a Gaelic name, from the old country. It means serp—ah, that is, *servant*." He shrugged. "Or *poet*. Take your pick."

What she wanted to pick was a safe spot, like her father's arms, and run there. And where was Adam? She gulped, uncertain of her emotions for the first time in memory. "Are you…from Savannah then, Devin?"

"Yes and no." The smile had returned. "You could say I'm from all over this part of the world. Tell me, Evie—you don't mind if I call you that, do you?—Evie, did your father really say you must never sit under any tree in the garden?"

She laughed, something like relief in her nervous trill. "No, silly! I may sit under any tree in the garden I care to. But Daddy did say I am not to sit under the live oak trees that circle the gazebo in the middle of the garden. He *did* say that." She diverted her eyes, an unaccustomed wave of shyness washing over her. "I'm not even to *touch* that gazebo," she added softly, "or I'll be…ruined!"

Devin let out a less-than-gentlemanly snort. "Ruined?"

"Ruined." She nodded emphatically. "Cut off without a cent. At least, I…well, I think that's what Daddy meant."

His laughter rolled across the lawn like tenpins on a bowling green. "Surely not! Your father loves you, child. He wouldn't dream of treating his only daughter in such a cruel manner."

He inched closer and slipped his arm behind her. When his gloved fingertips barely touched the small of her back, she flinched. They were inexplicably hot! If not for her gown, they might have singed her skin.

"Evie…you did say I might call you Evie, yes?"

She nodded, stunned. Her tongue suddenly felt dry and thick, as if she couldn't form words even if her life depended on it. Which for some very odd reason she thought it might.

One word kept sticking in her throat. *No…no!*

"The truth is, your sainted father knows something you don't."

She raised her eyebrows, still speechless. What could Devin possibly be talking about? Her father loved her, utterly and completely. There was nothing she needed to know that he hadn't revealed to her, nothing she desired that he hadn't provided.

A beautiful home. A perfect husband-to-be. A lovely garden.

Granted, that garden had a mysterious gazebo she couldn't explore no matter how much she might want to. But she didn't want to, did she? Well…did she?

"The minute you step inside that gazebo, dear girl, you'll make an eye-opening discovery—something your father knows all about, but you do not. Not yet."

She found her voice at last and rose to her feet. "No! I mean…he does? Oh! I don't? I…uh, that is…" It came out in one long, nonsensical phrase. What sort of man was this Devin, who could turn her thoughts inside out and tie her words up in knots she hadn't a prayer of ever untangling?

He stood as well, waiting patiently for her to gather her wits about her, it seemed. His smile didn't alter one inch. The fingers on her back returned, more insistent than ever, as if invisibly propelling her forward. Had she and Devin moved? It appeared they had, but in which direction? Her beloved garden was looking less familiar by the minute as the last rays of the sun cast long shadows across the lawn.

He hadn't taken his black eyes off her for a single moment since they'd met. Those eyes were full of knowing—a knowledge that made her pulse quicken. It was the only logical explanation for the strange sensations she was feeling in the pit of her stomach.

Perhaps if Devin shared this knowledge with her she could tell Adam as well. It would mean a special bond between them, a secret between husband and wife. *Yes!* That would please her father, wouldn't it? For her and for Adam to know everything that he knew?

She simply had to ask. "Wh-what will I discover in the gazebo?"

"Something delicious."

Delicious! Well, she *was* hungry. Adam had gone to find something healthy for her to nibble on. Now this Devin said *he* had something for her, waiting in the gazebo. Perhaps he'd gone to a great deal of trouble to prepare it. Devin didn't strike her as a man who did anything on a whim. She couldn't risk appearing impolite or unappreciative, not tonight of all nights.

"Something delicious, you say, in the gazebo? Is it fruit?"

He smiled his tiger smile. "It's every bit as sweet as fruit."

Ah, sweet! Yes, she'd enjoy that. *How nice.* But sweet things were usually fattening. "Does it have many calories?"

His voice was magnolia-petal smooth. "No calories at all."

Perfect! "But...how can something be good for me if my father says it's not to be touched?"

"That's exactly what we've come to the gazebo to find out, Evie."

They were there!

She hadn't realized they'd been walking in slow, deliberate steps toward the heart of the garden. A host of unfamiliar emotions, without names or adequate descriptions, surged through her. There wasn't time to sort it all out, not now when she was so close to making the discovery that Devin had promised. Only a curtain of Spanish moss separated her from the gazebo. She could almost touch the wooden supports, nestled in the arms of the live oaks that surrounded the ancient gazebo with an eternal embrace.

Why had it seemed so frightening from a distance? Close up it appeared cozy and inviting. Devin brushed aside the veil of moss, giving her an even better view of the verdant bower that awaited her mere inches away.

Her first surprise: It wasn't an elevated gazebo at all. It was sunken! And looked as if it had resided there since time began. *How enchanting!* Devin went down the three steps first, leading to the patterned brick floor of the gazebo. The bricks appeared slippery under his feet, and she wondered for a fleeting moment if they might soil her white silk shoes.

"Take my hand, Evie." He offered it with a gallant flourish. "You're quite safe with me."

She was grateful for her long, white gloves because his hand felt hot, almost feverish. "Don't let me fall!" she cautioned. "Daddy will skin me alive if I tear this dress." *Daddy.* Something tugged at the edge of her conscience, a feeling she'd never experienced in her lifetime and hoped she never would again.

Before she could stop him, Devin had captured both her gloved hands in his. They were standing face to face, making it difficult to get a proper look at the gazebo itself, the very thing she'd come to explore. There was no sign of food, of that she was certain. Not a table or chair, only lichen-covered wooden benches skirting the dim interior.

In a word, it was disappointing.

She noticed the fetid air around her growing darker as the shadowy corners of the gazebo faded to black. Oddly, the temperature was creeping up. Savannah flirted with temperatures near the eighties in April, but this felt even warmer than that, almost subtropical.

In the gloomy interior the only thing she could see clearly was Devin's face. For a reason she couldn't begin to grasp, he was looking more handsome by the second.

One of her many first-time sensations had a name: apprehension. A desire to go forward, all the while longing to pull back.

She should not be there.

She wanted to be there.

She *was* there.

This newfound apprehension tickled the hairs on the back of her neck. "What exactly did you want to show me, Devin?"

Expectancy hung heavily in the air. She sensed the weight of it pressing her down, down through the bricks, through the ground, to the darkest center of the earth.

She held her breath. Everything in the garden did too; she was sure of it.

Devin bent toward her, his eyelids slowly falling until his black eyes became beguiling slits that filled her senses to the brim.

She gasped when his lips touched hers.

It lasted only a second, whatever it was, but it tasted as sweet as the nectar from an acre of honeysuckle on a hot summer night. Every one of her senses blossomed with possibilities. So warm! So tender! So sweet!

He watched her as she struggled to put a name to it all. "That was a kiss, Evelyn. Aren't you glad you listened to me and stepped inside the gazebo?"

The gazebo! Oh, she'd truly done it, the one thing her father had asked her never to do. Still…nothing had happened, had it? She was alive and breathing; in fact, she felt wonderful, from the top of her blond head to her silk-covered toes. Although a quick glance down confirmed her earlier worry: Her once-pristine shoes were a muddy brown.

Oh, but a *kiss,* he'd called it. It *was* delicious, much better than plain old fruit. It was over so fast though. Would she remember enough to share her luscious discovery with Adam?

Adam! She really hadn't considered what *he* might think of her exploring the gazebo. That emotion she'd never wanted to feel again washed over her a second time. If she were inventing words, she would call it *guilt.* As if on cue, Adam's voice called out to her from the garden.

"Evie!" He sounded far away yet very close. "Evie!" The mossy curtain was swept aside to reveal her fiancé, dressed in pure white and utter shock. "Evie! You know you're not supposed to be here!"

She blinked, speechless for a moment, glancing around her in a daze. Devin was gone. *Wait.* Perhaps that was Devin lurking in the shadows. It didn't matter. Adam was there. *Dear Adam.* She had so much to show him.

With a peculiar sense of urgency, she stretched out a gloved arm to her betrothed. "Come! See what I've discovered, darling man. It's quite…ah, delectable."

He was beside her in a heartbeat, concern creasing his forehead. "Delectable? What are you talking about?"

"Taste and see for yourself." She half closed her eyes, just as Devin had, and pressed her lips against Adam's mouth, still agape. When she opened her eyes fully again, Evelyn gazed deep into Adam's wide, blue ones and spied something she'd never seen before. Love, yes, and trust, but more than that: She caught a wary look of vulnerability.

He seemed unable to speak, unable to breathe.

Ohhh! She realized in an instant he would never be able to resist her. The power she had over him overwhelmed her. She kissed him again, longer this time. A boldness seared through her veins, making her tingle to the tips of her soiled toes. She slipped one slim finger under Adam's neat bow tie, undoing it in seconds, then began unbuttoning his dress shirt, amazed that the tiny buttons gave way so easily.

After only three buttons she had to stop and catch her breath. What was happening to her? She and Adam had gone swimming all last summer in their bathing suits and thought nothing of it. Suddenly his bare neck was the most dazzling thing she'd ever laid eyes on! It was all she could do to keep from pressing her lips there. When she gazed up into his darkening eyes, she realized that Devin's "knowing" was starting to grow in Adam, clearly matching her own.

The faintest of breezes stirred the moss hanging over the gazebo entrance when a deep voice rang through the garden.

It was her father!

"Adam!" He was looking for them. "Where are you, Adam?"

Oh, Daddy.

Panic—had she ever felt that before?—had her fumbling with the buttons on Adam's shirt. The same ones that, moments earlier, had opened so quickly, now refused to respond to her trembling fingers.

"Where are you?" Her father was mere steps away from them.

The trembling in her hands turned to shaking all over. Her face was on fire. Was she ill? Had she caught whatever fever Devin had, with just one kiss? Her stomach felt queasy. When Adam stared down at her, she noticed his face was a startling red. The guilt she'd sensed for the first time only moments ago was now mirrored in her fiancé's own tear-tinged eyes.

"Oh, Evie..." Adam's whispered words seemed to stick in his throat. "When your father finds us, beloved, there'll be Hell to pay. Are you ready?"

She swallowed hard and tasted something like fear. "Y-yes."

Reluctance written all over his face, Adam turned toward the steps that led back to the garden. "Down here, sir..."

High Noon in the Garden of Good and Evil: Eve

> The LORD God took the man and put him in the Garden of Eden
> to work it and take care of it. *Genesis 2:15*

Thirty years ago Joni Mitchell wrote, "We've got to get ourselves back to the garden." Quite right, woman, but Woodstock isn't back far enough. Not thirty years but thirty *centuries* is more like it. Forty. Fifty. Waaaay back, all the way back to the Garden of Eden.

Eden is often translated as "delight" or, by way of a Persian word, "paradise." This wasn't some haphazard wildflower garden; it was a carefully designed and beautifully executed park of trees featuring cedars, cypresses, and figs, "the kind only planned by great kings."[1]

Such gardens don't maintain themselves; that was Adam's job. Even before the Fall, he was given the task of caring for the garden. It was far from hard labor though—remember, no weeds, no thistles, no thorns, no frost, no floods, no irrigation, no grub worms, and no "wascally wabbit" eating Adam's best carrots.

Adam was called to work, but it was a cushy gig.

The first man had everything a human needed to be happy in this garden of God's: water, food, warmth, shelter, and all-natural-fiber clothing...well, that came later. When God created Adam, he surrounded him with beauty that engaged all his given senses: shapes and colors for his eyes, fragrant flowers for his nose, a thousand textures for his hands to examine, the music of rushing streams to fill his ears, and endless tastes to try, all over the garden.

Okay…*almost* all over.

> And the LORD God commanded the man, "You are free to eat from
> any tree in the garden; but you must not eat from the tree of the
> knowledge of good and evil, for when you eat of it you will surely
> die." *Genesis 2:16-17*

There you are. A simple commandment. Not ten of them, just one:
"Thou shalt not eat." (Personally I wish the very first edict from God
hadn't involved dieting, don't you? If only he'd said, "You must not eat
anything with less than four hundred calories." Now *there* is a commandment I could live with.)

Knowledge is good, but it was the intimate "knowing" of evil that was
dangerous. Like any good parent, our heavenly Father built a hedge
around his child in order to protect the young man's innocence and to
keep him from learning things he didn't need to know.

Adam was obedient, but he was also lonely. Ask an only child, and he'll
tell you it's mighty quiet in the playroom all by yourself.

> The LORD God said, "It is not good for the man to be alone. I will
> make a helper suitable for him." *Genesis 2:18*

Immediately after giving Adam his look-but-don't-touch edict, the
Lord announced that his charge needed company. To keep Adam's mind
off the forbidden tree? To help with the gardening? Or simply in response
to Adam's very human longing for companionship?

One commentator voted for that last option: "Solitude is not good; man
is created for sociability."[2] Even those of us who cherish our quiet moments
alone get stir-crazy eventually. When I'm holed up in my writing loft, I last
about six hours before I wander downstairs or hit the Internet to check my
e-mail. It's a God-given drive, this need to connect with other humans.
People who have only a little of that drive are called "loners." People with
even less are labeled "hermits." People with none are put in straitjackets.

"People who need people" have God to thank for it.

First, though, God tried pets. Not just cats, dogs, and yellow canaries
but a whole beastly bunch of animals. Adam named them all, antelope to

zebra, yet no matter how he tried to fellowship with God's furry and feath-
ered creatures, there were too many of those basic irreconcilable differences.

But for Adam no suitable helper was found. *Genesis 2:20*

"Suitable" is elsewhere translated "comparable" (NKJV) and "right for
him" (ICB). God was looking not for a good fit but rather a perfect fit. This
wasn't *The Dating Game;* it was *The Match Game,* with one and only one
correct answer. And "helper" by no means suggested a lowly servant. It
meant an equal, a colaborer, a "suitable partner" (CEV).[3]

This partner had to be as valuable as Adam, as worthy of living in
God's glorious Garden of Eden, as equally created in God's image, and
yet…different. Adam was made from the dust of the earth. His partner
(truth be told) was made of finer stuff.

> So the LORD God caused the man to fall into a deep sleep; and
> while he was sleeping, he took one of the man's ribs and closed up
> the place with flesh. *Genesis 2:21*

(Say, two favorite movie titles in one verse: *While You Were Sleeping* and
Adam's Rib!)

Why a "deep sleep"? So that Adam wouldn't feel the pain of the Lord's
amazing-but-anesthetic-free operation, and so Adam wouldn't see the mystery of creation.

Why the man's rib? Perhaps because when it comes to the human skele-
tal structure, one rib isn't exactly a load-bearing wall. Plus, from an emotional standpoint, God wisely chose the bone nearest the man's heart as a
gentle reminder to keep his helpmate close by his side—physically, emotionally, spiritually.

> Then the LORD God made a woman from the rib he had taken out
> of the man, and he brought her to the man. *Genesis 2:22*

Oh the majesty of that moment when God brought the crown of his
creation to the one for whom she was designed!

Girls, you *know* she was a dish. She skipped childhood completely,
so no chickenpox scars. No adolescence meant no blemishes marred
her lovely face either. No genetic anomalies from weird Aunt Jane, nor

did she inherit her mother's flat feet. God did everything perfectly, including carving a woman out of bone (a *real* hard-body look) with ideal proportions.

She was also sinless. Her personality would have been utterly delightful. In *Paradise Lost* Milton wrote of her, "Grace was in all her steps, heaven in her eye, / In every gesture dignity and love."[4] Other writers in other centuries have called her "the best flower of the garden" and "Heaven's best, last gift."

Since she was the premiere edition and the only woman around, she didn't need to worry about competition from supermodels or centerfolds or the woman sitting next to her in church four sizes smaller than she. The first female was the very definition of womanly beauty. No one was taller, thinner, younger, or prettier. She was *it!*

I know what you're thinking: *Why did she blow this?* How could a woman with all this going for her ruin her life so completely?

Women do it every day. Men do too. We all throw away perfectly wonderful lives because our foolish, sinful appetites take us places we should not go.

But I'm getting ahead of myself. Things were still rosy in Eden.

> The man said,
>
> "This is now bone of my bones
> and flesh of my flesh;
> she shall be called 'woman,'
> for she was taken out of man." *Genesis 2:23*

One look at God's gift to man and Adam got positively poetic. "There is no doubt but Adam is saying, 'This woman, first, last, and always!'"[5]

In other words, "Ooh, baby. You got it right this time, Lord."

By no means was she to be Adam's "girl toy." She was created to be his partner for life.

> For this reason a man will leave his father and mother and be
> united to his wife, and they will become one flesh. *Genesis 2:24*

Marriage was instituted on the spot and ordained by God, "not as a civil contract but as a divine institution."[6] One man, one woman, one flesh. We need never doubt what God's perfect will is on this issue. One mate for life. How it behooves us to choose wisely!

> The man and his wife were both naked, and they felt no shame.
> *Genesis 2:25*

I don't know any practicing nudists, but I suspect more than one has pointed to this verse as justification for throwing caution and their clothes to the wind. Sorry, but that bird won't fly. This is a BF scene—Before the Fall. And there were only the two people, *and* they were married. When they rejoined their bones and flesh in sexual union, it was wholesome and natural, utterly enjoyable, and without embarrassment, shame, or hiding anything from each other.

Ah, but paradise was about to be lost.

> Now the serpent was more crafty than any of the wild animals the
> LORD God had made. *Genesis 3:1*

Make no mistake, it was a snake. A real, live, cold-bellied serpent—one of the animals God had created as part of his "Let's Find Adam a Friend" project. Satan isn't mentioned by name in this passage, but his slimy style was all over this snake-skinned charmer.

Various translations call the wild creature "subtle" (AMP), "cunning" (NKJV), the "shrewdest" (NLT), the "most clever" (ICB), and the "sliest" (TAB).[7] An animal ready-made for Satan's uses then. No doubt attractive to look at, with some colorful pattern on his sleek skin. He chose his words with care and saved his venom for later, showing the woman only his lightning-fast tongue but not his lethal fangs. As Shakespeare reminded us in *King Lear,* "The prince of darkness is a gentleman."

One word of comfort, sisters: The snake was a *he,* not an *it,* and definitely not a *she.*

> He said to the woman, "Did God really say, 'You must not eat from
> any tree in the garden'?" *Genesis 3:1*

Why Eve and not Adam? I wonder. Was she in the wrong place at the wrong time, or did the serpent go looking for her? And why, oh, why didn't she realize that if none of the other animals talked, this one shouldn't have either?

How I long for more information! Ah well. As Christopher Guest said in *The Princess Bride,* "Let's just start with what we have." What we have is one gullible gal and one sly serpent. When the devil comes a-tempting, he seldom goes in for group conversions. He waits until we're alone, then spins his web of deceit.

The only question I *don't* have is, "Why didn't she go find Adam and discuss all this with him first?" Get a grip. She knew he'd talk her out of it. A married woman knows better than to ask her husband a question like, "Shall I buy this outrageously expensive linen suit from Lord & Taylor?" She can bank on a negative response. It's the same reason women order stuff from catalogs and hope the UPS truck pulls up on a safe day.

Besides, we don't know where Adam was at this point. We left him back at the close of the last chapter, naked and not ashamed. Maybe he was taking a shower. In any case, the serpent was bending the woman's ear. She who will be called Eve by story's end makes (at my count) not just *one* colossal blooper but a *plethora* of mistakes, beginning with one that every child is cautioned against from the cradle: Don't talk to strangers!

Satan isn't called the Father of Lies for nothing. He opened his cozy chat with the woman using a deliberate lie—misquoting God, even putting words in the Lord's mouth. Satan has been doing that for millennia, sisters, and he's devilishly good at it. For that reason, whenever I hear a line of Scripture used to make a point—even by a well-meaning speaker or teacher—I go back to the Bible and see what the verse actually says in context.

By twisting the Lord's decree, Satan also tossed out one of the big stumbling blocks he still uses with great success today—making God look less than fair, kind, or loving. When tragedy strikes—a precious child is killed in an accident or a young mother dies of cancer—Satan tempts our faith with the same sort of opening line: "Would a good God allow *that?*"

Cunning doesn't begin to describe this wily serpent.

Author Jean Kerr, of *Please Don't Eat the Daisies* fame, shared a story about her son, Christopher, who'd been cast as Adam in his first-grade play and was less than enthusiastic about the role.

"Why, that's wonderful, that's the *lead!*" his mother assured him.

"Yeah," he replied gloomily, "but the *snake* has all the lines."[8]

Satan is full of lines, all right. He reeled in the first lady like an unsuspecting trout.

> The woman said to the serpent, "We may eat fruit from the trees in
> the garden…" *Genesis 3:2*

She meant well by correcting the serpent, but again, dialoguing with the creature to begin with was her first mistake.

"Like a theologian, she analyzes the serpent's arguments; like a lawyer, she enters into debate,"[9] goes one analysis of this scene. Plenty of theologians and lawyers have been made fools of by Satan. Whether we're innocent as doves or highly educated, the fact is, when Satan talks, the wise woman turns her back at the opening hiss and heads for the hills.

Naive Eve-to-be, however, tried to correct the serpent's misquote and instead made one of her own:

> "…but God did say, 'You must not eat fruit from the tree that is in
> the middle of the garden, and you must not touch it, or you will
> die.'" *Genesis 3:3*

Notice her second mistake: She added to the Word of God. The Lord never told her to "not touch it," just not to *eat* of the fruit. When we exaggerate God's Word, which literally means "to enlarge beyond the truth," we sow seeds of doubt in the minds of others—*Did God really say that other thing?*—and in our own mind—*Maybe God's words need my help.*

The crafty serpent didn't draw attention to her verbal blunder. The woman was already doing such a good job of deceiving herself, his assistance was hardly needed. Instead he picked the dire consequence of sin—death—and turned it upside down.

> "You will not surely die," the serpent said to the woman. *Genesis 3:4*

So far, this might have sounded like good news to her. It does to us. When Jesus said, "He who believes in me will live, even though he dies; and whoever lives and believes in me will never die,"[10] that was the best news in town. Still is.

What's the difference? Jesus prefaced that statement by saying, "I am the resurrection and the life,"[11] but the serpent made no such claim or promise. He didn't offer the woman life, let alone life after death; the serpent offered the woman *knowledge*—a knowledge which led to death. That was God's promise too, but the woman's eyes were no longer on God; they were on herself—another grave error.

"For God knows that when you eat of it…" *Genesis 3:5*

The serpent subtly shifted the conversation away from the Word of God and toward the desires of man, all the while invoking God's name. Not "God said" though; now it's "God *knows.*" Notice that the serpent left himself out of the discussion entirely. He always does. We never hear about how our actions will benefit him or his evil kingdom; he brings up only *our* perceived benefits.

In the Garden of Eden, he reminded Eve of two appetizing promises. First:

"…your eyes will be opened…" *Genesis 3:5*

Can't you hear our sweet girl now? "Gee, I didn't know my eyes were closed. Is there more of this lovely world to see? Am I missing something good?" It's easy to criticize her, but the fact is, her purity and innocence break my heart.

How well I remember, when I was truly "sweet sixteen and never been kissed," hooking up with a woman who was two years older than I was and infinitely more experienced in life. My eyes would literally open wider when I'd listen to her stories of sexual adventures that my virginal eyes had never even envisioned, let alone seen.

Oh, if only I'd known the Lord then and known where else to look! The two blind men by the side of the road outside Jericho knew exactly where to turn: "Lord, we want our eyes to be opened."[12] When Jesus did so, they rose and followed him. But the woman in the garden wasn't asking *God* to open her eyes. She thought this tasty-looking *fruit* was going to pop open her peepers.

Boy, did it ever.

The serpent added sugar to the fruit with the second promise:

"…and you will be like God…" *Genesis 3:5*

Satan still peddles this one today with great success. Most of the false philosophies and religions making the rounds have this lie at their heart: *You are God.* People are easily misled by semantics: "Why invite Jesus to live in your heart, when god already resides in all of us?" goes the sales pitch. (Note the small *g.*)

Since the woman pictured the Father of Creation as all-good, all-loving, and all-knowing—which he is, of course, but he's also all-powerful—she must have convinced herself that being like God was a grand idea.

"…knowing good and evil." *Genesis 3:5*

I doubt she even heard the "good and evil" part, especially since she was an innocent and wouldn't have known the difference. To her way of thinking, since life was all *good,* maybe *evil* was even better, right?

Let's face it, *that* bit of tripe sells well these days. Surfed the Internet lately?

When the woman saw that the fruit of the tree… *Genesis 3:6*

The tree that had been in the middle of everything yet obediently avoided—for how long we don't know—suddenly, that tree was *it.* The all-consuming, gotta-have-it thing. Like a child of Christmas past who put only *one* item on her wish list—Cabbage Patch Doll, Tickle-Me Elmo, Beanie Baby—Eve had a fixation about that tree.

She stopped looking to God for the truth.

She stopped looking to her husband for shared counsel.

She stopped looking at the good, wholesome fruit already available to her.

She even stopped looking to the serpent for direction.

Notice: *The serpent never said another word.* He didn't have to. His temptation was complete. The seeds of his deception had fallen on fertile ground. Now he stood back and watched the fruit fall from the tree into the willing woman's hands.

As Ralph Hodgson wrote: "Oh, had our simple Eve / Seen through the make-believe!"[13]

The problem here involved taking her eyes off what was good and acceptable, and putting them on what she *knew,* absolutely, to be forbidden.

Didn't that fruit look tasty though?

> …was good for food… *Genesis 3:6*

The witty Lord Byron once said, "Since Eve ate apples, much depends on dinner." True, but let's set the record straight on one thing: It was not an apple, Granny Smith or otherwise. Apples grow in Washington State, not in Mesopotamia. Historians have suggested three more likely suspects for the forbidden fruit: pomegranates, apricots, or figs.[14]

Personally I think it was Godiva chocolate.

Whatever the fruit, it appealed to her fleshly appetite. It made her mouth water and her stomach grumble and her taste buds stand up and pay attention. If she wasn't hungry before, she was now.

Bakeries that pump the aroma of freshly baked cinnamon rolls into the mall have utilized this old trick for years. So has Satan. Eve's mistake was listening to her stomach, not her heart.

> …and pleasing to the eye… *Genesis 3:6*

At first blush this seems a higher plane: the aesthetics of the situation. Instead of the base appetites of the flesh, she indulged in an intellectual appreciation of the fruit's artistic appeal. It was indeed attractive, a beautifully designed piece of fruit.

Of course it was—God made it!

But pleasing to the eye isn't the same as pleasing to God. Did God plant this lovely tree in the garden for the very purpose of testing the obedience and faithfulness of his created beings? No doubt in my mind whatsoever. The woman's test grade was a C- at this point, with a tough essay question coming up.

When my son, Matthew, was in first grade, his teacher used a tamer version of the tree of knowledge to teach her students right from wrong. On the wall in the back of the classroom was a floor-to-ceiling, construction-paper apple tree. It didn't look good to eat, but it *was* pleasing to the eye. Each child had an apple with his or her name neatly printed on it, dangling from the tree for every small eye to see.

When—not *if*—a child misbehaved in class, the apple fell into a basket at the bottom and lived there the rest of the day. Ugh. Serious peer pressure for a six-year-old. The next morning all was forgiven, and back on the tree went the apple. (Sir Isaac Newton would have argued about the gravity of such an object lesson, but it worked for the kids.)

It also made it easy for parents to do a quick obedience check: "Did your apple stay on the tree?" I'd ask Matthew.

Day after day, week after week, his answer was the same. "Yes, Mama." Until that fateful day months into the semester when he jumped into the car with tears rolling down his round cheeks.

"Let me guess, honey. Your apple fell down today, right?"

"Uh-huh." He nodded dejectedly, then hiccuped. "Sorry, Mama."

Oh, that sin nature. It was born in the garden, beneath the spreading leaves of an attractive fruit tree where a woman saw something so pretty she convinced herself it had no power to wreak destruction in her life.

...and also desirable for gaining wisdom... *Genesis 3:6*

Tasty as the fruit promised to be, it was the *fruit* of eating the fruit that really whetted the woman's appetite—the wisdom, the knowledge. Her ego longed to be equal with God, to have that much understanding and creativity and power.

Where was Solomon when we needed him to remind her that "the fear of the LORD is the beginning of knowledge"?[15] The book of Proverbs was eons away—but God and his Word were not. They were right there in the garden, walking with the two of them. If she desired wisdom, all she needed to do was ask, as Solomon did, and God would no doubt have given her all she could handle.

But our girl Eve wanted a shortcut to wisdom. We all do. One commentary phrased it this way: "With rationalization and justification Eve was soon in rebellion against God."[16] This translation of the verse says it all: "The woman was convinced" (NLT).

...she took some... *Genesis 3:6*

Everything stands in the balance right here. Touching it isn't tasting it—not yet. How often do we reach out for something we know to be wrong while our conscience is screaming, *No! Stop! You know better!*

Bet that happened to Eve, too.

Yes, she was innocent, but she also had one important piece of wisdom already tucked in the folds of her gray matter: God had said, "Don't eat of the tree." She knew that much to be fact.

Then why did she take the fruit?

Oh, the ink that's been spilled on that subject! One Bible scholar found her courageous: "It must have taken great daring to sin for the first time."[17] I have sympathy for the woman, but sorry, I can't see awarding her a Medal of Valor for being the first Good Girl to go Bad. Others have chalked up Eve's actions to "curiosity" and "ambition."

When those qualities—courage, curiosity, ambition—are aimed toward a lofty goal such as exploring a new mission field, they're admirable. But this woman had already demonstrated her goals and motivation, none of which honored God: "I'd enjoy the taste; I like the look of it; I'll be like God."

She could have quit, let go of the fruit, run the other way.

But she didn't. It was her last chance to remain innocent. At this point, no matter how noisy her conscience, the woman pressed on, perhaps assuring herself, "Hey, I'm not dead yet! Might as well take a bite."

> …and ate it. *Genesis 3:6*

Incredible. And devastating. The entire axis of human history rotated on six words: "She took some and ate it." In the original Hebrew, it is only three words: *wattiqqach mippiryo watto'cal.*

The fall of man. No high drama, no lightning bolts, no John Williams musical score full of kettledrums and trumpet blasts. Just the soft, juicy sound of the woman's teeth piercing the skin of the forbidden fruit. Milton wrote, "Forth reaching to the fruit, she plucked, she ate. Earth felt the wound."[18]

Hang your head, O ancient sister. You had no one to blame but yourself. Not a dysfunctional childhood, not a husband who led you astray, not abject hunger, not poverty, nor need of any kind. You couldn't even blame that serpent, though I'm sure the thought crossed your mind.

Speaking of which, where *was* the serpent, since he didn't offer an "attagirl"? Was he celebrating his victory in silence? Were the fallen angels rejoicing in some distant region?

And where was Adam during—? *Oh.* Look who showed up.

> She also gave some to her husband, who was with her... *Genesis 3:6*

The ten translations I studied all include the notion of Adam's standing next to her. None of them indicate when he arrived—whether it was early in the temptation scene, at midpoint, or after the fatal bite. If he'd been there, might he have tried to stop her? Would she have listened? Or would he have let her try it first, like an official food taster for the king?

We don't know and never will know, this side of heaven.

We know enough though. We know that not one word of protest or hesitation on Adam's part is recorded in Scripture.

> ...and he ate it. *Genesis 3:6*

It took the craftiest creature around to tempt the woman. All it took for the woman to tempt Adam was a question, posed with her eyes and extended hand: "Wanna bite?"

When Adam ate of the fruit as well, he became her partner in sin, even as he was in marriage; that is to say, they were equals. The woman took the rap for going first, but they both ended up in a prison of their own making.

Without the woman to offer him a bite, would Adam have tasted the fruit of that tree? Absolutely. Man is no less a sinner than woman just because he went second instead of first down the path of destruction. We are *all* sinners in need of a Savior. But, to be fair, because she offered her husband the fruit instead of doing the right thing and trying to talk him out of it, Eve adds another mistake to her growing list.

> Then the eyes of both of them were opened... *Genesis 3:7*

Interesting. God told them they would die, but the serpent told them their eyes would be opened. The serpent was still victorious. For the moment.

> ...and they realized they were naked... *Genesis 3:7*

This wasn't "Oh, boy!" This was "Oh, *no!*" To appear before the Lord naked was a major faux pas, and the Israelites who first heard this story would have known that. Even being naked with one another was embarrassing. As Mark Twain observed, "Man is the only animal that blushes. Or needs to."

> …so they sewed fig leaves together and made coverings for
> themselves. *Genesis 3:7*

To my way of thinking, this is proof that the forbidden fruit couldn't possibly have been a fig. Reach for a leaf from the one tree that spelled your doom? Talk about your dead giveaway!

Those leafy outfits resembled aprons, covering the bottom half of their naked bodies. A bit like hula skirts, perhaps, but with more coverage, since fig leaves are wider. Ah, but those figgy "puttings" couldn't hide their sin. Few things successfully do.

When I was a not-so-sweet-anymore seventeen-year-old, curled up in an overstuffed chair in my bedroom one summer evening, I was reading a book and—horrors!—smoking a cigarette. A major no-no. *Huge.* I heard my father coming up the steps and, in a panic, put out the cigarette, then tossed the whole ashtray out the window and sprayed perfume around me like a mad woman.

The one who was mad was my dad. "Have you been smoking in here?"

"Uh…gee, not exactly, Daddy."

"Then what exactly *have* you been doing?"

Sewing fig leaves, that's what.

I didn't get away with it. Neither did the two in the Garden of Eden.

> Then the man and his wife heard the sound of the LORD God as he
> was walking in the garden in the cool of the day… *Genesis 3:8*

"Late in the afternoon a breeze began to blow" (CEV), but for the first couple, it was an ill wind. They heard the footsteps of God, their creator and friend. They'd enjoyed a fellowship with him we can only begin to imagine. But sin had repercussions, and separation from God was the worst of all. For the first time, those fatherly footsteps struck terror in their hearts.

"You will surely die," he'd said.

He was a God who kept his promises.

Now fallen Adam, who had named every animal in the garden, had to find a name for what they did: *sin.* A name for what they felt: *shame.* A name for the consequences: *separation.*

> ...and they hid from the LORD God among the trees of the garden.
>
> *Genesis 3:8*

We delay the inevitable when we hide, but still we do it. Silly. Sad. And sinful.

> But the LORD God called to the man, "Where are you?" *Genesis 3:9*

God didn't call out to both of them, "Hey, where are you two love-birds?" He held Adam accountable first. To Adam's credit, the man responded immediately with three true statements:

> He answered, "I heard you in the garden, and I was afraid because I was naked; so I hid." *Genesis 3:10*

Before we pat Adam on the back for honesty, though, remember that when confronted with our sins, we often do the same thing: point out what we did right, or what was true, in the desperate hope it will mini-mize or divert attention from the ugly things we did wrong.

God saw right through that fig leaf.

> And he said, "Who told you that you were naked?" *Genesis 3:11*

We aren't smart enough to figure this stuff out ourselves, and God knows it. Knew it then, knows it now.

One wonders if perhaps a bit of fruity pulp was stuck between Adam's teeth.

> "Have you eaten from the tree that I commanded you not to eat from?" *Genesis 3:11*

It doesn't get any more direct than that. God asked a legitimate ques-tion about obedience, which produced one very circumspect answer.

> The man said, "The woman you put here with me—she gave me some fruit from the tree, and I ate it." *Genesis 3:12*

Three more statements from Adam. Two were totally true and without guile—she gave him the fruit and, yes, he ate it—but oh, that first response! Adam shifted the blame for his sin as far away from himself as possible. First toward "the woman"—he didn't even call her his wife, his beloved, his partner. Their separation from God had already led to a rift between them, a hairline fracture in the "bone of his bones."

But he didn't blame only "the woman." No, the one whom "you put here with me," Adam insisted. Oh, there's a novel idea. Blame the *Lord*. Adam was suggesting that left to his own devices, he'd never have eaten that awful fruit. It was her fault or God's fault. Not his fault.

(My own husband, Bill, thinks Adam would've been too distracted by the woman's charms even to *notice* the tree.)

> Then the LORD God said to the woman, "What is this you have done?" *Genesis 3:13*

It was the woman's turn. She didn't distinguish herself either. "Eve has always been a convenient peg on which men hung unflattering theories about women."[19] I'll point out it was a man who said that and not recently—1941. But the fact is, she followed her husband's example of not taking responsibility for one's actions and shifted blame faster than the late comedian Flip Wilson's Geraldine character could wail, "The devil made me do it!"

> The woman said, "The serpent deceived me, and I ate." *Genesis 3:13*

Her final mistake here was the classic of them all: "The snake tricked me" (CEV).

Why do we think we can get away with that "blame the serpent" stuff, when we who have the power of Christ living in us are told, "the one who is in you is greater than the one who is in the world"?[20] Satan may be cunning, crafty, and clever, but he is in no way equal with God.

In my own efforts to be blame-free, I've hidden behind that cloven-hoofed character more than once. I heeded Martin Luther's advice from 1521—"be a sinner and let your sins be strong"—without embracing the whole of it—"but let your trust in Christ be stronger." Before I had any relationship with God, I took singular pleasure in wearing a T-shirt that proclaimed, "Lead me not into temptation… I can find it myself." I was, as one writer eloquently described Eve after the Fall, "a changed being—a rebel—a sinner."[21]

Yes, I was. Yes, I am.

Eve was a rib, a woman, a wife, and a sinner. Finally the dear soul got a real name.

> Adam named his wife Eve, because she would become the mother of all the living. *Genesis 3:20*

When her firstborn, Cain, arrived—ooh, long story there!—Eve did not forget the Lord but acknowledged God's hand on her womb:

> She said, "With the help of the LORD I have brought forth a man." *Genesis 4:1*

Indeed, much later in Eve's life (you won't believe how much—like decades later), she gave birth to Seth, who stands in the lineage of Christ. Through her offspring, that old serpent would eventually be crushed forever.

Eve is unique among the Bad Girls of the Bible.

If she had been *Bad to the Bone,* she would have made the *serpent* eat the fruit, chopped the forbidden tree down to size, and charged Adam some serious coin for the privilege of enjoying her favors.

If she had been *Bad for a Moment,* she would have changed how she fixed fruit salad, not changed the course of human history.

If she had been *Bad for a Season, but Not Forever* she would have reveled in her sin for a long time, looking for more trees to nibble on, before she was invited to partake of the fruit of the Tree of Life—the Son of God.

She was instead the first woman God ever created. A one-of-a-kind Bad Girl.

When she was perfect, beautiful, and innocent, I found no toehold where I could connect with Eve.

When she was tempted by her flesh, humbled by her sin, and redeemed by her God, I could sing out, "Oh, sister Eve! Can we talk?"

What Lessons Can We Learn from Eve?

Don't get into a debate with Satan—get out!
We can't stop the Adversary from whispering in our ears, but we can refuse to listen, and we can definitely refuse to respond. No arguing, no debating!

Like Eve, we'll come out the loser. Let's stand and resist. "Just Say No." If he doesn't flee, we can take off running for the safety of the Lord's arms.

> Submit yourselves, then, to God. Resist the devil, and he will flee from you. *James 4:7*

Know God's Word so you won't be fooled.

When the serpents in our lives say, "Did God really say…?" let's be the first on our block to declare, "No, God did not!" Because Eve didn't remember the words of God's *one* commandment accurately, she left herself wide open for temptation to rush in. Studying, even memorizing, verses from the Bible gives us the strength to say no because we *know*.

> I have hidden your word in my heart that I might not sin against you. *Psalm 119:11*

Watch out for the Big Three.

Women are physical, emotional, and spiritual in nature, and all three areas have their weak spots. In Eve's case, the serpent sank his fangs into all three, by appealing to her physical appetite for food, her emotional appreciation of beauty, and her spiritual desire to be like God. Satan uses exactly the same tactics today. He's not creative in the least, just persistent. By identifying our weaknesses in all three areas, then arming ourselves with biblical defense methods, we can keep from experiencing our own daily (hourly!) reenactment of the Fall.

> For everything in the world—the cravings of sinful man, the lust of his eyes and the boasting of what he has and does—comes not from the Father but from the world. *1 John 2:16*

Let's avoid the blame game.

As one of six kids, I remember shouting at a very young age, "Not me! Not me!" Shifting blame is practically an American pastime. So whom shall we blame for our proclivity to sin? Our mothers? Our grandmothers? Wanna go all the way back to Eve? Or take a page from Adam's diary and blame God— "It's your fault, Lord. You made me this way!" No. God gave us his Spirit to empower us, his Word to strengthen us, and his Son to catch us when we fall. We have no one to blame but ourselves when we choose to sin. And no one to thank but our Creator when he chooses to save us from our sins...again.

> Who will rescue me from this body of death? Thanks be to God— through Jesus Christ our Lord! *Romans 7:24-25*

Good Girl Thoughts Worth Considering

1. Eve's first two mistakes involved getting into a discussion with the serpent about what God had and had not said. Have you ever walked into that kind of trap, either in your own heart or face to face with someone who doubted God's Word? Did it have the outcome you hoped for? What did you learn from the experience? What might you do next time?

2. Her next two mistakes weren't oral but visual: She was looking in the wrong place. Her eyes were on herself instead of God, and she wanted her eyes to be opened. Have you ever gone exploring with your eyes wide open and discovered more than you bargained for? What leads us into the temptation to look in the wrong places? What practical methods could we use to keep our eyes on God?

3. Eve wanted to be like God, knowing good and evil. "I can do it myself" and "I know best" often spill out of our minds if not our mouths. Find three verses in Scripture that emphasize why being like God is impossible and wanting to be so is sinful.

4. Eve couldn't stop looking at the tree or listening to her growling stomach or marveling at how pretty the fruit was or thinking how helpful it would be to have more knowledge. Our craving for *more* is manifested in every area of our lives. What do you want more of right now physically? Emotionally? Spiritually? Do any of those desires dovetail with the Word and will of God? If not, how can you adjust them to be Christ-centered rather than me-centered?

5. At the very point Eve could have stopped herself, she didn't. Been there? How do you feel when you don't stop? How do you feel when you *do* manage to control that urge to sin? What have you learned from those encounters? Eve *did* eat the fruit. What might you have said to her just before the first bite? What about *after* that fatal bite? When she offered Adam a taste, she sinned again. What thought processes do we need to go through to stop such a cycle of sin in our own lives and the tragedy of encouraging others to sin with us?

6. Eve's big cover-up came next. Hiding behind skimpy leaves, then hiding behind trees. Can you think of a time you physically tried to cover up the evidence of sin? Was it effective? Why or why not? Is covering up as "serious" a sin as the initial act of disobedience? Why or why not?

7. Her final mistake was one we all make: putting the blame on someone else. "The snake tricked me" was her ploy. Who or what do you tend to blame first when you sin: a friend? Your parents? Your husband or children? Your job situation? Your finances? The Adversary? The Lord? How can we stop playing the blame game? What's the biblical model for handling sin in our lives, step by step? Can you come up with a handy reminder for those important steps?

8. What's the most important lesson you learned from the story of this mother of all Bad Girls, Eve?

BORED TO
DISTRACTION

2

Heaven has no rage like love to hatred turned,
Nor hell a fury like a woman scorned.

WILLIAM CONGREVE

Mitzi leaned across the breakfast table toward her husband, making sure she was offering him an eyeful. "So…may I serve you something else before you head to the office?"

Apparently his eyes were too full of the morning news to notice.

"Speaking of the office, honey, you're gonna love the new guy." Christopher rustled the front pages of the *Indianapolis Star* with authority, not even glancing up to check if she was listening. "Hired him last month, and already I can see potential. Joe's a real go-getter but solid, too. The kind of man you can trust with the company bankbook." Chris lowered the paper long enough to give her a meaningful wink. "And everything else."

Buster, if you only knew. But he didn't know, couldn't imagine how lonely her days were, waiting for him to get home from work and give her the attention she deserved.

She rose from the soft tapestry cushions of one of her brand-new dining room chairs, an expensive addition to a house already crammed with pricey furniture from the best stores on Allisonville Road. They'd lived in Indianapolis for a dozen years, but no matter how much she decorated the place, it still didn't feel like home.

"Home is where your husband is," her mother-in-law had chided her more than once.

"Then tell *him* to stay home!" she'd snapped back.

Mitzi poured Chris a fresh cup of his favorite custom-blended coffee, then another for herself, enjoying the rich aroma and smiling to herself. Delicious, yes, but not nearly as appealing as the musky aftershave Joe had been wearing at the company picnic last weekend.

Did Christopher think she was blind? That she didn't see the handsome young guy with his lean muscles and big, brown eyes? *Fat chance I'd miss a hunk like that.*

She had eyed him at a distance, found an excuse to stand near him, then pretended not to notice him. *Noticing me.* Must have been the jumpsuit cut to *there* that caught his eye, precisely as she'd planned.

Oh, she'd heard the rumors. That he was a real do-gooder. Lived a squeaky-clean lifestyle. Was religious to a fault.

Perfect. She needed a challenge. Christopher was too easy to fool, too trusting. The man left her alone with no one to keep her company but a housekeeper, a gardener, and the UPS guy daily bringing her another box of flimsy lingerie ordered from one of her stacks of catalogs.

Not that Christopher ever paid any attention to what she wore. The dinner menu—now *that* garnered his interest. He pored over back issues of *Gourmet* and *Bon Appétit* as if they were Holy Writ. She, however, ate as little as possible. How else was she going to maintain her twentysomething figure with midlife knocking at her door?

She needed *Joe* knocking at her door. *That* would put a little pep in her step, a little glide in her stride. Mitzi knew exactly how to make that dream come true too.

Her voice dripped like honey. "Will you be home in time for dinner, Christopher?"

"Not tonight, sweetheart." Snapping the paper shut and tossing it aside, he stretched to his feet. "Meetings with the CEO all day. I'm his right-hand man, remember? Gotta be there to keep things on track. We're sponsoring a racecar in the 500 this May, which means a longer-than-usual meeting right through lunch, right through dinner."

The Indy 500. Fast cars. Faster men. A shiver of delight tingled up her spine.

He shrugged into his suit coat. "I hate those catered boardroom meals.

Taste like cardboard." He tweaked her nose. "Not like the feasts my wife arranges for me. Rack of lamb. Lobster bisque. Blackened trout." He groaned with pleasure. "Makes my mouth water just to think about it."

Mitzi forced a smile to her lips. *If only you knew how hungry I am, husband of mine.* "So," she sighed. "When should I expect you?"

He twirled the keys to his Porsche around his finger. "Probably won't get home until ten at the earliest. Why? Miss me already?"

Oh, I'll miss you, all right. Joe will come and go before you ever darken this door. "Not to worry. I'll be fine."

He bent down to press his lips lightly on her forehead. *Not even a kiss on the mouth!* Who could blame her for looking elsewhere for love and affection? She was a passionate woman. She deserved a lover who was her equal. Joe was apparently gung-ho about experiencing joy in the spirit. *Wait until he gets a taste of joy in the flesh!* Mitzi casually waved at Christopher's car backing down the drive as she composed a mental list of the tasks required for the hours ahead.

She made a few phone calls. Told the gardener to take the day off. Ditto with the housekeeper. Hung a note from the front doorknob asking UPS to leave any packages on the porch. No doorbells ringing, please. She might be napping.

Correction. She might be in bed if all went as planned.

And not alone.

Mitzi felt her palms sweating as she punched in the numbers for her husband's company. Not his private line. The switchboard. She inched her voice up a few notes and slipped in a southern drawl just to be safe. "Joe in Property Management, please." She didn't know his last name. For that matter, he didn't know her first name. *Better that way.*

When he came on the line, Mitzi dropped her voice back down to its usual husky pitch. "Joe? This is Christopher's wife." She could almost hear his ears perk up, his voice take on a tone of respect. "That's right," she purred. "We saw each other at the picnic. So glad to have you as part of our...family." She swallowed, stealing a quick glance at herself in the mirror to bolster her resolve. "I need a favor, if you don't mind. Chris has already driven off and won't be back until late tonight. Unfortunately he left behind his file on the racecar sponsorship, along with his cell phone, so I can't reach him. If he doesn't have this file for the meeting at ten…ah, I knew you'd understand."

She listened to his warm, confident voice, feeling a flush begin at her toes and move slowly toward her hairline. Yes, he assured her, he'd be happy to come over. Might she give him directions? *Oh, might she!* He'd be there in thirty minutes, since the traffic on Route 465 was bound to be heavy. Would that be soon enough? *Hurry, Joe, hurry!*

Moments later, she slipped into a steaming hot tub, brimming with fragrant bubbles. "Calvin Klein, take me away!" Her throaty laugh echoed around the tiled room. No, not Calvin. *Joseph.* Yes, she liked that. His given name. *His biblical name,* Mitzi realized with a sly grin.

Toweling off, she slathered her skin with a liberal dollop of lotion, heavy with the scent of Obsession, then flung open her closet doors. The scarlet gown, of course. Fit her like a silk glove. Left almost nothing to the imagination. Paired with a sheer, gauzy robe with a single clasp. Red slippers with little heels that made her legs look their shapeliest. Obsession sprayed everywhere.

She bent her head to brush her hair in long strokes from the nape of her neck to the tawny gold ends, then tossed it over her shoulders, enjoying the feel of it tickling her nearly bare back.

A brisk knock at the door sent her heart knocking in its cage.

Joseph!

She practically skipped down the stairs, then paused on the marble landing to catch her breath. *Not so eager,* she chided herself.

Assuming an air of youthful innocence, she pulled open the heavy oak door and let a look of surprise dance across her face. "Joe, you must be a man on a mission. I bet you made it out to my corner of the world in twenty minutes, tops."

The handsome, dark-haired man looked shocked, then shifted his gaze to the planters on either side of the entrance. She took in his freshly shaven cheeks, now pink with embarrassment. His eyes, fringed with long, dark lashes, paused at half-mast while he tried hard to look anywhere but at her.

Mitzi stretched out her hand to catch his, forcing him to meet her gaze. "Silly man! Have you never seen a woman in her pajamas? You merely got here too fast for me to change, that's all. The phone rang, and well...you know." How easily lies slipped from her well-oiled lips. "Come in, come in. Let me see if I can find that pesky file folder for you."

Clearly reluctant, he followed her in, pulling his hand out of hers as quickly as he could. "I'll wait here while you look." His voice sounded pinched; his expression was one of pure agony.

Closing the door behind them, she toyed with locking it, then thought better of it. *Too calculated.* She pretended to search for the imaginary folder, displaying her best assets as she knelt and stretched around every shelf and table in the foyer and hall.

Hmm. This might be harder than she'd thought. He looked so nervous! She offered him coffee, but he shook his head. "A bagel perhaps?" No, he didn't want that. Couldn't eat a thing, he insisted. "At least let me take your coat," she murmured, slipping it off his shoulders before he could protest, letting her hands brush against his shirt long enough to feel the tension in his muscles.

Subtlety was getting her nowhere, she decided. They were both adults. Why be coy? She fixed her eyes on his with a brazen boldness. "Joseph, do you know why I invited you here this morning?"

"It's becoming clearer by the moment, ma'am." His voice was steady, firm. So were the lines of his mouth.

"Good." She nodded, relieved. "Then we don't need to play games, do we? I want you, Joe. It's as simple as that."

He cleared his throat and took a step backward, pressing his broad shoulders against the massive front door. "Not simple at all. You're Christopher's wife. He gave me this job, promoted me to manager. He trusts me with...he trusts me with everything."

She watched him gulp and wipe his hands along the sides of his suit pants. *At least I'm making him sweat.* It gave her a perverse pleasure to see how she affected him.

Laughter spilled from her lips. "Come to bed with me, Joe. Believe me,

Chris not only won't know, he wouldn't care." *Not entirely true, but Joe obviously needs convincing.*

He groped for the knob behind him, then yanked the door open with surprising force. "You don't understand! It isn't only Christopher I'm worried about. This...this is a *sin.* A sin against the Lord. The Lord I love with all my heart."

"The Lord!" she sputtered. "What has God got to do with this?"

A grim smile moved across his face. "Everything."

Joe bolted down the stone path and into the company van before she could stop him, then started the engine with a grinding roar. The white vehicle careened down the driveway and backed onto the street, lurching forward with a squeal of tires.

"Well!" She slammed the door in disgust. *Now what?* Bad enough that she'd been made to feel foolish. Dirty even, blast his altar-boy heart. The morning had been a waste of perfectly good perfume.

Then it dawned on her. What if he told Christopher? Or blabbed to his coworkers and one of them told Christopher? *No, no, that can't happen!* It'd ruin everything.

As she looked down, a wave of relief washed over her. *His jacket!* He'd left behind his jacket. *Perfect.* All the proof she'd need to show Chris what had really happened. Joe had shown up out of nowhere. Caught her halfdressed. Forced his way into the house. *Yes!* Forced himself on her, but she'd refused, started screaming, and he took off in the van. *Yes!*

His word against hers. And which one of them would her husband believe?

His wife, of course.

Even as she hit the redial button, Mitzi could feel the sweet taste of revenge rising in her throat. *You'll pay, Joe. You'll pay. And more than a tithe of your income, you holier-than-thou jerk!*

Now it was time for serious damage control. When she heard the receptionist's voice on the line, Mitzi snapped on a teary sob the way most women flick on a light switch. "Uh, B-Betty? Is that you? Oh, I'm...I'm so...scared! Is Christopher there? Please. Tell him I need to talk to him.

Yes, yes, interrupt the meeting. Right away! The most unbelievable thing has happened…"

A Bad Girl in Pharaoh's Court: Potiphar's Wife

> Now Joseph had been taken down to Egypt. Potiphar, an Egyptian who was one of Pharaoh's officials, the captain of the guard, bought him from the Ishmaelites who had taken him there.… Joseph found favor in his eyes and became his attendant. Potiphar put him in charge of his household, and he entrusted to his care everything he owned. *Genesis 39:1,4*

The bored wife. The hired man.

It happened some thirty-five centuries ago, and still the story has the power to take our breath away at the audacity of a woman who thought she could ignore her marriage vows and graze in greener pastures.

She was known simply as Potiphar's wife.

The woman didn't even have a *name*. One of the major hussies of the Bible, and she didn't possess a simple moniker to call her own.

"The wife of." Period.

We can imagine her propped up against a stone pillar at one of Pharaoh's lavish feasts, adorned in her best plaited wig, drenched in her costliest perfume—the ancient equivalent of Obsession, no doubt—when a woman of higher station strolled by in her spun-gold sandals and pointed a ruby-ringed finger in her direction.

"Hmm. Potiphar's wife, isn't it?"

Potiphar. Her meal ticket. Undoubtedly a big guy, and not only in position. Potiphar was the head of Pharaoh's bodyguards, and as such was surely a large man—wide shoulders, bulging biceps, broad chest. The biggest and baddest of them all. Been around awhile. Past his youth but not past his prime in the bodyguard business.

Everyone knew Potiphar.

No one cared enough to remember his wife's name.

Many a man enjoys having a trophy wife to display on his arm. *She's mine,* his eyes say as he pats his wife's soft hand possessively. Who knows if Potiphar's wife saw herself that way? It's possible she liked the title, liked the flicker of admiration she saw in a stranger's eyes when she introduced herself as the proud wife of Potiphar, a man who had access to the Egyptian courts and to the ear of Pharaoh himself.

Or she may have grown weary of the limitations of the title, of having her entire being defined by her marriage to a powerful man. With a house full of servants, she clearly had too few responsibilities and too much time on her hands. As one writer put it, "Idleness became the soil that nourished her sinful thoughts."[1]

Potiphar's wife. Even without a name she has become synonymous with lust and licentiousness.

Did God know her name? Absolutely. Why is it not recorded in Scripture then? One commentator suggested, "There is no satisfactory answer to the silence of Scripture regarding the identity of its nameless women."[2] And there were lots of them, Good Girls and Bad Girls both, identified by what they did, whom they married or gave birth to, or where they hailed from. More than a hundred women are simply described in Scripture as the "daughter of," "wife of," "witch of," "woman of," "concubine of," "widow of," "nurse of," "Queen of" (well, *that* one has merit), and, naturally, the "mother of" someone more famous than she is.

I know that one well. At my children's schools, I'm the mother of Matthew, the mother of Lillian, or Carpool Mother #27. I have no name, no identity. They recognize my minivan but not my name.

"Aren't you Lillian's mother?"

Sigh.

Potiphar's wife would've understood. Though she's infamously *Bad to the Bone,* she's also one of the no-names of the Bible.

I'll bet Joseph knew her name. Joseph, the Hebrew boy sold into slavery by his jealous brothers, then chosen—purchased, that is—by Potiphar from the Ishmaelites.

Our man Mr. Potiphar was known for physical prowess certainly. Intellectual strength? Maybe not. Yet he did realize what a fine bargain he'd made in buying Joseph. In no time Potiphar moved Joseph up the ladder from lowly servant to right-hand man for one reason: God was faithful to Joseph because Joseph was faithful to God.

Potiphar knew a good thing when he saw it.

> So he left in Joseph's care everything he had; with Joseph in charge, he did not concern himself with anything except the food he ate.
> *Genesis 39:6*

Am I the only woman who sees a red flag waving here? Potiphar's only concern was...dinner? Breakfast and lunch, too. Snacks, maybe? One scholar suggested that Mr. P's preoccupation with food might have been due to the ritual separation outlined in Genesis 43, "because Egyptians could not eat with Hebrews, for that is detestable to Egyptians."[3] Or, that Potiphar "worried really about nothing any longer except his own food."[4]

Consider Potiphar himself. The beefy bodybuilder, the head of the guards, the musclebound bouncer. A man with an oversized appetite, busy caring for the needs of his stomach while ignoring the needs of his wife, who we'll see in a moment had a few hungers of her own that required tending.

Make no mistake. She *is* the Bad Girl in this story. But her inattentive husband, with his belly full of food and a busy work schedule, unquestionably contributed to her wandering eye.

And Joseph gave her plenty to gawk at.

> Now Joseph was well-built and handsome. *Genesis 39:6*

Stop right there, girls. Most of our Bible heroes and heroines are not described in any physical detail. That makes these few words about Joseph— incidentally, the precise words used to describe his mother, Rachel—take on even more importance. Call Joseph what you will—beefcake, hunk-o-rama, stud muffin—the man had serious curb appeal. He was young, attractive in form and face, bright, a fast learner, eager to serve, a natural leader.

He was also in waaay over his head.

Joseph, fresh from the fields and thrust into the corrupt luxury of city life in Egypt, had his faith and fidelity to God tested in short order. Hebrew to the core, he was nonetheless soon dressed "in the white pleated garments of his adopted country, shaved and perfumed, an Egyptian in all save his blood."[5]

Oooh baby.

Joseph not only looked good, he *knew* he looked good. Beautiful Rachel, who had waited so long to have a child, must have lavished her son with praise, as did his father, Jacob, who called Joseph his favorite son. A label which, as we know, bugged his brothers plenty.

Joseph. A handsome young man, a slave in name only, confident of himself and his God. Paraded before an older woman who was neglected, needy, and hungry for attention.

Honey, could anything but this have happened?

> And after a while his master's wife took notice of Joseph and said... *Genesis 39:7*

Hold it.

"After a while"? *How long?* we wonder. What was she doing in the meantime? Spending time with another lover? Decorating her finely appointed rooms? Getting fitted for a collection of new, more revealing linen tunics?

Or was she resisting temptation? Looking the other way? Hanging around the clay ovens in the kitchen, longing to be near her famished husband, hoping he'd drop his bowl of lentils long enough to give her the time of day?

The truth is, we can't tell at this point in the story. This is her one big scene, after which Mrs. P is never mentioned in Scripture again.

She made quite an entrance, though, with her eye-popping opening line.

> "Come to bed with me!" *Genesis 39:7*

The woman was not subtle. As the wife of a powerful man, she was clearly accustomed to getting exactly what she wanted. And what she wanted was Joseph, hubby's handsome slave. As a foreigner, Joseph was forbidden fruit, and Potiphar's wife knew that. It was undoubtedly part of the attraction. They were complete opposites. She was older; he was younger. She was married; he was single. She was Egyptian; he was Hebrew. She had no morals; he had high morals. She worshiped the flesh; he worshiped in spirit.

Opposites *do* attract. Here, however, the electricity was flowing in only one direction, as his response indicates.

> But he refused. *Genesis 39:8*

Details, we want details.

We can picture her draped across a fifteenth-century B.C. version of a king-size sofa bed, batting her kohl-rimmed eyes in his direction. We can picture this chick-magnet with arms folded, chin held high, shaking his handsome Hebrew head.

But such pictures are left to our imaginations. We only know that he refused. Period. Then Joseph explained why.

> "With me in charge," he told her, "my master does not concern
> himself with anything in the house; everything he owns he has
> entrusted to my care. No one is greater in this house than I am."
> *Genesis 39:8-9*

Well, I guess he told *her.* Perhaps there'd been other slaves before Joseph who'd said yes to her advances. This one said no, not because he found *her* unappealing but because the very idea of abusing the trust of his master and the laws of his Lord made his freshly shaven Hebrew skin pale.

> "My master has withheld nothing from me except you, because you
> are his wife. How then could I do such a wicked thing and sin
> against God?" *Genesis 39:9*

There is no suggestion that Joseph was genuinely tempted by her offer. Remember, we know that *he* was comely; we know nothing of *her* appearance. Was she herself beautiful, used to having young lovers falling at her feet? Or was she a plain woman who, by propositioning her own slave, was willing, in essence, to pay for his services? Or—a third possibility—was she suffering an Egyptian midlife crisis, wondering if she still had what it took to catch the eye of a younger man?

The "why" really matters not. Adultery was a major no-no in ancient days, one of the most serious crimes. Only death was considered a suffi-cient penalty.[6] For Joseph, it went deeper than that. He saw it as a sin against his God, Yahweh.

Ten points for Joseph. Zero for Potiphar's wife.

If she'd quit there, apologized, and begged his forgiveness, she'd undoubtedly have been relegated to our list of *Bad for a Moment* Girls. But as "the first sensualist in the gallery of scriptural women,"[7] she pressed the point. Scorned by a slave—an uppity slave, at that!—she persisted in her pursuit of the stubborn lad.

> And though she spoke to Joseph day after day, he refused to go to
> bed with her or even be with her. *Genesis 39:10*

As the song (sort of) says: "And here's to you, Mrs. Potiphar; Joseph loathes you more than you will know. Whoa, whoa, whoa."

"Whoa" is right! Stop already with the come-hither glances and the languid smiles, Mrs. P.

But she didn't stop.

"Day after day" means we could hardly chalk this up to a weak moment on her part. She was morally corrupt and persistent to a fault.

She did lower her sights though, seeking a compromise with Joseph. "Just be with me then? Keep me company?" The words of a forgotten woman. Honestly, where was old Potiphar? Still banging together those pots and pans while his wife tried to get something cooking in their bedroom? Guarding Pharaoh when he should have been guarding his wife's reputation?

Hers was a sin of commission; her husband's, one of omission. He should've paid more attention to her, we might argue. Spent his time building hedges around their marriage with vines of love and affection instead of building a name for himself in Pharaoh's court.

But the worst sin Potiphar can be accused of is ignorance.

His wife, however, stands accused of sinning against a foreign God she didn't comprehend, one who has a moral interest in his people. What a concept for an Egyptian! Her only god was her body and its physical appetites. Though she didn't know Yahweh, her adulterous behavior still broke one of the cardinal rules of her age. Men of the time could have many wives, but a wife was bound to absolute fidelity and could belong to only one man.[8]

Mrs. P was *Bad to the Bone* indeed. She didn't give a fig or a grape leaf about Joseph's God or his morals. In fact, she no doubt found the challenge appetizing.

We don't know her heart, black as it appears. We don't know her history. We don't know if she was ruled by her lust or lonely to the core. We *do* know that her pride wouldn't let her take Joseph's no for an answer.

> One day he went into the house to attend to his duties, and none
> of the household servants was inside. *Genesis 39:11*

Uh-oh. An empty house? At whose doing? "None" of the servants? It's hard to believe *that* wasn't arranged.

Enter Mrs. P, who might aptly be portrayed the way actress Tallulah Bankhead once described herself: "Pure as driven slush."

> She caught him by his cloak and said, "Come to bed with me!" But
> he left his cloak in her hand and ran out of the house. *Genesis 39:12*

Don't let that cloak thing fool you. Other translations call it his garment, which was actually an *under*garment, a long shirt tied at the hips. After all, he was inside the house in a dry, hot land—no coats required.

Let's ask the obvious question: Why was Joseph close enough for her to grab his unmentionables in the first place? Was she hiding behind Curtain Number Three, waiting to grab him as he strolled by on his master's business? Or did Joseph get closer than he should have, then abruptly change his mind?

Since he faithfully refused her "day after day," we'll assume it was Mrs. P's antics all the way. Clearly she set Joseph up, caught him by surprise, and left him no choice but to flee into the courtyard, as one scholar noted, "completely undressed, at once disgracefully and honorably."[9] Many a man has left evidence of his indiscretions, but poor Joseph was merely trying to get away with his virtue intact, if not his wardrobe. He could hardly risk going back, even though he surely knew where all this would lead.

Perhaps Paul was thinking of young Joseph when he wrote, "Flee the evil desires of youth, and pursue righteousness."[10] Joseph, righteous to the end, took off running. Try as we might to look at all viewpoints in this dramatic scene, there's no question that Joseph did right in the eyes of God and Potiphar's wife showed her true colors. Unlike Joseph's coat of many colors, hers came in one shade: solid black.

> When she saw that he had left his cloak in her hand and had run
> out of the house, she called her household servants. "Look," she

said to them, "this Hebrew has been brought to us to make sport of us!" *Genesis 39:13-14*

She hollered to her household servants, eh? The same ones she had sent outside while she pitched her woo? My, how this woman loved to order people around! She didn't succeed in committing adultery with Joseph, but she was very successful in lying, pinning the blame on "this Hebrew," insisting he shamed not only her but "us." Scorned by the upright slave, she turned her passion into a prejudicial put-down.

> "He came in here to sleep with me, but I screamed. When he heard me scream for help, he left his cloak beside me and ran out of the house." *Genesis 39:14-15*

Gee. *I* didn't hear a scream. Did you hear a scream?

Any scriptwriter worth his salt would flag such a glaring oversight. If Mrs. P had *really* screamed while Joseph was still there "making sport of her" as it were, wouldn't the servants have come running and stumbled over the hotfooting-it Joseph? Instead, after the young man was long gone, *then* she had to yell for them to come in.

They were servants, yes, but they were not fools. If the boss lady said she screamed for help, so be it. Notice, not a single response from the servants is recorded. Maybe they saw through her lies. Maybe they saw the fleeing Joseph—without his cloak, he would have been hard to miss, tearing across the courtyard. Maybe they'd all succumbed to her demands themselves at one time or another and now served as her kangaroo court, ready to pass judgment on the innocent Joseph, "that Hebrew."

Besides, she *did* have the man's cloak in hand. That was proof enough for anybody, even Mr. P.

> She kept his cloak beside her until his master came home.
> *Genesis 39:16*

Any lingering drop of sympathy for the woman dries up with this single-line scenario. You can imagine her sliding her hands over the threads of the cloak next to her, perhaps even holding it to her face, breathing in the scent of Joseph's body, letting her lust turn to anger, then revenge, then a bald-faced lie. She accused the innocent Joseph of the very behavior of which she herself was guilty.

An evil woman scorned is frightening to behold. One writer noted, "How quickly the heat of her passion hardened into hatred."[11] The vitriol of Mrs. P's dark soul echoes through the ages. *How dare he reject me, the fool! Wait until Potiphar hears about this.*

Might Mrs. P be the woman mentioned in Proverbs? "For the lips of an adulteress drip honey, and her speech is smoother than oil; but in the end she is bitter as gall, sharp as a double-edged sword."[12]

One smooth lie always begets another.

This lie was so smooth it sailed right over poor Potiphar's head.

> When his master heard the story his wife told him, saying, "This is
> how your slave treated me," he burned with anger. *Genesis 39:19*

Oh, that's rich. "Your slave." In other words, it was Potiphar's fault for bringing this Hebrew into her presence in the first place. I'm reminded of Adam's answer to the Lord's question about why he'd tasted the forbidden fruit: "The woman you put here with me..."[13] In other words, "*You* gave her to me, Lord. Your fault! Your fault!"

Adam didn't get away with that one.

Did Mrs. P's blame-shifting work for her?

Potiphar got angry, but at whom? Joseph was the obvious target of his wrath, although if Potiphar had been truly convinced of the young Hebrew's guilt, the punishment would've been clear and swift: death for the foreigner. Wasn't Potiphar the chief guard? All would've believed Potiphar.

But Potiphar believed Joseph, the man he had entrusted with all his worldly goods. He couldn't kill a man he knew in his heart to be innocent.

> Joseph's master took him and put him in prison, the place where
> the king's prisoners were confined. *Genesis 39:20*

Prison, yes. Death, no. In fact, Joseph was soon put in charge of the prison, started interpreting Pharaoh's dreams, and...well, you know the rest.

But what of Potiphar's unfaithful wife? One author suggested that Potiphar's "fierce, possessive love blinded him to the wickedness thinly veiled to all but him."[14]

That veil isn't thin, babe; it's transparent. I think Potiphar had sufficient gray matter to see through his wife's lies, enough to spare Joseph and, in truth, to avoid adding to his own shame.

The innocent got hauled off to jail. The guilty got away with murdering a young man's reputation. In one fell swoop, Potiphar's wife managed to commit a whole host of sins without blushing, let alone repenting. Sadly, "she was not only a sensualist but a coward who could not admit her own guilt."[15]

This one's for you, Mrs. P:

> There are six things the LORD hates,
>> seven that are detestable to him:
>>> haughty eyes,
>>> a lying tongue,
>>> hands that shed innocent blood,
>>> a heart that devises wicked schemes,
>>> feet that are quick to rush into evil,
>>> a false witness who pours out lies
>>> and a man who stirs up dissension among
>>>> brothers. *Proverbs 6:16-19*

Seven points for Mrs. P—all on the losing side.

While Yahweh stood by Joseph, in jail and everywhere else, Potiphar's wife was left alone in her own sort of prison, its iron bars forged from lust, revenge, and lies. Her warden? Hubby dearest, his eyes smoldering with a lingering distrust.

What Lessons Can We Learn from Mrs. P?

We gotta stay on our toes.

We never know when temptation will arrive at our doorsteps. We can't assume that because we're happily married or content in our singleness a hunky delivery guy or a cute carpenter working on our new guestroom can't possibly shift our fertile imaginations into overdrive. It happens to Christian women every day, with tragic consequences. Stretch those toes, girls!

Be very careful, then, how you live—not as unwise but as wise, making the most of every opportunity, because the days are evil. *Ephesians 5:15-16*

It's smart to surround ourselves with support.

Mrs. P sent the servants away. Bad move, honey. Let's leave the office door open when we meet with a male coworker. Take the kids with us when we sit outside to chat with the handsome handyman. Not to mention making sure we're appropriately dressed! Carry along a photo of hubby when we travel, and display it on the nightstand. We're one-man women, right? Married to an earthly husband *or* a heavenly one, our motto is: Never leave home without him foremost in our hearts and minds.

Put on the full armor of God so that you can take your stand against the devil's schemes. *Ephesians 6:11*

Let's seek out our husbands before not after.

If movie stars and paperback heroes are filling our minds with images that don't honor God or our husbands, suppose we find those men of ours—in the kitchen, the garage, wherever—wrap our arms around their broad shoulders and whisper the same words that Mrs. P first said to Joseph. If you're married to the man, it's not only legal, it's biblical! Trust me, Joseph may have refused, but your hubby will undoubtedly be delighted with your invitation, however unexpected it may be.

"Your desire will be for your husband." *Genesis 3:16*

When we stumble, confession beats a cover-up.

How easy it is to blame someone else when we're tempted to sin. It's "his" fault, "her" fault, or when all else fails, it's God's fault. Potiphar may not have seen through his wife's lies, but the Lord we love looks straight into our hearts. Instead of going for a cover-up, let's confess and repent. The snazziest lipstick in the world can't compete with clean lips…and a clean heart.

Save me, O LORD, from lying lips and from deceitful tongues. *Psalm 120:2*

Good Girl Thoughts Worth Considering

1. How do you feel when people refer to you as "the wife of," "the mother of," "the daughter of," or "the secretary of"? Is there a tactful way to share a wider view of your identity, for their sake and your own?

2. What are some ways you can take pride in your various roles, without letting them become a wall you hide behind?

3. The story of the scorned adulteress is a common one in movies and literature. Can you think of any examples? Do the stories ever have a happy ending? What are the repercussions?

4. Was Potiphar at all to blame for his wife's wandering eye? If so, how did he fail her? What could she have done to garner his attention? In your own life, if you're married, does your husband ever behave like Potiphar? How might you get *his* attention? Might a woman make the same mistake, ignoring her husband and pushing him into another woman's arms? If you're single, how can you avoid "catching" such a man and convincing yourself that if his wife can't make him happy, you can?

5. How can we fill our idle time (if we have any!) with appropriate thoughts? Are there specific things you need to avoid, such as R-rated movies? Internet temptations? Graphic novels? Make a list, then make a commitment to steer clear of those things that appeal to your flesh at the risk of your spiritual growth.

6. Could Joseph, the godly man in both the fictional and biblical stories, have taken any steps to avoid the revenge-filled conclusion? How should a godly person handle such an unfair and false accusation?

7. Though her obvious sin was lust, perhaps the root of Mrs. P's sin was anger. How does that same sin rear its ugly head in your own life, and what could you do to surrender that specific sin to the lordship of Christ?

8. What's the most important lesson you've learned from the tragic, timeless story of Potiphar's wife?

PILLAR OF THE COMMUNITY

3

Dust in the air suspended
Marks the place where a story ended.

Thomas Stearns Eliot

The first day of spring, huh? Could've fooled me."

Lottie gathered her wool cape tighter around her shoulders, holding the chilly March winds at bay while she gazed across the icy expanse of Spirit Lake. The surface, still frozen solid, was riddled with hairline cracks. Had she noticed them yesterday?

"What's the difference? I'm not likely to strap on a pair of ice skates anytime soon now, am I?" Her voice was a sharp knife, cutting through the frigid afternoon air.

Lottie was speaking to no one. Or to anyone who would listen.

Her solo hours perched on the steep terrain surrounding the lake were a source of amusement to her family. To her, they were sanity itself. As the wife of a gregarious salesman who talked incessantly on the phone and the mother of two teenage daughters who giggled nonstop, Lottie found peaceful solace wherever she could.

Today she embraced the cold serenity of her surroundings, even as they wrapped her in a welcome cocoon of silence. The only voice she heard was her own. *What a relief!* She laughed out loud for the sheer joy of it.

After standing to brush aside a fallen branch, Lottie turned back and released a soft murmur of satisfaction, her warm breath visible in the frosty air. She never wearied of gazing at her lakeside cabin nestled in the sheltering arms of the Cascades. Hadn't she designed it herself after years of thumbing through dog-eared copies of *Architectural Digest* and *House Beautiful*? Its graceful wooden lines seemed at one with the environment, exactly as she'd planned.

"You'll have to carry me out of here in a pine box," she'd informed her builder after the last nail was hammered home. "At the very least I want my ashes scattered over the lake." When everything else in life disappointed her, Lottie always had her dream house, her pride and delight.

She glanced at her watch. *Quarter to four.* Should she keep walking or head back and start dinner? The girls wanted pasta. Again. Her husband was on the road for—

Her mental monologue ended abruptly, cut short by an eerie sound, like the low rumble of faraway thunder.

What in the world...?

Beneath her feet the ground began to shake. *An earthquake?* It hardly seemed possible, but the evidence was all around her. Swaying trees above. Jostling rocks underfoot. Across Spirit Lake sharp reports resembling gunshots echoed as the ice splintered in jagged cracks.

Stunned, Lottie dropped to her haunches, feeling dizzy and disoriented. Seconds later the tremors stopped as quickly as they'd begun. Her internal shaking, though, kept going. She rose slowly to her feet, her knees trembling, her breathing ragged. Other than the cracked ice, all appeared normal again, as if nothing had happened.

But something *had* happened. Something more significant than the minor rumblings they'd had over the last few days. Those were barely mentioned in the six o'clock news. This would be the lead story. Probably four-something on the Richter scale.

She stumbled toward the house, keeping her eyes on her beloved wraparound porch. Behind and above it loomed a massive, snow-covered giant stretching nearly ten thousand feet into the southern Washington sky.

Mount St. Helens. The quietest of all her neighbors.

Exactly one week later the no-longer-silent mountain made news again. This time an explosion of steam blasted out the top vent. In the days that followed, smoke and sulfurous gases spewed from the peak at odd hours without warning.

Around the lakefront, rumors flew like falling ash.

"Lottie, they're saying the government is gonna make us evacuate." Brigid's piercing blue eyes sparked with anger. The older woman had lived on Spirit Lake longer than any of them. "It's on account of those scientific geeks crawling all over our mountain, measuring every little hiccup. What do they know? St. Helens could go on like this for years, decades, and never hurt a soul."

Lottie nodded, letting the woman blow off her own head of steam. She'd heard similar complaints from the handful of Spirit Lake residents and vowed not to get caught up in their whirlwind of anxiety. No matter who came knocking on her door, Lottie was staying put with her house, her family, and her dogs. She wasn't easily intimidated, especially not by smoke and rumors.

Come April, the ominous rumblings were fewer and farther between, but when they came, they were significant. Lottie spent her mornings on the porch, stitchery in hand, an Irish setter on each side and one eye trained on the north slope of the mountain. Curiosity seekers soon started arriving, poking their four-wheel-drive vehicles into everyone else's business and trampling the wildflowers before the tiny beauties had the slightest chance to blossom.

In the afternoons, to escape the circus atmosphere Lottie stayed inside and counted. Counting things gave her a sense of peace and control. She never counted money—how vulgar!—but an inventory of her possessions never failed to push away her fears and give her a measure of comfort.

She started with big things—couches and chairs, of which she owned eight—then her prized antique oak sideboard, the black deacons bench from back East, the old spinning wheel that had belonged to her grandmother. Her quilts numbered nearly two dozen—twenty-three, in fact—and her handmade baskets totaled twice that. Last year she'd gone through the two-story cabin with a video camera, cataloging each item, secretly pleased when her agent cluck-clucked over the additional insurance she'd have to buy to cover her potentially steep losses.

Well, that was what insurance was for, wasn't it? In case something unexpected happened?

The knock at her door that May afternoon wasn't unexpected…just unwelcome. Her husband's look of apprehension quickly gave away the identity of the two men on their doorstep. Not that their uniforms left any doubt.

"L-Lottie, these are…"

"I know who they are." She released a heavy sigh, swinging the door open wider. "Come in. And wipe your feet if you don't mind."

The two strangers knocked the ash off their hats and boots and stepped inside, following her into the living room with its oversized windows and wide oak beams. She watched their eyes, taking a small amount of pride from their expressions. Clearly they were impressed.

She waited for them to speak, dreading what they would say.

The older of the two cleared his throat. "Ma'am, we need you to pack a few things for yourself and your family."

"You're evacuating us then."

Her husband, standing behind the two men, nodded slowly.

"Fact is, Mrs…uh…"

"Call me Lottie." She'd known their visit was inevitable. The increasing clouds of smoke and ash and the acrid smell of sulfur told her all she needed to know. The reality of it seared her throat and stung her eyes. Blinking hard, she spoke her mind through clenched teeth. "The fact is, gentlemen, the Robertsons left last week and took most of Spirit Lake with them." *Even Brigid.* "We're the last family left."

"That's right, ma'am. The volcanologists are telling us St. Helens could blow any minute."

She felt her nerves snap like a bent twig. "And what if she doesn't blow? What if I abandon my home to looters and thieves who'll carry away everything we've worked so hard for?" The blood pounded in her throat and forehead, making her lightheaded.

The man's raised eyebrow suggested he was losing patience. "If a pyroclastic flow pours down this mountain at eighty miles an hour, Lottie, you won't have to worry about your hewn-log cabin or your expensive furniture. The thirteen-hundred-degree heat will incinerate everything in seconds, then bury it in fifty feet of volcanic debris." His rough voice softened slightly. "Look, I'm sorry to be the bearer of bad tidings. Every minute we're standing here is risky. Now pack some clothes for yourself and your family. We'll be waiting outside with a vehicle to get you to safety. But we gotta move fast. Understood?"

She nodded mutely, not trusting herself to speak without sobbing. *Her house!* Her precious home and all it contained, mere fodder for an angry mountain.

Hearing her daughters whimpering behind her, Lottie whirled around. "Enough of that, girls! I want each of you to pack a suitcase. One dress, one pair of jeans, then anything else you like. But *one* bag each, tops." She waved toward the stairs that led to their bedrooms. "Go on! We can't keep these fellas waiting." Aiming a pointed look at the front door, Lottie added, "They might get a pumice stone in their eyes standing out there."

Her husband hurried after the girls, no doubt planning to pack his own bag full of electronic gear and CDs instead of the slacks and socks he'd be whining for within hours.

No problem. Lottie would pack those herself since she had no intention of leaving. When everyone got in the van, she'd wave them off, then stay behind and hold down the fort, keep an eye on things. They'd be back in a week or two, tails between their legs. In the meantime she'd read a few novels, do some spring cleaning, and enjoy the solitude.

But thirty minutes later when she tried to send them off, the two government types wouldn't hear of it.

"Ma'am, this is not an optional evacuation. We're to get everyone off this mountain, like it or not."

She folded her arms across her chest. "*Not,* then."

He yanked open the door to the vehicle with a groan. "You can't fight us on this. We have our orders, and trust me, they're from the very top. Get in."

Jerking her chin to the side, she threw herself in the backseat next to her wide-eyed daughters and stone-faced husband. The official closed the door behind her with a bang, then settled into the passenger seat in front as the engine roared to life.

His expression grim, he leaned over his left shoulder. "Do yourself a favor, Lottie. Don't look back. It'll only make it worse."

"Oh, right," she fumed, deliberately turning around to stare out the window behind her. "It can't get any worse than this."

They rode in silence while her thoughts turned along desperate paths. Their home was as good as gone. *Gone!* Her lovely things, a lifetime of memories, left behind for no good reason. If the mountain really blew her top, they'd have time to get out, wouldn't they? Surely the lake would quickly cool that pyro-whatever mess. Yes, it was risky, but life was all about risk. Wasn't it hers to take?

Despondent, she turned back around to face forward, her heart broken by her last sight of home now blanketed with a fine layer of ash. Another sobering thought struck her: Would their homeowner's policy cover volcano damage? She almost laughed aloud at the ridiculousness of it all, until a sickening realization washed over her.

The video! She'd forgotten the video, the one with their detailed house inventory, left perched on the bookshelf in her chef's dream of a kitchen. It was the only record she had, her only hope for a fair settlement if it came to that.

"Wait! I need to go back." Lottie gripped the headrest, pulling herself forward. "Please! I forgot the one thing we'll need for our insurance. It won't take me a second to get it, honest. You can leave the engine running if you need to. I promise I'll hurry."

Grumbling under his breath, the driver maneuvered the van around on the narrow, forest-service road, downshifted, then took off with a jarring lurch. Lottie smiled to herself as her home came into view once more, the rocking chair on the porch offering a tantalizing respite from all the doom and gloom around her. Shoving open the van door, she hurried up the steps, catching a glimpse of their own Chevy truck out of the corner of her eye.

Of course! She had her own wheels; she'd get herself out, if and when the time came to flee the mountain's wrath.

Lottie spun on her heels and hurried back down the steps toward the officials, now glaring at her from the front seat. She leaned on the open van window and forced herself to sound sincere. "Fellas, this may take a little while after all. I'm...I'm not sure where I stuck that insurance video. Why don't you go ahead, and I'll follow you in the truck?" She pointed at it with casual indifference. "It has a full tank and four-wheel drive, all ready to go. I won't be long. Deal?"

As expected, her family protested.

"Mo-ther! We gotta *go*—now."

"Lottie, honey, this is *not* the time for arguments."

"C'mon, Mom! That...that *dragon* up there is ready to blow."

Lottie held up her hands, determined to have her way. "I'll be fine. Go on, take off. I'll be along before you miss me. All I need to know is where we're going to meet later."

His lips drawn into a narrow line of frustration, the driver spat out directions to their rendezvous point. "This is highly irregular, ma'am," he insisted. "I hope you won't regret it."

"Nothing to worry about. Now go. I'll see you shortly."

She stood on the bottom porch step, waving as the vanload bumped their way toward uncomfortable motel beds. A slight smile moved across her lips as she turned and climbed the steps. The May evening was warm, the sky smoky but quiet. She'd almost grown accustomed to the faint smell of sulfur in the air.

Dropping into the inviting porch chair, Lottie pointed herself toward the mountain and began rocking in a steady rhythm. "St. Helens, old girl, suppose you do the talking for a change, and I'll just sit here and listen." As the sky darkened, Lottie was lulled to sleep by the sounds of nature all around her and the assurance that when the sun rose, so would she...

> May 18, 1980, 8:32 A.M. PDT: A magnitude 5.1 earthquake occurred one mile beneath Mount St. Helens, releasing an avalanche of rock and ice down the north face of the mountain, completely overtaking Spirit Lake. The resulting tsunami swept water as high as 820 feet, followed by a volcanic eruption of pumice and ash covering 230 square miles. The death toll stands at 57.[1]

She Left Her Heart in Sodom and Gomorrah: Lot's Wife

"It was the same in the days of Lot. People were eating and
drinking, buying and selling, planting and building." *Luke 17:28*

In the days of Lottie, in the days of Lot, in the days immediately preceding the revelation of the Son of Man—all such days Jesus described as ordinary days. People going through the mundane motions of life. Nibbling Pop Tarts for breakfast, buying CDs on the Internet, spraying the rosebushes for bugs, flipping burgers on the grill. Days straight out of *Better Homes and Gardens.*

Until suddenly…

"We didn't know, Lord! We weren't expecting *that!*" No one is ever prepared for disaster to strike.

Lot's wife wasn't ready, not even when she was warned.

"But the day Lot left Sodom, fire and sulfur rained down from
heaven and destroyed them all." *Luke 17:29*

All were destroyed *except* Lot and his two daughters, as we'll soon see. Lot's wife, though, wasn't counted among the survivors.

She's another of the no-name Bad Girls, married to a man whose chief claim to fame was his uncle, the great patriarch Abram (soon to be renamed Abraham).

"Neither Lot nor his wife was a bad character," one commentator insisted.[2] Next to the other residents of Sodom—Lot's lethal city of choice—Lot and his wife no doubt looked pretty good. But Lot was selfish. When he and his uncle went their separate ways, Lot chose the best land for himself.

Lot looked up and saw that the whole plain of the Jordan was well
watered, like the garden of the Lord. *Genesis 13:10*

"Aha!" Lot must have thought. Hassle-free gardening, unlike the experience of his unfortunate ancestor Adam. "This land is my land, Uncle." And so it was.

> Abram lived in the land of Canaan, while Lot lived among the cities of the plain and pitched his tents near Sodom. Now the men of Sodom were wicked and were sinning greatly against the LORD.
> *Genesis 13:12-13*

The land was good, but the people were not, and Lot knew that from day one. He deliberately chose to dwell among a people who flaunted their sins in God's face. Very repugnant stuff too. The word "Sodom," like the name "Jezebel," has come into our modern language as a noun of ill repute: "sodomy."

Ugh. Let's not go there.

Lot pitched his tents near sinful Sodom, knowing full well the city's nasty reputation. Sodom was also a place of opportunity and easy riches, and that's what drew Lot closer and closer until he'd built himself a fine residence within the city walls, thoroughly immersing himself in his adopted urban home.

A gentle reminder: Disaster is right around the corner.

Lot's famous uncle tried to avert that disaster by pleading with God to reconsider his plan to destroy Sodom and Gomorrah. "What if there are fifty righteous people in the city?" Abraham wanted to know.[3] God agreed. He'd spare all of Sodom for the sake of fifty souls.

Abraham rethought that one and dropped the number to forty-five, then forty. Abe the Auctioneer begged the Almighty, "Do I hear thirty? Twenty?" Clearly the man knew there was only one family in all of Sodom worth saving, and that was his greedy nephew, Lot, and his wife and children. "What if only ten can be found there?"[4] Good thinking. Lot had at least two betrothed daughters and a spouse. The Lord agreed to be merciful to all of Sodom for the sake of only ten.

Grace unspeakable! That the Lord valued even the imperfect Lot was clear. Two realizations leap into my heart at this truth: (1) God's mercy stretches further than we can imagine, and (2) he is withholding fire and brimstone even now, for *our* sake, that we might let others know that judgment awaits them...and so does grace.

Two angels, who'd already visited Abraham, were now dispatched to the sleazy metropolis, perhaps to find those ten worthy souls.

> The two angels arrived at Sodom in the evening, and Lot was
> sitting in the gateway of the city. *Genesis 19:1*

We know they're angels, because the Word of God tells us so, but to Lot they appeared as mere men.

The gateway of the city was where the civic leaders met, a place of honor and leadership. Life among the Sodomites had clearly lined Lot's pockets—as well as his wife's—all the while coating the walls of their hearts, preventing God's truth from piercing and convicting.

Ouch.

I'm sitting in my writing loft, surrounded by possessions that bless my soul every time I look at them. A tiny silver heart-shaped box from a dear friend's trip to Spain, a basket from an antique barn in North Carolina, a quilt crafted by a master quilter from Paris, Texas.

They give me joy. And a sharp stab of guilt.

Could I walk away from it—all of it—taking nothing but the clothes on my back? That's the question Lot and his wife faced before the cock crowed.

There's no doubt Lot's wife enjoyed her husband's prosperity right along with him. In fact, maybe—just maybe—she was the one who unintentionally urged him along the crooked path toward affluence and spiritual apathy to begin with. As Solomon would write of such women centuries later, "her paths are crooked, but she knows it not."[5]

Behind many a successful man is a materialistic woman with one hand on his back and the other on his wallet. Would Mrs. Lot fit that description? Hard to know for sure, considering not one word from her lips was recorded in Scripture. (Girlfriend, this will *not* be written on *my* tombstone: *She Never Said a Word…*)

Since we're given plenty of clues about her husband's character, though, and the two were married long enough to have grown daughters, we can confidently assume a few things about her from what we know of Lot.

For starters, let's see what Lot did with these angelic gate crashers.

> When he saw them, he got up to meet them and bowed down with
> his face to the ground. *Genesis 19:1*

They were strangers to him, but perhaps they were what our British friends call "quality"—persons with commanding stature or fine attire or a regal demeanor. *Something* made Lot fall to his knees.

> "My lords," he said, "please turn aside to your servant's house. You
> can wash your feet and spend the night and then go on your way
> early in the morning." *Genesis 19:2*

Hospitality was a big deal to these ancient desert dwellers. Lot's Bed-and-Breakfast was open 365 days a year, and smooth-talking Lot had his sales pitch ready: clean feet, a clean bed—y'all come. Of course, you and I know who probably handled foot washing and breakfast—Mrs. Lot and the girls. But still, Lot offered.

> "No," they answered, "we will spend the night in the square."
> *Genesis 19:2*

The *square?* Sleep in public in that wicked town? Were they crazy? Lot must have thought so. He didn't know they were angels on a mission to track down ten people worth saving. For them, safety wasn't even an issue; in fact, the town square was an ideal place to case the joint.

Lot, however, wouldn't hear of it.

> But he insisted so strongly that they did go with him and entered
> his house. *Genesis 19:3*

He was a persuasive man, skilled at using words and getting his own way. And guess who did the cooking?

> He prepared a meal for them, baking bread without yeast, and they
> ate. *Genesis 19:3*

Photocopy *that* verse and stick it under hubby's nose the next time he brings home unexpected company! Well, it does say "he," doesn't it? No sign yet of Lot's wife.

> Before they had gone to bed, all the men from every part of the city
> of Sodom—both young and old—surrounded the house. *Genesis 19:4*

This was *not* a Welcome Wagon bearing a basketful of household supplies for the out-of-town visitors. This was *all* the men of the city—literally every one of them, the Hebrew says—of all ages. They surrounded the house, but it was hardly a prayer circle. Shift the music to a minor key.

> They called to Lot, "Where are the men who came to you tonight?
> Bring them out to us so that we can have sex with them."
> *Genesis 19:5*

Sorry. There just isn't any polite way around this. I checked other translations to see if they might render this passage in a more genteel way. "Get familiar with them" (TAB), "have relations with them" (NASB), and "know them carnally" (NKJV) are an improvement, but the *International Children's Bible* tells it like it unfortunately was: "We want to have sexual relations with them."

Brother Lot had a problem on his hands.

> Lot went outside to meet them and shut the door behind him and
> said, "No..." *Genesis 19:6-7*

Oooh, brave and honorable Lot, right? Keep reading.

> "...my friends. Don't do this wicked thing." *Genesis 19:7*

"Friends?" These sodomists were Lot's *friends?* Maybe he was using the word as appeasement, trying to cool their anger—and their ardor—before he mentioned what he really thought their plans were: wicked.

That's why Lot's next offer boggles the mind.

> "Look, I have two daughters who have never slept with a man. Let
> me bring them out to you, and you can do what you like with
> them." *Genesis 19:8*

Do...do...*what?* (I'm sputtering here.) *"Do what you like?"* It was clear what they liked. Unspeakable things. And *every* man of the town against two young girls? Did Lot's pure, virginal daughters have no value, not even to their own father? They would surely be raped and abused like the poor concubine of Judges 19, who died stretched out by the front door, her hands on the threshold, begging for mercy.

Oh, Lot. Your shame stinks to high heaven.

"But don't do anything to these men, for they have come under the protection of my roof." *Genesis 19:8*

You're still thinking about those innocent daughters beneath his roof, aren't you? Me, too. Weren't *they* under his protection? Granted, hospitality required that he protect his guests at all costs…but at *that* cost?

Obviously God saw something worth saving in this man, but my advice would have been, "Smite the jerk!" For which the Lord would have reminded me, "But if you do not forgive men their sins, your Father will not forgive your sins."[6] Okay, okay.

Still not a word from Lot's wife, the mother of two vulnerable daughters offered as a living sacrifice to a bunch of lascivious louts.

"Get out of our way," they replied. *Genesis 19:9*

Not good, not good. Was there a Jordan Valley version of 9-1-1?

And they said, "This fellow came here as an alien, and now he wants to play the judge! We'll treat you worse than them."
Genesis 19:9

No, not *that* kind of alien with six eyes and green gills. Another translation handles it better: "You're an outsider. What right do you have to order us around?"[7] Imagine many voices here. Men were shouting accusations and loathsome suggestions by the dozen, bullying their way forward, shoving Lot against his own sturdy door.

They kept bringing pressure on Lot and moved forward to break down the door. *Genesis 19:9*

Lot surely feared for his own life even if he didn't seem to give a flip about his family. Blessed was he among men, however, since someone else was watching out for his well-being.

But the men inside reached out and pulled Lot back into the house and shut the door. *Genesis 19:10*

Boy, that was fast! Miraculous, in fact, considering the mob could have easily pushed open the door while they had the chance.

Grace again—still—for the undeserving Lot and his silent wife, who was also spared. If these depraved men had pushed down the door and abused him, Mrs. Lot and her daughters would have been next in line. Thank goodness for our angelic heroes.

> Then they struck the men who were at the door of the house,
> young and old, with blindness so that they could not find the door.
> *Genesis 19:11*

This blindness was literally a "blinding flash emanating from angels."[8] For a nanosecond the two men abandoned their human disguise and rendered the men of Sodom temporarily blind with their dazzling brightness, just like the glare from sunlight on fresh snow.

A second miracle then—one not explained away by fast reflexes. Mrs. Lot couldn't ignore the supernatural powers these men displayed. Hadn't they saved her husband? Struck the crowd blind? Spared her daughters, which is a *lot* more than Lot did?

And they were willing to do even more.

> The two men said to Lot, "Do you have anyone else here—sons-in-
> law, sons or daughters, or anyone else in the city who belongs to
> you?" *Genesis 19:12*

Remember our magic number: ten righteous souls. Since *every* man in Sodom had gathered outside to have his way with these visitors, the angels needed to search no further for godly men in Sodom. There weren't any. In any case, time had run out for the Sodomites.

Do you smell smoke? Sulfur maybe?

> "Get them out of here, because we are going to destroy this place.
> The outcry to the LORD against its people is so great that he has
> sent us to destroy it." *Genesis 19:12-13*

Lot was probably shocked...but not surprised. The last time the Lord had destroyed the land he had covered every inch of it with water. Lot knew God's patience was awesome but not endless. If these two men said destruction was at hand, why disagree?

> So Lot went out and spoke to his sons-in-law, who were pledged to
> marry his daughters. *Genesis 19:14*

Wait. The same two daughters he'd offered to the angry mob? Oh, wouldn't these men have been pleased, especially if they'd already paid a bride price for them! A few translations suggest these men were married to two *other* daughters of Lot and his wife. Either way, they were already considered family.

One note here: Lot had allowed his daughters to be betrothed to men of Sodom—to be unequally yoked, the righteous to the unrighteous. Lot may not have been born in Sodom, but he was as close to being a Sodomite as one could get without the birth certificate.

I'm often asked, "Are you from Kentucky?"

To which I respond, "I married a Kentuckian and gave birth to two, so I'm three-quarters Kentuckian (and one-quarter proud Pennsylvanian)!" That's how it was with Lot—except Kentucky is a slice of heaven, and Sodom was a wide wedge of the other place.

Nary a sound from Lot's wife yet.

Her husband, however, was still talking.

> He said, "Hurry and get out of this place, because the LORD is about to destroy the city!" *Genesis 19:14*

Not unlike Noah telling his sons, "All aboard!" Lot urged his sons-in-law to head for the gates. Noah's family members were smart enough to act on his advice. Lot's relatives were just amused.

> But his sons-in-law thought he was joking. *Genesis 19:14*

Think of Lot as Chicken Little—"The sky is falling!"—or as the boy who cried "Wolf!" He was the sort of person whom others didn't take seriously. Lot, with his glib tongue and clever speech, was undoubtedly a storyteller, prone to exaggeration, which may explain why his sons-in-law thought Lot was pulling their legs.

In this case the joke was on his unbelieving listeners. How callous the men of Sodom had become, thinking they were above the law, above punishment, above reproach!

> With the coming of dawn, the angels urged Lot, saying, "Hurry! Take your wife and your two daughters who are here..." *Genesis 19:15*

Finally his wife was mentioned along with the two daughters, who lifted their sleepy heads to find their houseguests dragging them from their beds at first light.

"…or you will be swept away when the city is punished."

Genesis 19:15

So far they've said "hurry" two times and "destroy" three times. An intelligent person would *hurry* and get out before he was *destroyed,* yes? Not this guy.

When he hesitated…*Genesis 19:16*

Don't tell me. Let me guess. He who hesitates is Lot.

Groan.

Surely he wasn't dragging his feet because of his family—they were going with him. His sons-in-law had laughed in his face, so it's unlikely he felt much sympathy toward them. Even Lot found the ways of Sodom to be wicked, so he wouldn't care about leaving that wretched place. Which means the only thing he might have been hesitant about abandoning was his…stuff?

Nah. Really?

What's a sofa compared to survival?

To Lot, Mrs. Lot, and the little Lots…a lot.

His wife tarried too, finding it equally hard to say good-bye to a lifestyle of luxury. She was "marinated in her pleasant present,"[9] rooted to her riches and her wealthy way of life.

All four of them were having a hard time deciding what to haul across the desert, it seemed, until the two angelic men grew weary of waiting.

> …the men grasped his hand and the hands of his wife and of his
> two daughters and led them safely out of the city, for the LORD was
> merciful to them. *Genesis 19:16*

Grace at work once more—and they fought it tooth and nail. Lot went first—it was Eastern custom for the man to walk ahead of the woman—followed by his wife, then his daughters. One can picture them mumbling and grumbling, dawdling through the murky city streets, avoiding a few pointed stares from their neighbors, all the while slowing down the angels' well-planned destruction.

And still not a squeak in the Scriptures from Mrs. L.

> As soon as they had brought them out, one of them said, "Flee for
> your lives!" *Genesis 19:17*

Once they cleared the city gates, the patient angels were ready to light some holy fires. "Flee," they said—a combination of "get out" and "hurry" in one nice, short word. The message, however, was not getting through. As one writer phrased it, "What is it about the word 'Flee!' that you don't understand?"[10]

"Don't look back..." *Genesis 19:17*

A new command was given, and a clear one. *Do not look.*

"...and don't stop anywhere in the plain!" *Genesis 19:17*

A second, definite directive. *Do not stop.*

Even a young child grasps the meaning of these words: "Go to jail. Go directly to jail. Do not pass Go. Do not collect two hundred dollars." The angels addressed the foursome like obstinate kids.

"Flee to the mountains or you will be swept away!" *Genesis 19:17*

A destination was offered, and a warning. And another *flee.*

But Lot said to them, "No, my lords, please!" *Genesis 19:18*

"But..."? Listen, Lot, the angels didn't say talk; they said walk, preferably very fast. Was Mrs. Lot married to a man who wouldn't let her—or anyone else—get a word in edgewise?

"Your servant has found favor in your eyes..." *Genesis 19:19*

There goes Mr. Persuasive again.

"...and you have shown great kindness to me in sparing my life."
Genesis 19:19

Grand. Give 'em some chocolate and flowers then, but get going, man! And besides, didn't the men spare your *family's* lives, too?

"But I can't flee to the mountains; this disaster will overtake me,
and I'll die." *Genesis 19:19*

"*Can't* flee"? Was he lazy? Slow? A whiner? A slacker? Afraid of heights? Scared of mountain lions? Why was *flee*-bitten Lot dragging his feet again?

"Look, here is a town near enough to run to, and it is small. Let me
flee to it—it is very small, isn't it? Then my life will be spared."
Genesis 19:20

If Abraham sounded like an auctioneer, then Lot sounded like a used-car salesman: "Don't worry about that scratch. You can barely see it, it's so small. Sure it runs the length of the car, but look how thin it is. Very thin, don't you think?"

He was selling this tiny town for all it was worth, almost as if he knew about the ten-person rule. If Lot and his family fled to the town, its inhabitants would be spared as well. But Lot wasn't thinking about them. He was thinking about that long haul up the mountain.

Why those angels put up with Lot I'll never know.

Probably the same reason God puts up with my own stubborn foolishness.

> He said to him, "Very well, I will grant this request too; I will not
> overthrow the town you speak of." *Genesis 19:21*

"Overthrow" suggests an earthquake, an upheaval in the land.

Do you hear a faint rumbling?

> "But flee there quickly…" *Genesis 19:22*

This story has more *flees* than a circus!

> "…because I cannot do anything until you reach it." (That is why
> the town was called Zoar.) *Genesis 19:22*

The angels of the Lord were holding all the forces of nature back until Lot—heel-dragging, barely righteous Lot—and his family were safely out of danger. "Zoar" meant "little," and the town was "very small," precisely as Lot insisted.

> By the time Lot reached Zoar, the sun had risen over the land.
> *Genesis 19:23*

They'd started at dawn and walked until high noon. But it wasn't lunchtime; it was *crunch* time.

> Then the LORD rained down burning sulfur on Sodom and
> Gomorrah—from the LORD out of the heavens. *Genesis 19:24*

Twice we're told it came down out of the heavens from the Lord. It was divine judgment, not a geological surprise—not as far as God was concerned. It was intentional and specific. The innocent did not perish; God made sure of that. Traditionally it's described as "fire and brimstone," but "burning sulfur" gives us a better sense of the excruciating pain and stench of it.

Every living thing in the plains of Jordan perished.

> Thus he overthrew those cities and the entire plain, including all those living in the cities—and also the vegetation in the land.
> *Genesis 19:25*

At thirteen hundred feet below sea level, the Dead Sea is full of chemicals, salt, and the smell of sulfur. Archaeologists place Sodom and Gomorrah at the north end of the Dead Sea. Legend places those cities at the south end.[11]

God placed them *gone*.

Now, don't blink or you'll miss this:

> But Lot's wife looked back... *Genesis 19:26*

She was behind her husband all along, remember. Perhaps she was lingering even farther back than necessary. The sounds of destruction and horror must have been deafening, frightening. "But his wife, from behind him, looked back."[12]

Why did she look back? That's what has stumped scholars for centuries. It's this one mistake that made her a Bad Girl. It's what earned her a place in Scripture, both Old Testament and New. It's what killed her too.

Even the volcano movie *Dante's Peak* used the same familiar warning as an advertising hook: "Don't look back!"

Rather than "judge Lot's wife 'guilty' on the slimmest of circumstantial evidence,"[13] let's consider ten practical reasons she might have looked back.

1. She **missed the warning** over the wailing of her daughters.
   "Sorry, Officer, I didn't hear the siren. The kids were screaming in the backseat and...well, you know how it is."

2. In her grief she simply **forgot** the angel's dire prediction.
   If she was anywhere near forty, that old short-term memory probably took a long-term hike.

3. She **was curious.**
   People who rubberneck when they drive past a car accident sometimes manage a three-car collision of their own.

4. She **dropped** something and turned to pick it up.
   I wish I had a dollar for every time I've dropped my car keys when my arms were full of grocery bags.

5. She **tripped** over her tunic in her haste.

    Blame the hem, the heels, the sand—something.

6. She **heard a cry for help** and was moved by compassion to look.

    "Was that a cat? I distinctly heard a cat in those bushes."

7. She **mourned** her family and friends, lost to her forever.

    What if she did indeed have two married daughters, left behind to incinerate in Sodom? Imagine the pain of losing them!

8. She **longed** for all the material goodies she had left behind.

    If we'd seen the couch, we'd understand.

9. She clung to memories of the past and **dreaded her future.**

    Mrs. Lot was a sandwich-generation woman, not sure what life might hold for her—scared of going forward, frightened of going back.

10. She **didn't trust** her husband's God.

    Lot gave the Lord lip service, but then again, Lot gave everyone lip service. If his God caused all that fire and smoke, who wanted to hang around with a deity like him?

Hubby Bill insisted I include two more possibilities: She left the coffeepot on—one of us usually does—or she and Lot had an argument, and out of habit she whipped her head in the other direction to show the man who wore the bloomers in *that* household.

None of the above quite hits the mark.

As with Eve, the key is this: She was disobedient. Mrs. Lot wasn't singled out for punishment—"one wrong move and the woman gets it"—but rather, she chose her fate by choosing to disobey the clear command of the Lord.

Sodom didn't see judgment coming, nor did Lot's wife. She merely turned to look back. But "what she saw, the rest of them never knew."[14]

    …and she became a pillar of salt. Genesis 19:26

Mrs. Lot not only looked, she hesitated, perhaps long enough for the edge of the maelstrom to reach her and wrap her head-to-toe in sodium chloride. At the southern end of the Dead Sea are literal mountains of salt.

Such is the substance that whipped itself around Lot's wife, smothering her in seconds as it "encrusted her and built round her a sarcophagus."[15]

This wasn't a unique punishment, separate from the one that leveled her city. By lingering behind and looking, she chose to identify with her neighbors who also were doused with salt and peppered with sulfur. But unlike them, she had had the chance to escape. She was offered salvation yet turned away from it. In doing so, Lot's wife "became a shrine of unbelief."[16]

Oh, sisters! How many times in my young adult years did God take me by the hand and lead me away from my destructive lifestyle, urging me not to look back but to press on to something better?

I didn't believe him. I didn't *trust* him.

I liked my pitiful, party lifestyle and my apartment full of stuff—most of which has since been thrown out or sold at a yard sale for a quarter. What was I hanging on to? Why, at the last minute, so close to a clean, new life in Christ, did I turn back toward death again? And again?

Stubborn pride. Foolish youth. Willful disobedience.

I deserved what Mrs. Lot got. I deserved to die for my sins, just as the Word cautions, "For those who are self-seeking and who reject the truth and follow evil, there will be wrath and anger."[17]

But because God loves us so completely, he shoves us forward toward safety and light and life…then turns back and faces the heat on our behalf. What a hero! What a Savior!

We're turned into salt, all right. But not the kind that kills. The kind that gives life. "Let your conversation be always full of grace, seasoned with salt, so that you may know how to answer everyone."[18]

> Early the next morning Abraham got up… *Genesis 19:27*

Stop right there! No reaction from Lot? From the girls? That's it for Mom the Saltshaker? The poor woman truly had "the shortest biography in literature."[19]

My friend Sara admitted she'd always felt sorry for Lot. "Imagine trying to explain to people offering their sympathy! 'Did your wife pass away? I'm so sorry. What happened?'"

"Well…"

If the angels had never commanded her specifically *not* to stop and *not* to look back, we would feel nothing but empathy for her. *Poor thing*. She didn't know it was wrong. She didn't understand the consequences. She was merely a victim of a cruel God's wrath.

But she *was* told. She *did* know. We do too.

When a woman dies apart from God, wrapped in her sin like a shroud, life continues without her. One might question if she ever really lived at all, since the woman "who lives for pleasure is dead even while she lives."[20]

The sad tale of Mr. and Mrs. Lot and the destruction of Sodom is valuable for one reason: Jesus used it as a sermon illustration.

"It will be just like this on the day the Son of Man is revealed."
Luke 17:30

Just like what? Like the destruction of Sodom.
Unexpected. Destructive. Absolute.

"On that day no one who is on the roof of his house, with his goods inside, should go down to get them." *Luke 17:31*

But wouldn't a person have to go back down into his house to get out? Not in those days. Throw a rope over the edge of the roof and climb down, buddy. More on that when we get to Rahab's story in chapter 7. The message for twenty-first-century believers is clear: Don't look back!

"Likewise, no one in the field should go back for anything."
Luke 17:31

In other words, drop your plowshares (or your laptop or your cell phone) and haul tunic!

"Remember Lot's wife!" *Luke 17:32*

This is why the example of Lot's wife is important. Not because a woman was turned into salt, however strange and fascinating the concept. But because Jesus employed it as a teaching tool—a history lesson—to help prepare his followers for his future revelation.

The Lord's message, then and now, is the same one the angels delivered: "Don't stop. Don't look back. Take my hand and walk with me to safety."

What Lessons Can We Learn from Lot's Wife?

Actions speak a lot louder than words.
For all his endless questions, Lot was, in the end, obedient. But for all her silence, when decision time came, Lot's wife disobeyed. The Lord can handle our questions. What grieves his heart is our poor choices. O Father, help us see that every time we turn the wrong way we risk losing something of greater value—our close walk with you.

> "The LORD is a God who knows,
>   and by him deeds are weighed." *1 Samuel 2:3*

When God says walk, walk!
The angels gave clear commands. So does God's written Word. Yet Lot and his family hesitated, as if waiting for the angels to suggest a different idea, something they'd find more appealing. The Lord already knows the best itinerary for our lives. When he shines a light on the path by his Spirit and hands us a map in his Word, let's stop hesitating and start walking!

> I have kept my feet from every evil path
>   so that I might obey your word. *Psalm 119:101*

The escape route is clear: Jesus Christ.
The Lord used Mrs. Lot's story to make a point. When he returns, we are to be ready to follow without hesitation, forsaking everything. Salvation is offered freely but at a price: our old lives in exchange for new lives in Christ. His grace has no limits...except time. The day will come when we must abandon all and follow. Since we know neither the day nor the hour, the question is, could we drop everything and go right now?

> How shall we escape if we ignore such a great salvation? *Hebrews 2:3*

Stuff is temporary. Life in Christ is eternal.
Okay, I admit it. I like stuff. Over the years I've collected several items that have great value to me, mostly because of where they came from, not what they cost. Even those are tarnished junk compared to what we have waiting

for us in heaven. Pray with me to let go of the power that material things hold over our hearts. Pray for a clear vision of the future, when the stuff, like dross, will burn away, and only that which is gold—faith, hope, and love—will remain.

> "What good will it be for a man if he gains the whole world, yet forfeits his soul?" *Matthew 16:26*

Good Girl Thoughts Worth Considering

1. Do you know women like Lot's wife—exceedingly quiet, willing to let their husbands make the important decisions? What is the plus side of such reticence? What are the dangers? Where do you fall on the scale of quiet to noisy? How does the quieter approach help or hinder our relationship with God?

2. Why did God spare Lot and his family? Did they deserve such grace? How can you explain God's patience with Lot and his wife? Do you try God's patience at times? Do you deserve God's grace? How can you accept it?

3. This business of Lot's offering his daughters to the men of Sodom—how do you handle a story like that? Turn away from it? Hide it from your children? Get angry about it? Learn something from it? Is that story only suited to ancient times, or do we see anything similar happening today? If so, how are we to respond?

4. Lot's sons-in-law laughed at him—why? Have you ever told someone bad news and had him or her laugh? We all have people in our lives who are headed for eternal punishment. Should we tell them and risk being laughed at, as Lot was? How do you handle people who ridicule your sincere attempts to show them an escape route?

5. Has the Lord ever given you directives as clearly as the angels did to Mrs. Lot—"Don't look!" or "Don't stop!"? Were they difficult to obey? Is a "don't" harder to obey than a "do"?

6. Why did Lot ask to run to Zoar rather than the mountains? Do you ever bargain with God like that? What are we to learn from Lot's example of asking for another option?

7. Of the suggested reasons Lot's wife turned back toward Sodom, which one makes the most sense to you? Why aren't we told more about Lot's wife in this story and, in particular, about her decision to turn back? Did she want to perish, or would she have seen it as an accident? Or...as punishment?

8. What's the most important lesson you've learned from the salty tale of Lot's wife?

DYING FOR A DRINK

4

*I knew then that "w-a-t-e-r" meant the wonderful cool
something that was flowing over my hand. That living
word awakened my soul, gave it light, joy, set it free!*

HELEN KELLER

Hey, blondie! Pour us another round, will ya?"

Crystal wiped her hands on a damp dishtowel and tossed it in
the direction of the tiny sink tucked under the bar. "Hold your horses,
Wayne. I'm coming." Grabbing a round serving tray, its cork surface
stained with every kind of libation the Oasis had to offer, she sauntered
over to a pair of tables that'd been shoved together to accommodate half a
dozen men. One by one, they turned to give their waitress a once-over.

Nothing new there.

"Attagirl." Wayne winked one bloodshot eye at her. "There's a big tip
waiting for ya at closing time, honey." His leer stretched above a beard-
stubbled chin that begged for a razor. "That is, if you get my drift."

She gave him a withering glance. "The only thing drifting around here,
Wayne, is your memory." Snatching two dirty glasses off the table, she
banged them onto her tray. "We used to be married, or have you forgotten? I know for a fact there ain't a thing worth waitin' for past closing
time." She paused for effect. "If you get my drift."

His buddies around the table howled at that one. *Serves him right.* What
was he doing there anyway? He knew she tended bar every Monday night
except during football season, when too many people came in and chances
were good that more than one bad memory would stroll through her door.

Crystal liked things quiet.

Tonight was just right. Wayne's table, two or three couples—that was it. No hassles. Except for Wayne, and he was hardly a threat. Now if Lowell showed up, *that* was a problem. Another ex-husband, but not nearly so tame. Life'd be a lot easier if Lowell would go ahead and marry that red-haired hussy instead of dragging the girl around town from one wobbly barstool to the next.

Jimmy had married again. Why couldn't Lowell?

Or at least skip town, like Richard had. *And good riddance to you, fella.*

Or drop dead, like poor Bart Jackson. The only one of the five who hadn't sued for divorce. The sucker died before he'd gotten the paperwork together.

Balancing her tray on one bony hip, she offered the motley crowd a cool, practiced stare that never failed to keep her male customers in line. "What's everybody drinking?"

They mumbled their orders—a Dewar's, two bourbons and branch, a Miller Lite, Johnny Walker Black Label on the rocks. She nodded and turned toward the bar, narrowly missing a playful pinch from Wayne.

Good thing Mick wasn't around to see that. They weren't married—after five trips to the altar, what was the point?—but Mick had a jealous streak as wide as the Columbia River and every bit as wild. When storm clouds showed up in the man's eyes, she got out of the water fast.

Pouring the orders with a steady hand, Crystal kept one eye trained on the door. For no reason she could get a handle on, a sense of expectation hung in the air, thicker than the smoke from Wayne's Marlboros. Mick was working at the Bonneville Lock and Dam until midnight, so he wouldn't be darkening the Oasis door anytime soon. But something—or someone—was coming, she was sure of it.

Stooping to pick up a bottle cap, she slipped a loose strand of hair behind her ear, making a mental note to call Glenda in the morning and set up an appointment to get her hair chopped off. *You're forty-seven, sister!* Too old to be wearing her hair all over her shoulders. Who knows, she might even work up the nerve to go back to her own color.

Minus the gray, of course. *'Nuff's enough.*

Glenda was one of her few female friends. Women with husbands, boyfriends, and the like—they flat out didn't trust her. Maybe they figured if she'd been through five men, their beau could easily be number six.

Like another man could solve all her problems.

Fat chance there.

With the tray carefully balanced on one hand, she grabbed a stack of fresh cocktail napkins and headed for Wayne's table. They were a thirsty bunch tonight. Was this their third go-round or their fourth? *Whatever.* She was at their service until last call and not one second longer.

The minute Wayne's glass touched the table, she heard the door close softly behind her. *Lawdy, don't let it be Lowell!* She turned slowly, slipping the empty tray under one arm, her senses on full alert.

The man was already at the bar. Crystal released a soft sigh of relief. *Not Lowell, thank somebody.* This guy wasn't one of her regulars. A stranger, in fact, dressed in plain clothes that'd seen a lot of wear and needed a trip through the washer—yesterday.

He was thirsty, no doubt. Probably lonely, too. Most of 'em were.

Moments later she wiped the bar and slapped a square white napkin in front of him. "What'll it be, sir?"

He lifted his eyes to hers, and she shrank back, startled by the depth of his gaze. He had dark hair and eyes, swarthy skin, and was younger than she by fifteen years, easy. Not handsome—not hardly—but she found it impossible to turn away. His eyes looked right through her, as if he could see down inside her soul. As if she had one.

Truth was, the guy gave her the creeps.

"Will you give me a drink?" His voice sounded oddly familiar. *Impossible.* She'd never laid eyes on him before.

"That's what I'm here for, buddy." She felt the corners of her mouth begin to lift in an unaccustomed grin. "Unless, of course, you don't want your liquor poured by a woman. Some customers are funny like that."

He shook his head, his features softening. "If you knew me, you'd know that's not something I'd ever worry about." His gaze dropped to the nametag on her navy-and-white striped blouse. "I see you don't have a name."

She glanced down and let out a nervous excuse for a laugh. "Guess I lost it somewhere." The plastic tag merely read "The Oasis," with a blank space below it. "One of those stick-on labels, you know." She shrugged, busying her hands drying glasses. "Anyway, it doesn't matter."

"It matters to me."

Oh brother. She knew where this was leading. "If you…uh, don't mind, I've got other customers, mister. So…um, what'll you have?"

He inclined his head toward the glass by her elbow. "Whatever you're drinking."

"Oh! Well…that's just bottled water with a twist of lime."

"Perfect. I'll have one too." He smiled. "On the rocks."

Crystal knew her sigh sounded impatient. "Sure you don't want me to add something from the well?" She pointed to the bargain-label whiskeys in the trough beside the sink.

When he shook his head, she reached for a tall glass and thumped it on the bar. Who had time for games? Not her, not on a night with one of the regular waitresses out sick and another rowdy group stumbling through her door at that very moment. If the stranger wanted water, he got water. Two dollars a glass, the same thing everybody else paid for well drinks.

He tossed his money on the counter and downed the full glass, pushing it toward her again.

She laughed in spite of herself, in spite of the way he studied her so closely. "Liked it, huh?"

His shrug was noncommittal. "I've had better."

"Better *water?*"

"Real water." His smile transformed his features. Maybe he wasn't so homely after all. "Water that never leaves you wanting more, that quenches your thirst completely. Forever."

"Is that right?" She poured him a second glass, waving the newcomers toward an empty pair of tables. "Suppose you toss down another one while I get this group set up with drinks." She moved in their direction, then turned to send him a saucy wink. "Don't forget, buddy. Two dollars a holler."

Her four new arrivals had each commandeered a small cocktail table and chair, filling up an entire corner with their long, blue-jeaned legs, mud-caked boots, and bright orange coats and vests.

"Been fishin' today, fellas?"

"Got that right, sweetheart!" The obvious leader of the group flashed her a toothy smile. "Didn't catch diddly-squat, so we're here to drown our sorrows in your cheapest beer."

She took their orders, half expecting to find the stranger's barstool vacant by the time she returned. It was vacant, all right. He was behind the bar, helping himself to a fresh glass.

"Hey!" Snatching it out of his hands, she dropped his tumbler in the tepid dishwater, splashing suds on both of them. "What do you think you're doing?"

"Serving." He straightened and dried his hands on her towel. *Her* towel! "It's what I do best."

"Fine." She yanked the towel out of his hands. "Be sure and fill out an application. The next time we need a waiter, we'll give you a call."

Before she could drive her point home any further, a couple in their twenties slid onto two nearby barstools and motioned him over. His words rang with sincerity. "May I offer you something to drink?"

She jabbed an elbow in his side and shot him a nasty look, but he merely smiled and turned back to the couple, who ordered gin and tonics with a twist. As smoothly as if he'd been tending bar all his life, he pulled down two clean glasses, scooped up shaved ice, and sliced two slim wedges of fresh lime.

Crystal peered at him through narrowed eyes. "You've done this before."

"As I said, I was born to serve." Pouring the contents of a sparkling pitcher of water into the glasses, he slid them in front of the couple, who toasted one another and lifted the drinks to their lips.

What in the...? She grabbed him by the elbow and dragged him to the far end of the bar, making sure her back faced the customers. "What are you *doing?*" she hissed, heat rising to her cheeks. *The nerve!* "These people didn't order plain water; they ordered gin and tonic. Are you trying to get me fired?"

"You haven't even tasted it yet."

"The water?" It was almost a shriek. "I know what water tastes like, for God's sake."

"Exactly." He was utterly calm. His eyes gave away nothing.

"But that's not what they ordered!"

"No. But that's what they need. They're thirsty."

"Look, I..." She raked her hands through her hair. "Nobody...I mean..." She groaned. "Nobody comes in here because they're thirsty."

He handed her an icy glass, as if out of nowhere. "Why don't you sample some while I see if these two need anything else?"

Crystal held it, too stunned to drink, as he chatted with the smiling couple who were standing to leave and stuffing a ten-dollar bill in his hand. "Best drinks we've ever had," she heard the young man say. "What did you call it again?"

Curiosity finally brought the glass to her lips. She sniffed, keeping an eagle eye on the impromptu bartender, who was pouring another round of ice water for the fishing party. "Oh no, you don't!" She lunged at him, nearly spilling the liquid all over her blouse. "They're Pabst drinkers, the whole lot of them."

"Let's see if this doesn't do a better job of quenching their thirst."

Clearly there was no stopping him. The man was on a mission and certifiably crazy besides. She watched as the gang in orange and blue tossed down their drinks, laughing and nodding their approval.

What is going on here?

She lifted her glass again, sniffing it suspiciously. It smelled fresh, like the air up on Mount Hood. Holding it toward the meager glow of a nearby Coors sign, she could see the water was crystal clear. *Hardly dangerous.* She took a hesitant sip and was amazed at its purity, the sweet clarity of its taste.

"Well?" He was by her side again, smiling broadly.

"Well!" Shaking her head, she exhaled, then downed her glass in a greedy gulp. "That's really something." She held out the glass, half expecting it to magically refill itself. "What is it?"

"Life."

"*Life?*" She wrinkled her brow. "Is that something new from Anheuser-Busch?"

His laugh was genuine. "Not quite, Miss…uh. I'm sorry, what did you say your name was?"

"I didn't say." She flipped her hair over her right shoulder, suddenly embarrassed.

"It is 'Miss'; I'm sure of that." He was looking through her again. "Though it would've been 'Mrs.' last month."

It wasn't a question. Her eyes widened. *How could he know?* Folding her arms, she leaned back slightly, trying to put some distance between them. "I don't have a husband."

He folded his arms as well. "That's true. Not anymore. You've had five, though…"

She gasped.

"…and the man you're living with now—Mick, right?—he isn't your husband either."

"Mister, I…I'm…" Her face was on fire. Her tongue was glued to the roof of her mouth, refusing to budge. *Was he a psychic? Employed by the court system? Or your everyday, garden-variety madman?*

"Uh…" *Get hold of yourself, Crystal!* "It's obvious that you…know some…things about me." *Everything, probably.*

The warmth in his eyes was unmistakable. "Would you like more water?"

"Yes, I…I think I would." She stuck out her glass with a trembling hand. Had she ever been this thirsty in her entire life? He wrapped his strong fingers around hers, steadying her hand as he poured while she watched, mesmerized. "So…what did you say *your* name was?"

"Ahh." The warmth in his voice was unforgettable. "I thought you'd never ask…"

Known by Her Location but Not by Her Name: The Woman at the Well

So he came to a town in Samaria called Sychar... John 4:5

Lord, with all due respect, surely you made a wrong turn somewhere. What was a Jew like you doing in a place like this? True, when someone travels from Judea to Galilee, it's hard to skip Samaria, but most Jews at least tried to avoid a group of colonists they saw as less than honorable members of the house of Israel.

Jews and Samaritans had one thing in common though. On a hot day, they all developed a powerful thirst.

Jacob's well was there... John 4:6

It still *is* there, as a matter of fact. Visit the Holy Land and see the ancient well of Jacob for yourself, once a welcome source of water in a parched parcel of ground that Jacob bequeathed to his son Joseph.

But it was the *women* of the land who spent time at the wells. Rebekah was wooed at a well by Eliezer on Isaac's behalf. Rachel was courted by Jacob at a well at Haran. Now we find another well in the wilderness where a woman's arrival was imminent.

Anticipation hung over the scene like the desert heat, unseen but palpable. By all that was considered right and holy, Jesus shouldn't have been there. But he was.

...and Jesus, tired as he was from the journey, sat down by the well. It was about the sixth hour. John 4:6

By Roman time, it was six o'clock in the evening; by Jewish time, twelve noon. Since most women went to the well at eventide and there wasn't a water pot in sight yet, we'll stick with the conventional reading and assume it was noon, the heat of the day. Jesus had been traveling all morning. Finding a watering hole, he dropped there in an exhausted heap. His spirit was willing to press on, but his flesh was too weak to move another step. Though he's fully God, Jesus' utterly human nature in this scene always tugs at my heart.

Would someone get this man a drink, please?

> When a Samaritan woman came to draw water... *John 4:7*

There she was, just a-walkin' down the street. She had two strikes against her already: (1) She was a Samaritan, not a Jew, and (2) she was a woman, of all things. John, the only gospel writer to record this story, didn't even include her name.

Non-Jew, non-male, who cares?

Jesus cared.

> Jesus said to her, "Will you give me a drink?" *John 4:7*

He cared so much he spoke to her directly. No doubt he looked her in the eyes when he said it, might even have touched the sleeve of her garment to get her attention.

Oh, it gives me shivers just to *think* of it! The Lord reaching out to someone who was in all ways a social reject. Notice he didn't command her; he asked her. His words were polite and forthright, the start of a lengthy conversation—the longest found in Scripture between Jesus and *anyone,* let alone a Samaritan.

Let alone a woman.

Let alone *that* kind of woman.

Her gender and her nationality are not incidental to the story; they are integral, because they drive home the universal truth of God's fountain of grace: Its refreshing waters are meant for every human being willing to hold out his empty cup.

What was she doing there in the scorching heat of midday? She must have been mighty thirsty to risk the sting of the sun *and* the neighborhood gossips. Alas, water's a necessity of life, then and now. Forced by that need, she chose the one time other women from Sychar wouldn't be likely to show up and ventured toward the outskirts of town where a well—and a wise but weary man—waited for her.

The woman wasn't expecting him, but clearly Jesus was expecting her. Otherwise he might have joined his disciples.

> (His disciples had gone into the town to buy food.) *John 4:8*

Instead, he met her one-on-one, the single best way to approach any-one about spiritual matters. Classroom teaching has its place, and small-group studies are wonderful, but when Christ speaks to my heart, it's always just the two of us. With you, too?

> The Samaritan woman said to him, "You are a Jew and I am a Samaritan woman. How can you ask me for a drink?" (For Jews do not associate with Samaritans.) *John 4:9*

The parenthetical explanation says it all: *Jews + Samaritans = No Go.* Jesus, however, blew off the Jewish custom of steering clear of Samaritans. He even asked to share her water pot… Germ City, Lord! Clearly he did-n't allow anything as trivial as religious tradition to get in the way of her genuine journey toward faith.

(And she thought she was merely walking toward a well.)

> Jesus answered her, "If you knew the gift of God and who it is that asks you for a drink…" *John 4:10*

The subtle shift from temporal thirst to eternal satisfaction had begun. "If you knew" left the door wide open. He didn't say, "Duh! Don't you know who I am?" He didn't put her on the spot or demand that she iden-tify him…or herself. Ever the gentleman, this Rabbi merely suggested that he had the means to quench her obvious thirst.

> "…you would have asked him and he would have given you living water." *John 4:10*

Water from a well was dead water—rainwater mostly. Far from pure or refreshing, it was more suited to sheep than people. Well water was com-mon, everyday stuff, but *living* water? What a concept! The Lord's words, full of mystery and intrigue, got her attention.

> "Sir," the woman said, "you have nothing to draw with and the well is deep. Where can you get this living water?" *John 4:11*

The woman was polite but gutsy. Observant, too. Jesus didn't have a bucket, barrel, or bowl, and they both knew it. No Web site either—*www.livingwater.org*. Still, he seemed confident enough. She pressed her point, tossing in a bit of history, perhaps to impress him.

> "Are you greater than our father Jacob, who gave us the well and
> drank from it himself, as did also his sons and his flocks and herds?"
> *John 4:12*

It's the standard argument: "Hey, if it was good enough water for Jacob,
it should be good enough for the likes of you." One scholar called the
woman "skeptical, intelligent, irrepressible."[1] In the vernacular, I'd label
her a *pushy broad*.

Maybe that's why I like her so much.

> Jesus answered, "Everyone who drinks this water will be thirsty
> again…" *John 4:13*

Stated like a promise, one she could hardly refute. *She* was back for
another drink, wasn't she? When you're really thirsty, you can down a huge
tumbler of icy water in one gulp and quickly thrust your empty glass out
for more.

Unless Jesus is the one holding the pitcher.

> "…but whoever drinks the water I give him will never thirst.
> Indeed, the water I give him will become in him a spring of water
> welling up to eternal life." *John 4:14*

Many Sunday afternoons in my childhood my parents drove to the
outskirts of our small Pennsylvania town, to a gushing spring that shot
straight out of a crudely made pipe lodged in the side of a mountain. It
was spring water—cold as snow and fresh as sunshine, full of natural min-
erals and absolutely free. People brought empty milk jugs, gallon jars,
whatever would hold the crystal-clear liquid. My mouth waters at the
memory of it!

The water Jesus spoke of was even more delicious. An endless supply of
holy, cleansing water awaited the Samaritan woman—a personal fountain
of spiritual youth that could well up inside her forever.

> The woman said to him, "Sir, give me this water so that I won't get
> thirsty and have to keep coming here to draw water." *John 4:15*

It's obvious she'd like nothing better than never to visit that well again.
Never risk public ridicule, never admit she had a need so basic as water.

Too bad, my dear. We simply can't live without it. The average woman's body is 50 to 60 percent water, which requires constant replenishing. A few hours without H_2O in some form and our mouths turn to cotton, dark circles appear under our eyes, and our lips grow chapped. A few days without water and serious dehydration sets in, producing weakness, lethargy, exhaustion.

A week without water and we're dead.

One look at her and Jesus knew she was parched with thirst in both body and spirit. The first was easily solved with a dip in the well. The other thirst needed to be brought out in the open before it could be sated.

> He told her, "Go, call your husband and come back." *John 4:16*

Jesus wasn't being rude, just bowing to the custom of the day. Women—Good Girls, that is—didn't speak alone with a man in a public place. By asking her to call her husband to join them, the Lord was honoring her, saying in essence, "I know you're not a harlot." By inviting her to come back, he was assuring her of his interest in her welfare, rather than in something more carnal.

No, she wasn't a harlot. Nor was she married, at the moment.

> "I have no husband," she replied. *John 4:17*

We can hear the hesitancy in her voice, sense the blush that might have crept up her neck and across her cheeks. *Does he know? Will he assume the worst about me?*

First he affirmed the accuracy of her answer.

> Jesus said to her, "You are right when you say you have no
> husband." *John 4:17*

For one beat she must have inwardly breathed a sigh of relief.

> "The fact is, you have had five husbands, and the man you now
> have is not your husband." *John 4:18*

Her heart surely sank. *He knows!*

Our hearts sink too. *Five husbands!* No wonder she was so comfortable speaking with a strange man. How could any woman survive five husbands? Between warfare, famine, disease, pestilence, and fatal injury, men in those days didn't have lengthy life spans. Since a woman in that society was doomed to poverty or worse as a widow, it behooved her to keep remarrying.

Oh, but *five* weddings… Think of all the toaster ovens!

Clearly she wasn't a young woman, nor had life been kind to her. We can imagine the premature lines on her face, her skin leathered by the sun, her hands dotted with age spots and calluses. We can fathom the hope that was born in her heart five times, only to be crushed again and again, sending her on yet another search for someone to love her, support her, comfort her, and protect her.

Five husbands was one thing. Excessive but not illegal. But living with a sixth man who was not her husband…well, that was fornication. No getting around that.

"What you have just said is quite true." *John 4:18*

Interesting that Jesus affirmed a second time that she'd spoken the truth. He did not accuse her of lying or twisting the facts. This wasn't one of those hairsplitting, "it depends on what your definition of 'is' is" sort of debates. He was merely pointing out what *was* true, perhaps to give her the courage to admit what was *not* true.

So…did she confess her sin? Rend her garments? Reach for sackcloth and ashes? Beg for forgiveness? No way, not this feisty female. She looked Jesus straight in the eye and, denying nothing, offered an astute observation:

"Sir," the woman said, "I can see that you are a prophet." *John 4:19*

Talk about your funny one-liners! This woman was ready for HBO or Showtime with that zinger. It's almost as laughable as Aaron's explanation to Moses of why he'd fashioned a golden calf in his brother's absence: "They gave me the gold, and I threw it into the fire, and out came this calf!"[2]

Harrrr!

Like Aaron, this woman wasn't trying to be funny. She was merely grabbing for something, anything, that would divert attention from the sin that'd just been uncovered. I've done it myself. Caught with my hand in the cookie jar, as it were, I'll toss out some line meant to conceal my embarrassment, which usually has the opposite effect—I end up drawing even more attention to my foolishness.

Notice that the Samaritan woman neither denied nor affirmed the Lord's prophetic word about the six men with whom she'd been intimate. Instead, she cleverly shifted their conversation in a completely different direction.

You're a prophet, eh? Then let's talk shop.

> "Our fathers worshiped on this mountain, but you Jews claim that
> the place where we must worship is in Jerusalem." *John 4:20*

Been there, honey. Before I knew Jesus as my Savior, if someone steered our conversation down a spiritual path, I veered off toward religion. Less personal, more debatable. It's always easier to talk about church than to talk about Christ.

Jesus had struck a nerve, so the woman reacted by pushing him away using words that divided them (*"our* fathers" and *"you* Jews"), concepts that were corporate ("worship") rather than personal, and places that were safely distant ("Jerusalem") rather than frighteningly close. As close as her own soul.

The Lord might have been physically drained, but spiritually he was fully prepared to handle her diversionary tactics.

> Jesus declared, "Believe me, woman, a time is coming when you
> will worship the Father neither on this mountain nor in Jerusalem."
> *John 4:21*

Note the strong language. "Believe me, woman." Ooh, I can hear that! Wake up and smell the coffee, sister. Jesus was trying to get her attention. And never mind Jerusalem or Samaria. The Father had another throne of worship in mind altogether: her very human heart.

Even with his own agenda in mind, Jesus listened carefully to her questions and responded to them first.

> "You Samaritans worship what you do not know; we worship what
> we do know, for salvation is from the Jews." *John 4:22*

Oh, Lord, you name-dropper! Sneaked the word "salvation" in there and pointed toward your very own name—Jesus, "Jehovah is salvation."

> "Yet a time is coming and has now come when the true worshipers
> will worship the Father in spirit and truth, for they are the kind of
> worshipers the Father seeks." *John 4:23*

The Father is not the only one who's in a seeking mode. This Samaritan sister-in-waiting had been watching the horizon herself.

> The woman said, "I know that Messiah" (called Christ) "is
> coming." *John 4:25*

Aha! The first mention of the Messiah—the Anointed One—and it
came from her lips, not his own. Having pointed to the prophecy, she
backed off again.

> "When he comes, he will explain everything to us." *John 4:25*

Had she grown weary of all the discourse? Was she suddenly anxious to
dismiss both the topic and this stranger who knew too much, who saw too
much? "He'll fill us in when he gets here," she insisted, perhaps thinking
that would be the end of it.

Jesus refused to let her off the hook. Instead he did an extraordinary
thing: He revealed his calling and his ministry to her.

> Then Jesus declared, "I who speak to you am he." *John 4:26*

Wait, Lord! What were you doing? Casting your pearls before swine?
She was a...*she!* And a *Samaritan.* And a *fornicator!* And she was...

Thirsty is what she was. Thirsty for the truth.

Jesus saw past her hardened exterior to the parched interior of her soul
and "respected her enough to fill her with the living water of faith."[3]

What a storyteller the apostle John was. At this crucial point in the nar-
rative, he suddenly shifted the spotlight to stage right.

> Just then his disciples returned and were surprised to find him
> talking with a woman. But no one asked, "What do you want?" or
> "Why are you talking with her?" *John 4:27*

Way to go, fellas. For once the disciples didn't insert their dusty feet
firmly in their mouths. They were surprised, but bless them, they were
quiet. Such questions would have ruined everything. A former Bad Girl
was about to make the decision of her life.

Did she challenge this stranger who'd called himself—*gasp!*—the Messiah? Did she shake her water pot at his followers and label them fools?

No, she did not. She believed. *Believed!* Having made such a leap of faith, she abandoned her search for plain water.

> Then, leaving her water jar... *John 4:28*

Like an old wineskin, that earthen jar couldn't begin to contain the refreshing water she'd just tasted. Did she leave it on purpose or simply forget it in the excitement of the moment? It doesn't matter. She'd discovered something better, which enabled her to leave her sinful life behind her, forgotten in the dust, and move on.

Filled with living water, she sought other thirsty souls, eager to offer them a drink too.

> ...the woman went back to the town and said to the people,
> "Come, see a man who told me everything I ever did. Could this
> be the Christ?" *John 4:28-29*

Yes, it could, woman!

I think of the evangelistic bumper stickers in the midseventies that proclaimed, "I Found It!" This woman must've been sporting a dozen of them, stuck all over her tunic. Not only had she found the gospel for herself, she wanted everyone else to find it.

"Come, see..."

Two things happen when we meet the Christ and see him for who he really is: (1) We confess our sins openly, and (2) we share the good news of forgiveness freely. That confession—testimony, if you will—comes effortlessly. It's the fragrant aroma of a heart set free.

After that, sharing with others the who-what-when-where-why is only natural. We'd call a friend if we discovered retired Beanie Babies on sale, right? Then why wouldn't we tell the whole world if we found the gift of grace at the best price—free?

People often ask how I can share my past without blushing. No problem. The shame is gone because the *sin* has been forgiven and (thank you,

Lord!) forgotten. As to sharing the gospel, I try not to make a nuisance of myself, but when joy bubbles up, it has to go somewhere.

Sometimes I manage to stifle it though, and then I *am* ashamed. On a live television appearance one December morning, the co-host turned to me with thirty seconds left in the show and said, "Since you're an encourager, Liz, who encourages you?"

The door was wide open to share my faith. Did I smile and say, "Jesus encourages me" or "My trust in God gives me strength"? Oh, nooo. I was too worried about how that secular media personality might react, too concerned that I might look like some religious nut to the viewers.

Good grief, Liz, you *are* a religious nut! Why fight it?

Anytime I get my eyes off Christ and focus on myself, I'm in trouble. I drove home that gray winter morning, grieved and despondent, vowing I wouldn't ignore my next opportunity to gently, firmly honor God publicly.

The woman at the well didn't wait for a door to swing open; she kicked it down herself. "Come, see..." Why did the men of her city listen to her, a woman with a shady lifestyle? Simple: She had seen the Christ. Now the people of Sychar saw the Christ in her.

A changed life gets people's attention every time.

> They came out of the town and made their way toward him.
>
> *John 4:30*

Here they came, a little knot of people, expectant, even apprehensive. All their lives they had heard the centuries-old prophecies about the Messiah. Was it *really* him? What did he look like, sound like, act like? And what was he doing in their neighborhood?

Good old John wove his story well, leaving those questions unanswered to spin the camera back to Jacob's well, where Jesus and his disciples were discussing lunch.

> Meanwhile his disciples urged him, "Rabbi, eat something."
>
> *John 4:31*

They'd gone to town for food, remember? I wonder if they bothered to mention to folks that the Messiah they'd all been waiting generations to meet was sitting by their well, in their very midst. *Nah.* Too busy with the menu.

It doesn't say so in the text, but I think I heard Jesus let out a big sigh of resignation here.

> But he said to them, "I have food to eat that you know nothing
> about." *John 4:32*

The Lord was at it again, baiting them with a tantalizing mystery, using their physical appetites to teach them about spiritual hunger. With the woman it was water; with his followers, it was food.

> Then his disciples said to each other, "Could someone have
> brought him food?" *John 4:33*

Oh, puh-leese! Guys, you're the *disciples.* You're supposed to pick up on this stuff. We'll cut the woman some slack—she didn't know his identity yet—but *you* of all people should've known that Jesus meant something other than tacos and refried beans.

> "My food," said Jesus, "is to do the will of him who sent me and
> to finish his work." *John 4:34*

At this teachable moment, the Lord segued into a lesson on reaping and sowing and the fields being ripe for harvest. I can see the disciples as they struggled for a theological toehold, wondering if they should head back into town to buy hayseed, hoes, and fertilizer—bless their befuddled hearts.

Five verses later the camera suddenly shifts back to the seeking Samaritans, so abruptly that one almost wonders if something hit the cutting-room floor. Except you'd be hard-pressed to find a better example of reaping what you sow. Jesus sowed the seeds of faith in this woman and *watered* them thoroughly (sorry, couldn't resist). The harvest that followed was bountiful.

> Many of the Samaritans from that town believed in him because
> of the woman's testimony, "He told me everything I ever did."
> *John 4:39*

Another writer said it best: "The woman herself, then, becomes a teacher."[4] The Samaritan woman taught not with books but with her life. Her faith couldn't be contained. It flowed through every crack and crevice of her being.

Her neighbors, who knew her best, were utterly convinced she'd encountered the Messiah. Now they wanted to hear from the man himself.

> So when the Samaritans came to him, they urged him to stay with them, and he stayed two days. And because of his words many more became believers. *John 4:40-41*

How our sister must have loved being part of that two-day revival meeting in Sychar! She was no longer treated as an outcast; she was part of the community. She was no longer seen as a foolish female; she was a wise woman. Hadn't she been the first to meet the Messiah? Hadn't she cared enough to include others in the excitement?

> They said to the woman, "We no longer believe just because of what you said; now we have heard for ourselves, and we know that this man really is the Savior of the world." *John 4:42*

Her neighbors weren't being critical. Rather, they were confirming her original testimony: "You were right! He's everything you said he was and more."

The camera crew departed with Jesus for Galilee, so we're left wondering what happened next. My guess is, our woman evangelist won the heart of her man for the Lord and married him. No doubt everyone went home to share stories and search the Law and the Prophets to look for clues that pointed to the man they'd just met.

Whatever the story line, of this we can be sure: The woman with no name left behind not only her discarded water pot, but her shame as well, never to embrace it again.

What Lessons Can We Learn from the Woman at the Well?

Never be afraid to ask questions.

The Samaritan woman wasn't shy about pressing for answers and didn't hesitate to ask for clarification. Sometimes we're afraid to wade into theological waters with someone more knowledgeable than we are for fear we'll ask the wrong questions or appear foolish. Take the risk. Find out what you need to know. If the Lord has provided a teacher, be a willing student. If she hadn't asked all her questions about living water, the woman at the well would have gone home with nothing but a pot full of lifeless liquid and a dozen unanswered questions burning in her heart.

> If any of you lacks wisdom, he should ask God, who gives
> generously to all without finding fault, and it will be given to him.
> *James 1:5*

Not lying isn't the same as telling the truth.
The Lord knows us intimately, just as Jesus knew everything about this woman. She didn't confess her sexual sins; instead, he had to gently point it out to her. God used her subterfuge to reveal his true identity as prophet and Messiah. For those of us who already know the Lord—and are known by him—such word games are no longer appropriate. Wise is the woman who, when her sins are revealed, confesses, repents, and rejoices in the knowledge that even though Jesus sees through our smoke screen, he loves us completely. It's our sins that bring us humbly to our knees, exactly where the Lord wants us to be, so he can shower us with grace.

> Then I acknowledged my sin to you
>   and did not cover up my iniquity.
> I said, "I will confess
>   my transgressions to the LORD"—
> and you forgave
>   the guilt of my sin. *Psalm 32:5*

Thirst is a gift from God.
The woman was eager to find a way around her daily trips to the well, perhaps to avoid the labor and nuisance of it and most certainly to escape the raised eyebrows of her neighbors. Yet it was her thirst that put her in the path of the Messiah. It was her bodily thirst that led to a spiritual quenching. Just as in the physical realm, thirst is a God-given safety measure that

sends us reaching for the nearest glass of water, in the spiritual realm, thirst is a sign we need a time of refreshment with our only source of living water. Let's not ignore that thirst…let's quench it!

> My soul thirsts for God, for the living God.
> When can I go and meet with God? *Psalm 42:2*

Water is meant to be shared, not hoarded.
The Samaritan woman could have tried to keep the good news about the Messiah to herself, conjuring up convincing arguments about how unkind and judgmental the townspeople all were. But the reality was, she *couldn't* keep it a secret even if she'd wanted to. Her joy was too full. Her face was too radiant. Her heart was too changed. Sharing her faith with others wasn't a Monday night missions requirement; it was the unavoidable outpouring of a woman whose spiritual cup suddenly ranneth over.

> "I consider my life worth nothing to me, if only I may finish the race and complete the task the Lord Jesus has given me—the task of testifying to the gospel of God's grace." *Acts 20:24*

Good Girl Thoughts Worth Considering

1. Why is this woman never named in Scripture? Does the omission of her name make her story more or less believable? More or less powerful?

2. Have you ever felt judged by people who aligned themselves with the church? Ever felt "less than"? How did you handle it? Avoidance? Confrontation? Begrudging acceptance? A gentle attempt at reconciliation? Who should reach out first, and why?

3. The woman at the well was thirstier than she realized. What are you "thirsty" for, spiritually? Have you been reaching for something other than the living water Christ offers? Has it quenched your thirst? Why or why not?

4. Jesus spoke first. What prompted the Samaritan woman to respond to this stranger—a man, and a Jew at that? Was it courage? Curiosity?

Contempt? Courtesy? Chutzpa? Have you ever been in a similar situation? What does it take to reach beyond our comfort zones?

5. Look back at their conversation. At what point did the woman realize they were talking about more than mere well water? Did she ever seem uncomfortable with the way their discussion was going? What does that say to you?

6. When the disciples arrived, why didn't they intervene? Look at Jesus' brief teaching on sowing seeds, recorded in John 4:35-38. How does that connect to the Samaritan woman's story that surrounds it?

7. List all the reasons—whether righteous or selfish—the Samaritan woman hurried back to the town to tell everyone she'd met the Messiah. Have you ever shared your faith with people who know you well? What were your reasons? And what were their responses?

8. What's the most important lesson you've learned from the life-changing story of the unnamed woman at the well?

THE FIRST CUT IS THE DEEPEST 5

There is a lot to say in her favor,
but the other is more interesting.
MARK TWAIN

Lila!" The receptionist's voice was just short of a bray. "Your six o'clock manicure is here."

"Shh." Lila shot the woman a look of aggravation. "You'll wake Sam." She watched as the man, now sprawled across her barber's chair, twitched in restless slumber, his dark lashes feathering across his rugged cheeks, his massive shoulders more than filling the chair.

It happened every week. Judge Sam Nazar would show up for a shave and a trim, and within minutes his chin would fall to his muscular chest, his eyelids would droop, and a gentle snore would come rumbling from Lila's corner of the salon. Sometimes he even talked in his sleep, sharing the latest courtroom intrigue in a low murmur only Lila heard and never shared.

The other stylists found it amusing. "Slumbering Sam" they called him—when he was fast asleep and out of earshot.

Wide awake, seated behind the bench in his flowing black robe, Judge Sam was a formidable sight. Only a fool would poke fun at such a giant in the Dallas judicial community. One of the youngest on the bench, Sam had a hard-earned reputation and a hard-driving style. Hadn't he tossed drug dealers behind prison walls for life without parole? Didn't he routinely send greenhorn attorneys running from his courtroom, their tails tucked between their trousered legs, afraid of disbarment or worse?

And the death penalty? An easy call for Judge Sam. He'd sentenced dozens of men to their deaths without blinking an eye or shedding a tear—if his countenance could be trusted.

The legends that swirled around Sam Nazar were legion, though how accurate the stories were—well, that was anybody's guess. Like that rumor about his wife burning to death in a tragic fire soon after their wedding. Somewhere in West Texas, people said, though nobody had newspaper clippings to prove it. Or the old yarn that he'd chased off a dozen gang members with a bone. A *bone?* Folks were crazy.

Then there was the tale about Sam killing a runaway lion at the Dallas Zoo. Witnesses said he didn't even have a gun, just wrestled the lion to the ground and broke the animal's jaw.

One look at his hands—twice the size of most men's—and Lila believed that one. Judge Sam was the law, and everybody in the Metroplex knew it. Judge Sam was also in love with her, and nobody even suspected it.

Me! Lila! Not a society type in sequins and furs—a stylist at a downtown salon. A nice place, sure, but she'd hoped for better someday. When Sam strolled into her life, she thought she'd found her ticket to riches and comfort. Even if he did talk about his God more than she liked, his tailored suits and designer ties told her there was gold underneath his high-and-mighty exterior.

But he didn't give her money or gifts. He only gave her his love. At least that's what *he* called it. She'd heard the word before, plenty of times, and it usually meant something else altogether.

He didn't offer her his name or promise they'd have a future together. He only offered his head in her capable hands every Thursday and his arms wrapped around her slim waist every Saturday night.

"Liii-laa! Your next appointment is here."

Ignoring the insistent voice of the receptionist blaring over the salon speakers, Lila slid a styling comb through Sam's hair and cast an admiring professional gaze on the natural body and dark, generous waves beneath her fingers. He wore his hair longer than any judge in Texas and didn't care who complained about it. Instead, he'd fix his piercing black eyes on hers and issue an order: "Comb it any way you fancy, but take no more than an eighth of an inch off the ends. Hear me, gal?"

She looked down at him now, her scissors flashing in the artificial light of the Cutting Edge, and sleeked a damp clump of hair flat between her fingers, sliding the sharp blade along the edge. *Snip.* One-eighth inch fell to the black-and-white vinyl squares beneath her feet. *Snip.* Another cascade of wet ends drifted to the floor. Lila worked in silence, blocking out the hubbub around her in order to concentrate on the man who'd come to mean much more than a greenback tip in the soda glass propped by her salon mirror.

She'd never told a soul how she felt about Sam. Wasn't sure she knew herself. He was surly and unpredictable and—truth be told—dangerous. He also had a charisma about him that hinted at old money, serious social connections, and Texas roots that went all the way down to molten rock, best she could tell.

Of this she was certain: If she'd met Sam a few years earlier, he might have kept her from chasing after all the wrong sort of men—the kind Sam threw behind bars every chance he got. They'd all been physically strong but morally weak, every one of those men, and their weaknesses had proven to be their undoing. Problem was, when they fell, they never failed to drag her down another notch with them.

Sam rolled his broad shoulders, trying to get more comfortable in her chair even in his sleep. The innocent action sent a cool shiver tripping up Lila's spine. Strength in a man always got her attention. It made her skin tingle and her breath catch and her imagination run wild. Sam Nazar was all about power. Powerful muscles wrapped around a powerful mind acquainted with powerful friends in high places. He scared her almost to the point of fainting when he dropped in her chair every Thursday afternoon. Maybe it was better that he snoozed while she snipped. It made her less nervous that way. Even if he did occasionally tuck love notes in her smock pocket or whisper endearments in her ear when she bent over him with conditioner in her palms, the man was definitely less threatening when his eyes were closed.

Sliding the comb beneath the long hair on the back of his neck, she smoothed the hair upward and felt a rough line of scar tissue underneath the black strands. *What's this?* She'd never noticed it before. *Hmm.* Intrigued, she ran a fingertip along the jagged length of it.

Without warning, Sam jerked, making her jump and accidentally jab his thick neck with her scissors. In an instant he was sitting up straight, fully awake and looking none too happy. She'd barely broken the skin, but still a dot of blood blossomed into a tiny stream running down the back of his neck.

"Wh-what the—!" His eyes were angry storm clouds as he pressed an expensive handkerchief against the wound.

"Judge, I'm...so sorry!" She watched him stanch the small red blotch while she swallowed a lump that was climbing up her windpipe with alarming speed.

He lowered his hand and glanced at the red spot; then his eyes met hers and cooled as quickly as they'd heated. A wry smile stretched across his face. "Just a tiny scratch, sweetheart, judging by the blood."

"W-well, you're the judge." A wave of relief left her lightheaded, giddy. "I'm truly sorry, Sam." She gently touched the edge of the scar tissue hidden under his hairline. "When I found this—"

He yanked her wrist with a rough twist. "Don't touch that."

"Oh! I didn't...you never..." Her relief dissipated like hair spray. She shrugged, hoping to appear nonchalant. "It just surprised me, that's all."

"Well..." He tossed her hand aside as if to dismiss the subject. "No problem, Lila. Just a sensitive spot, that's all. Finish cutting while my hair's still wet, will you?"

Her hands were shaking as she gathered up another section of hair. "Sensitive, you say? That scar tissue looks like it's been there awhile. Does it still hurt?"

His voice dropped to a murmur. "Some wounds never heal."

Oh. She guided her shears around his collar, pressing her lips shut until her curiosity got the better of her. "It's a mean-looking line. Good thing your hair covers every bit of it. How...how did it happen?"

He turned to fix her with a steady gaze, giving nothing away with his eyes. "Three guesses, beautiful girl."

Her cheeks warmed, exactly as a girl's might, even though she'd seen three dozen hot Dallas summers come and go. "Gee, Sam. Another one of your guessing games?" She sighed in mock exasperation. "All right, first guess: Did you land on barbed wire on your daddy's ranch?"

He laughed. "Try again."

"Have a close encounter with a barstool in some Lone Star honky-tonk?"

"You know better than that." Sam never touched the stuff.

She paused, considering. "Did you find yourself at the wrong end of a jealous husband's straight-edge razor?"

The flicker in his ebony eyes was so slight she decided she must have imagined it. "I give up, Sam. What really happened?"

His grin was a loaded weapon. "A big dog bit me."

All day Friday Lila couldn't get the mystery of Sam's scar out of her mind. There wasn't a dog in the world with a bite that wide or that lethal. Sam was hiding something from her, the creep. Didn't he trust her? Who was she gonna tell? It wasn't the scar that mattered, not really. The fact that he'd lied to her, *that's* what pushed her buttons.

Late Saturday afternoon she was finishing up her last client, whipping off the teal vinyl cape with a flourish, when she noticed three men filling the archway into her corner of the salon. Big men, well dressed, with smiles that suggested they wanted something from her.

The minute her customer was gone the men made their move. She watched them, wary. Who were these guys—vaguely familiar and more than a little scary? She swallowed hard and waited while they circled around her.

The stocky man, jangling a set of keys in his hand, spoke first. "Lila, isn't it? From Mesquite?"

She nodded, barely breathing. Was her foolish youth coming back to haunt her? What else did they know about her?

The man's voice was a measured growl. "It's come to our attention that Judge Sam Nazar sits in this chair every Thursday."

"Yeah," another one chimed in. "Falls asleep like a baby, we hear." His laugh was ugly. "Must have some kinda magic in those hands, miss."

Lila bristled. "How I serve my clients is my business."

"Not when he's the most influential judge in Texas." The tallest of the three stepped closer, automatically sending her body heat spiraling.

Power. Her instincts never failed her on that count.

His eyes regarded her with a sinister glint. "We've also heard he talks in his sleep."

How can they possibly know that? One of her coworkers must have spilled the beans. *The jerks.* She raised her chin defiantly. "So? Lots of people talk in their sleep."

They closed ranks on her, blocking her view of anything except their wide-brimmed Stetson hats and predatory smiles. The tall one leaned over and whispered, "We'll get right to the point, Lila. We have reason to believe that Sam Nazar killed a man. Maybe more than one."

The blood in her veins turned to ice. *Sam, a murderer?* It wasn't possible. She told them as much.

"You're wrong, miss. Dead wrong. Once the good voters of Dallas hear about this, Judge Nazar will be done in this town. Off the bench and off our backs for good. It's his one weak spot, that history of his. Did you happen to notice a scar above the back of his neck?"

Her eyes widened. The puzzle pieces were falling together. *Of course!* The scar was put there not by a dog's teeth but by a knife, no doubt wielded by a man who got himself killed in the process.

The men exchanged knowing glances. "All we need is his sleep-talking confession on this little microcassette recorder." A small black box was shoved her direction. "That's where you come in, Lila. You and your pretty face should be able to coax a confession out of the judge, right? Ask a few questions, lull him off to sleep. Bingo."

The tall one slipped a bulging envelope out of his pocket and opened it briefly, waving the contents under her nose. "As you can see, we'll make it worth your while."

She didn't have to count it to know it was a huge sum of money. Thousands. Hundreds of thousands maybe. Enough to build that better life she'd been dreaming about. Enough to start over.

"Have we made our point, Lila?" He shoved the envelope back in his pocket and patted it with a rough-knuckled hand. "You're seeing Lover Boy on Saturday night as usual, yes?"

So they know about that, too. She shrugged, then realized she'd given herself away. Clearly they knew the score, knew she was interested in their money, too. Sam was a nice guy. No, not nice—strong. Masculine. But there was no future there. Not for a girl like her.

Sam was a murderer, plain and simple. Who was to say she wouldn't be his next victim? Sure, she'd miss his soul-stirring kisses, but there was enough cash in that envelope to keep her warm for decades of chilly Dallas winters. Besides, all his talk about God got on her nerves, and she was growing weary of changing the subject.

The truth was, the opportunity of a lifetime had just marched through the doors of the Cutting Edge, and she wasn't about to throw it away.

An image flashed across her mind and disappeared just as quickly. An image of Sam waking up not in her lap but in prison. Shackled. Ridiculed. Stripped of his power. The big man cut down to size.

By her.

Sorry, Sam.

Lila took a deep breath and shoved her shaking hands into her smock pockets. "I'm listening. Tell me what you want me to do…"

A Truly Bad (Girl) Hair Day: Delilah

A woman like Delilah is the last person a devoted mother would choose for her only begotten man-child. But if Samson had fallen in love with a nice girl from home, there would have been no story. And my, my, was there ever a story.

> The woman gave birth to a boy and named him Samson. He grew and the LORD blessed him, and the Spirit of the LORD began to stir him. *Judges 13:24-25*

"He" would be Samson, a man in no way like the godly Joseph of chapters past, despite Samson's auspicious beginning. A Scottish scholar of the twentieth century found Samson "more like Rob Roy and [Robert] Burns than he is like the mighty prophets and leaders of Israel."[1] Rob Roy? Aye, I canna help but hear the skirl of bagpipes when I clap me eyes on his tartan-swathed thighs…

Well, maybe not. Surely such attire would have been an affront to Samson's Nazirite vows—outlined in the sixth chapter of Numbers—which included no fruit of the vine (not even raisins), no contact with dead bodies, and definitely no haircuts.

For a guy who was supposed to avoid dead bodies, Samson surely created a ton of them. The Scotsman called Samson a "frolicsome giant." Giant, yes. Jolly and green, no. Samson's larger-than-life exploits in Judges 14 and 15 depict a rather mean-spirited, biblical Paul Bunyan who wielded his vastly superior strength like an ax on the necks of the Philistines.

His enemies had good reason to fear Samson, of whom the banner headline in the *Timnah Times* might have proclaimed, "He-Man Tears Apart Lion with Bare Hands." A feat, by the way, which he managed to do on the way to his own wedding feast.

"I am Samson; hear me roar."

His stunts were legendary. When his bride, a foreigner, was given away to his best man instead, Samson tied the tails of three hundred foxes together in pairs, attached a flaming torch to each set of tails, and sent them running into his enemy's grainfields, destroying everything in their path. (Think of the special effects it would take to create *that* panorama for the silver screen.)

The Philistines retaliated by burning Samson's wife and father-in-law to death. Not as flashy as the fox fiasco but much more personal. Samson eventually took revenge by striking down a *thousand* men with the jawbone of a single donkey, a move that was flashy *and* personal. No question, the entire book of Judges should carry a warning sticker—"For Mature Audiences Only." The murder and mayhem quotient, already high at that point in the story, got worse.

Samson found his way to a prostitute's bed in Gaza while his enemies slept at the city gate, waiting to kill him in the morning. Our hero outsmarted them by jumping up in the middle of the night, lifting that very gate onto his broad shoulders, and carrying it to the top of a hill nearly forty miles away. Clearly even a night of passion couldn't deplete the superhuman resources of this herculean man. Arnold, Sly, and Jean-Claude at their bench-pressing best wouldn't stand a chance against this musclebound brute, though Samson needed *someone* to cut him down to size.

It took a woman to accomplish the task.

A woman named Delilah.

> Some time later, he fell in love with a woman in the Valley of Sorek whose name was Delilah. *Judges 16:4*

In Hebrew, "Delilah" is variously translated as "languishing" or "weak." In Arabic, "Delilah" means "flirt" or "coquettish woman."

By any definition, this valley girl's charms worked on poor, besotted Samson, who not only trusted her, he loved her. We are never told that she loved him in return, yet it's clear that he cared deeply for her. She was not a one-night stand, like the woman in Gaza. Or an abandoned wife, like the woman in Timnah. He "fell in love" with the woman. Period. The other two women are not named in Scripture, but this mysterious woman of whom we know so little—no past, no nationality, no family—had a name, and a delectable one at that.

We know very few facts about Delilah, but the things we do know raise more questions than they answer. She lived in the Valley of Sorek, between Israelite and Philistine lands, which tells us where her home was located but not where her allegiance dwelled. Was she Philistine or Israelite? The scholars can't agree on that one.

She had a house of her own, a rare distinction unless she was independently wealthy (meaning the bribe that followed wouldn't have had nearly as much appeal). Or she could have been a widow. Or a prostitute. Though if that was the case, why wasn't she so named, since the harlot in Gaza sported that label?

Besides, if Delilah regularly sold her services, when did she find time for this long, hairy affair with Samson?

One commentator called her "The Undesirable Woman."[2] The *what?* That was one attribute of Delilah that goes without saying: desirability. Obviously that writer never laid eyes on the lady, who must have been quite a looker to capture Samson's eye and heart. That she was a fallen woman of loose morals we have no doubt, since Samson spent time alone with her in her inner chamber—something Good Girls didn't do.

Powerful Samson could have had any woman he wanted, and he wanted Delilah, even though we see no evidence that she had a charming personality, great wit, boundless compassion, or gentle affection. Only one explanation remains: She was an extraordinary beauty who knew how to display her body, hair, and face to snare a man's heart. Even strong men can harbor a hidden weakness. For Samson, that vulnerable spot wasn't his long hair; it was Delilah herself.

Over the centuries commentators have slung buckets of mud in Delilah's direction. Though referred to merely as a "woman" in the Scriptures, she's since been labeled "a harlot," "a heartless seducer," "a temptress," "dark and sinister," "a temple prostitute," and "one of the lowest, meanest women of the Bible—the female Judas of the Old Testament."[3]

The way I see it, the operative word for Delilah might be *pawn.*

The rulers of the Philistines went to her and said… *Judges 16:5*

This snippet of the story reveals an important fact: Betraying Samson wasn't Delilah's idea. Yes, she bought into it—literally, as we'll see in a moment—but conventional wisdom says, "Follow the money." In this case, the money led directly back to the Philistine heads of state. They were the ones who planted the seeds of betrayal in her heart.

If Delilah were on the witness stand, I'd have only one question for her: "Delilah darlin', did you choose to be with Samson for your own pleasure and *then* hear from the Philistines, or did those bad boys set you up to tear Samson down from day one?" Such a technicality would merely satisfy my own curiosity, since as far as the outcome of the story is concerned, it really doesn't matter. Either way, sooner or later Delilah was summarily used by powerful politicos with payback on their minds.

She might get our sympathy vote, though, if we knew she was coerced into it.

> "See if you can lure him into showing you the secret of his great strength and how we can overpower him so we may tie him up and subdue him." *Judges 16:5*

The reputation of Delilah as one who could lure a man must have been known far and wide. The Philistine leaders appealed to her vanity and her confidence in handling the opposite sex. They realized Samson's strength was superhuman, that its source was a "secret," not just a healthy diet, daily workouts, and a dose of steroids. The man's weakness was already obvious—women. It was his mysterious strength his enemies wanted to subdue.

Most translations say "afflict" him; it literally means "tie, bind, imprison, bring low." Yet during his tryst with the prostitute in Gaza, the Philistines waited at the city gate to *kill* him.

"Subdue" him? Oh sure. That's what they told Delilah.

In truth, they wanted to bring Samson to his knees, humble him publicly, and *then* kill him. As with another legendary leader centuries later—William Wallace of *Braveheart* fame—the powers-that-be would not be appeased with a *dead* hero. They wanted a *humiliated* hero, and they needed Delilah to help them do their dirty work.

Notice they went to her directly. Not to her father, her brother, her husband, or her son, as would have been customary. Straight to Delilah. Our twenty-first-century ears don't perk up at that, but they should. Women of the time weren't famous for their financial acumen. Something shady was going on, and the fewer people involved, it seemed, the better.

Think Watergate. Contragate. Monicagate.

Notice that they didn't appeal to her intellect or her sense of patriotism. No "this is for the good of the country" speeches. They didn't entreat her with promises of physical pleasure. No "give us your lover, and we'll find a man ten times his equal." They didn't aim for her tender woman's heart either. No "if he really loved you, he'd marry you" innuendos.

They trained their oil lamps on her own weakness—greed—and took careful aim with a loaded coin.

> "Each one of us will give you eleven hundred shekels of silver."
>
> *Judges 16:5*

Honey, this is some major money. Thirty-four pounds of silver multiplied by several men. A fortune, considering a Levite might work an entire year for a paltry ten shekels.[4]

A woman could live like a queen for the rest of her natural life on such an astounding sum. Before we condemn Delilah for the actions that followed, we might ask ourselves which we would choose: (1) the company of a violent man with a rocky reputation and shocking track record with women, who was neither a husband nor a father and who might disappear without a word of regret, *or* (2) the comfort of cold, hard silver that would keep a woman well fed and finely dressed for a lifetime?

Not an easy decision, then or now.

Unless the woman truly loved him.

Grab your daisies, sisters, and let's pull off the petals, one by one. "She loved him. She loved him not. She loved him. She loved him not…"

Not, it seems. Delilah made her choice without hesitation.

> So Delilah said to Samson, "Tell me the secret of your great strength and how you can be tied up and subdued."
>
> *Judges 16:6*

Give the woman credit for one thing: She didn't water down her request. Didn't appeal to his male ego by asking simply, "What makes you so strong, big boy?" Delilah laid the grisly goal right out there—"so you can be subdued." At times like this I long for an adverb or two. Did she say it coquettishly or brazenly or teasingly? With a playful wink? With a kittenish pout? The Lord knows, but we do not.

I vote for the playful wink. After all, Delilah knew Samson well. Exceedingly well. He'd played riddles and verbal games his whole life. In fact, it was a riddle that led to his first wife's death, so this bold question from Delilah might have struck him as mere pillow talk from his lady love, nothing more. As one commentator phrased it, "Nowhere is woman's craft seen in its naked cruelty more clearly."[5] Thinking it a simple game, Samson played along.

> Samson answered her, "If anyone ties me with seven fresh thongs
> that have not been dried, I'll become as weak as any other man."
> *Judges 16:7*

It didn't work, of course. The Philistines brought her fresh thongs—*not* skimpy bathing suits but narrow leather strips—which she used to tie Samson down, to no avail.

> But he snapped the thongs as easily as a piece of string snaps when
> it comes close to a flame. *Judges 16:9*

Delilah was getting a little hot under the necklace herself, especially since the Philistines were hiding in the room when it happened, waiting to subdue him. Whether a minute later or a day or a week, she brought up the subject again.

> Then Delilah said to Samson, "You have made a fool of me;
> you lied to me. Come now, tell me how you can be tied."
> *Judges 16:10*

It's strange that Delilah is always the one accused of deception, since she was the straightforward one in this scene and Samson the one whose answers were false. The difference? Their opposing motives.

He told fibs for sport.

She spoke truth for silver.

They went through this exercise twice more. He insisted that new ropes would hold him, then proceeded to break the ropes as if they were mere threads. He declared that if she wove his seven braids into the fabric on a loom, he'd be helpless. When he awakened from his sleep, he pulled up the entire loom—braids, fabric, and all.

Three lies. Three surprises. The third time *wasn't* the charm. But Delilah—like Mrs. Potiphar, her sister in seduction—was nothing if not persistent. Notice how carefully she did not profess love for *him* but used his love for her like a cruel cattle prod.

> Then she said to him, "How can you say, 'I love you,' when you
> won't confide in me?" *Judges 16:15*

"If you really love me…"

Stevie Wonder may have had a top-ten hit with that title in 1971, but women have been singing that refrain for thousands of years.

"How can you say, 'I love you,' when…"

Delilah's true nature, if not already obvious, was revealed here. No adverbs are needed to discern the tone in her voice in these lines. It's clear the woman was *whining*.

Try it. Say Delilah's words aloud. See? The only delivery that works is a pronounced nasal whine—served with cheese and a nice, crusty Philistine bread.

The same fare was on the menu for breakfast, lunch, and dinner.

> With such nagging she prodded him day after day until he was
> tired to death. *Judges 16:16*

Proof once again that the Lord has a sense of humor. Other translations render it, "annoyed to death" (NASB) and "vexed" (AMP), but I like this version, written for children, best: "He became so tired of it he felt like he was going to die!" (ICB)

Nag, nag, prod, prod, whine, whine. It was enough to wear the man down to the nub, exactly as his first wife managed to do two chapters earlier:

> Then Samson's wife threw herself on him, sobbing, "You hate me!
> You don't really love me.…" So on the seventh day he finally told
> her, because she continued to press him. *Judges 14:16-17*

It was déjà vu all over again. Samson clearly had a hankering for whine, women, and song. Hundreds of years later one of the writers of Proverbs might have had Samson in mind when he penned:

> A quarrelsome wife is like
>> a constant dripping on a rainy day;
> restraining her is like restraining the wind
>> or grasping oil with the hand. *Proverbs 27:15-16*

Sam the Sham was ready to throw in the towel. No more parlor games. No more clever riddles. His physical strength was still intact, but his emotional strength had shriveled up and blown away, thanks to Delilah's endless nagging.

So he told her everything. *Judges 16:17*

Oh, to be a fly on the tent flap for *that* pivotal moment in history! Delilah, scented and sultry, waited eagerly to hear the truth at last. Samson, his long, black braids flying, his dark eyes snapping, his sandaled feet thundering along the hard-packed earth, ground out his answer.

"All right, woman!" we can imagine him shouting. "You want to know the secret of my strength? Fine. I'll tell you. Anything to get you off my back." When the truth was spoken, his doom was sealed.

> "No razor has ever been used on my head," he said, "because I have
> been a Nazirite set apart to God since birth. If my head were
> shaved, my strength would leave me, and I would become as weak
> as any other man." *Judges 16:17*

The man was so trusting. Make that dense. Didn't he see where this was leading? Was he so blinded by love—or lust—that he didn't care? Why didn't someone read him his Miranda rights, since his testimony could and definitely would be used against him?

One almost feels sorry for Samson.

Almost.

> When Delilah saw that he had told her everything… *Judges 16:18*

Wait. How did she know it was "everything"? A woman's intuition perhaps. The agonized expression on Samson's face. Or maybe because it made sense. Hair that had never been cut would be exceedingly long and most unusual, at any time in history. Think Rapunzel. Lady Godiva. Samson's floor-length tresses would have been the cause of much conjecture. *Of course.* Cut his hair, and his power is history.

Delilah didn't feel sorry for him. She felt rich.

> …she sent word to the rulers of the Philistines, "Come back once
> more; he has told me everything." So the rulers of the Philistines
> returned with the silver in their hands. *Judges 16:18*

The comparison to Judas is hard to avoid. Not thirty pieces of silver for Delilah though. Thousands of shekels. Still, it's not the amount that counts when it comes to sin, treachery, and deceit. Delilah was a Bad Girl, at any price. She put no value at all on Samson's love, life, or loyalty to her.

The truth is, the silver didn't represent Samson's price; it was *her* price. She was the one who was bought and sold. Her pride, her name, her reputation, however soiled they may already have been, were now shamed for eternity.

We might not trust a girl named Delilah, but Samson did, resting his head on her lap, the picture of submission. Or stupidity, after a line of questioning like hers.

> Having put him to sleep on her lap... *Judges 16:19*

My first thought was a sleeping potion. Some nefarious drug of the time that would have rendered him unconscious. But the Hebrew word means she literally *lulled* him to sleep, no doubt using every wile of womanhood. Her soothing, hypnotic voice whispered words of comfort and ease. Her gentle fingers drew circles on Samson's scalp in an ever-widening pattern until his eyes drooped to half-mast, then closed completely.

At our house this is known as "Mama Magic." I practiced it on our children when they were tiny babies fighting sleep. After every other base was covered—clean diaper, full tummy, warm blankie—it was time for my secret weapon: making circles on their downy heads. Round and round I went to the tune of "Hush Little Baby, Don't Say a Word." Indeed, I didn't have to say diddly-squat. My soft voice and sleepy circles took care of everything.

Here, though, we have an adult man and woman who were sexually intimate, so undoubtedly Delilah had more devious ways to be sure her man was thoroughly exhausted. Whatever her methods, they seemed most effective, sending Samson off to Lullaby Land with his head on her knees and his life in her hands.

> ...she called a man to shave off the seven braids of his hair, and so began to subdue him. And his strength left him. *Judges 16:19*

Why did she call a man to do the dirty work? Because she didn't dare risk moving this giant of a man from her lap while she reached for the scissors? Because at the last minute she couldn't bring herself to do it, knowing that she was not only ending his life but their relationship as well?

It sho'nuff wasn't because her cosmetology license had expired.

My guess is that if Samson awoke midsnip, Delilah didn't want to be the one caught cutting off his source of power. She did call out a warning of sorts, but it was more likely her cue to the Philistines: "He's out like a light! Make your move!"

Samson awakened, thinking the occasion would be like the last three, that he would shake off the ties that bound him and raise his arms in victory once more.

> But he did not know that the LORD had left him. *Judges 16:20*

He found out soon enough. We won't dwell on the gouged-out eyes and the bronze shackles and the prison sentence that followed. Suffice it to say that Samson learned the hardest lesson of all about the consequences of sin: separation from God.

At this point in the story, Delilah disappears from Scripture, slinking off to an ignominious end, we assume, resurfacing through the ages in paintings by Rubens and Moreau, in the writing of Milton, and even as the title of Tom Jones's 1968 hit record about a cheating woman named—what else?—Delilah. She's a legend, a household word, a one-name wonder about whom history and the Bible reveal nothing more. As Victor Mature said of Hedy Lamarr in Cecil B. De Mille's 1949 classic, *Samson and Delilah,* "The name Delilah will be an everlasting curse on the lips of men."[6]

Good exit line, mister.

Samson, however, made one more earthshaking appearance when his enemies gathered to celebrate their triumph over him. Why, oh why, didn't they give him a haircut for the occasion, just to be on the safe side?

> But the hair on his head began to grow again. *Judges 16:22*

His dependence on God was growing right along with his dark locks. All he needed was the right time and place to put his growing strength to the test.

The temple was bulging with Philistines that day. From their viewpoint on the roof, three thousand watched as Samson was dragged out to "perform" for the assembly. Did he entertain them with marvelous demonstrations of muscle? Or with clever riddles, for which he was renowned far and wide? Perhaps seeing him led there by the hand, blind and weakened, was sufficient sport for their jaded palates.

The most intriguing question of all: Was Delilah in the audience? One wonders how she could resist the spectacle. Surely her presence would be expected. We can imagine the necks craning around the temple courtyard and hear the whisper of gossips who'd found a tasty morsel to chew on.

"Is that her? Is it Delilah, in the flesh?"

"Look at that tunic, will you! Must have cost a fortune."

"If you ask me, silver is *not* her color."

Would Delilah be hailed a heroine for bringing down the mighty Samson? Or would the Philistines despise her for not standing by her man but handing him over to the authorities for a heartless reward of silver?

If she was on hand for the festivities, Delilah left her riches behind for her survivors, because few if any walked away that fateful day. Samson managed to save his reputation, if not himself, when he called on God for one last show of strength and pulled down the pillars of the crowded temple around him, killing "many more when he died than while he lived."[7]

The prophet Zechariah's words, penned nearly a millennium later, would have served as a fitting epitaph for Samson's grave:

> "Not by might nor by power, but by my Spirit," says the LORD
> Almighty. *Zechariah 4:6*

Samson, despite causing his parents unending grief by choosing a Philistine wife, then a Gaza prostitute, then a vapid valley girl, still made the Hebrews honor roll.

> And what more shall I say? I do not have time to tell about Gideon,
> Barak, Samson, Jephthah, David, Samuel and the prophets, who
> through faith conquered kingdoms, administered justice, and gained
> what was promised; who shut the mouths of lions…whose weakness
> was turned to strength. *Hebrews 11:32-34*

Samson in the company of David and Samuel? Impressive, big guy. Even with all his failings, he still had a heart for God, while our Bad Girl Delilah had a heart only for herself and for money. The Lord used her treachery for good nonetheless, bringing Samson to his knees in humility and the Philistines to their death.

A century ago a commentator concluded, "Delilah rises suddenly from darkness…and goes down in a horizon of awful gloom."[8] Maybe Delilah left town long before that disastrous day. Or maybe the last thing she saw before her eyes closed for eternity was the strong hero she'd once brought to her knees, lifting up his eyes to the heavens, calling on a God she would never know. Of all Delilah's shortcomings, this was by far the greatest: not that she was rich in silver but that she was poor in spirit.

What Lessons Can We Learn from Delilah?

The love of a man is to be treasured.
Oh, when I think of the hearts I trampled rather than treasured in my foolish youth! Yes, my heart got mashed plenty of times as well, but it was my own heartless tendencies that needed curbing. When men declare their love for us, we should handle them with utmost care, even if the feelings aren't mutual. For the sake of future marital happiness, or to leave their hearts intact for another woman down the pike, let's be gentle and trustworthy with their brave declarations.

The heart of her husband trusts in her. *Proverbs 31:11* (NASB)

Silver and gold aren't very good company.
What Delilah gained in goods she surely lost in relationships. The same thing can happen to us when we pursue a materialistic life style and leave behind dear friends in our frenzy of accumulation. Money separates people more often than it joins them. Remember when we were Brownies and we sang about friendships—"one is silver and the other gold"? Let's pull our sit-upons up to the campfire and choose warm, golden memories over the company of cold silver.

To be esteemed is better than silver or gold. *Proverbs 22:1*

Weaknesses need to be strengthened, not exposed.
On purpose or by mistake, the people we're closest to eventually reveal their vulnerable spots and weaknesses. We need to fight the urge to use that

knowledge against them as a weapon for public embarrassment, even in jest. Does that person have an unusual mannerism, a phobia, a quirky private habit, a deep-seated concern? Zip those lips, girls! Keeping someone else's limitation a secret between the two of you will knit you closer together. In the workplace, it's a step toward friendship and respect. In marriage, it's a tool for intimacy. In all things, it's a way to honor the Lord.

> That is why, for Christ's sake, I delight in weaknesses.... For when I am weak, then I am strong. *2 Corinthians 12:10*

For a happy home, keep your scissors out of reach.
We might not chop off all seven braids at once, thereby reducing our man's power to nil, but how many among us have snip-snip-snipped at our man's sense of worth and value by undermining him with not-so-gentle jabs at his masculinity?

"If only you could provide more for our family..."

"Well, *my* father could fix anything..."

"Is that the best you can do?"

(*Ouch!* Stabbed my *own* self with the scissors.)

The world cuts our men down enough. Even as we enjoy it when they build *us* up, so should we be ready with emotional bricks and mortar for their edification.

> The wise woman builds her house,
>> but with her own hands the foolish one tears hers
>> down. *Proverbs 14:1*

Good Girl Thoughts Worth Considering

1. What weaknesses other than his attraction to the wrong sort of women do you find in Samson? Do you see any of those same weak spots in your own life? In your man's life?

2. What weaknesses did Delilah have? Did they ultimately serve her well or poorly? Is a weakness the same thing as a besetting sin?

3. Samson was often depicted as taking revenge for one wrong or another. Could Delilah have been seeking revenge too? For what perhaps? Is revenge ever a legitimate motive? Why or why not?

4. Climb into Delilah's heart. What do you see there? An angry woman? A hurt child? A deserted wife? A greedy harlot? Think of all the ways you might describe her, based on the scriptural story and your own experiences as a woman.

5. How much did the reward of silver influence her decision to deceive Samson? Have you ever taken a job simply for the money or in any way been influenced by monetary gain? What did you learn from those experiences? Are there potential Philistines in your life now, tempting you with easy money?

6. Why was Samson so easily deceived? Was that Delilah's fault or his? Are there blind spots in your own life where you can be swayed more easily? At work? With your children? With certain friends? What could you do, specifically, to avoid being ensnared like Samson?

7. What was Delilah's root sin? Lust? Greed? Idolatry? Selfishness? How does that same sin rear its ugly head in your own life, and what could you do to surrender it to the lordship of Christ?

8. What's the most important lesson you've learned from the dark, disastrous story of Samson and Delilah?

GENEROUS TO A FAULT

6

That money talks I'll not deny,
I heard it once: It said, "Goodbye."

RICHARD ARMOUR

ofia opened the creamy white envelope with a single slice of her
grandmother's heavy brass letter opener. A cherished and valuable
item on her writing desk, it featured an intricately carved handle and
sleek, polished blade. Quite the thing to use whenever she had an audience. At the moment only her husband, Aidan, was nearby, absorbed in a
book, giving little thought to the morning mail.

No matter. That would change in ten seconds.

Her hands trembled as she slid out the embossed card inside. The first
few lines launched her heart on a merry dance. *Finally!* It was an invitation they'd waited years to receive. Sofia's lips pursed in a satisfied bow, as
if she'd just tasted a bite of tangy lemon pie.

"Aidan, it's here." She waved the invitation at her husband of two
dozen summers, pleased to see a smile crease his handsome face when the
card came into focus. Aidan understood what this meant to her, what it
would mean for both of them.

"Read it to me, darling." He tossed his book aside, offering her his
undivided attention.

She cleared her throat with a drama that suited the occasion, then
began to read aloud: "The Three Rivers Philanthropic Society requests
your presence at their 100th annual awards dinner. Black tie only, please."
Sofia practiced her most sophisticated laugh. "Naturally. Who would dare
appear in anything else?"

Noting the request for a response, she reached for the phone, then paused. *Too eager, Sofia.* After waiting this long to be included among the notable attendees, she'd hate to ruin her chances for future invitations with near-desperate enthusiasm. She would wait until tomorrow at least. In the afternoon. *Perfect.*

A dozen details flitted through her mind, demanding immediate consideration. Her dress would have to be elegant, conservative. Haute couture, of course. Preferably European. If it complemented her emerald necklace and earrings—the ones that matched the deep green of her eyes—so much the better. Aidan's formal wear, freshly returned from the cleaners, would never do. Something updated and understated would be more apropos. Would a corsage for her be over the top? Should they rent a limo and driver for the night? Oh, but that *would* be overdoing it.

Aidan's deep voice penetrated her reverie. "Don't spend all our money on appearances, beloved." His smile assured her he was only teasing, though he added, "Your eyes are filled with shopping bags. Expensive ones. We're supposed to be giving our money away, remember?"

Sofia pushed out her lower lip in an exaggerated pout which never failed to amuse her husband and loosen his hold on her purse strings. "I simply want us to present ourselves to this group in the most flattering light possible."

He shook his head, clearly not convinced. "It isn't fancy attire that will impress them, dear. It's an exceedingly generous check to the foundation that will win their approval." He tipped his silver-streaked head, assessing her. "It *is* their approval you're after, isn't it, Sofia?"

No point arguing. Aidan had her there, and she knew it. Ever since they'd relocated to Pittsburgh twenty years earlier—struggling newlyweds on their way up financially and socially—Sofia had eyed the altruistic elite from a distance. Theirs was a quiet dignity that reeked of money, but even more, of respectability. As Aidan's business acumen in the Golden Triangle grew, so did Sofia's desire to be part of the city's *old* money. Not for her the circle of young movers and shakers, spending their hard-earned dollars on exorbitant trappings. It was the established families, living off wise investments, that appealed to some place deep inside her.

Andrew Carnegie had set the pace in 1900 when the Three Rivers Philanthropic Society was established. Along with Carnegie, Andrew Mellon used his wealth and personal art collection to enrich the city, as did industrial magnates like Henry Phipps and Henry Clay Frick.

In jest, Aidan whispered privately about "keeping up with the Andrews."

"Or with the Henrys," Sofia reminded him with a wink, though she knew it was the Mellon family that garnered the most respect these days.

Such names filled the Pittsburgh phone directory: The Carnegie Museum of Art, Carnegie Science Center, Carnegie-Mellon University, Phipps Conservatory, the Frick Art Museum.

Sofia and Aidan were prepared to wait their turn. It might be another decade before the two of them managed to donate the sort of funds that would put their name on a building. In the meantime they had moved to an impressive home in Fox Chapel, made investments that involved both higher risk and higher profit, and finally had enough tucked away to offer a donation of some merit at the awards dinner.

That was the point of the evening. Each couple or individual was expected to contribute at least one million dollars to the foundation. It was never stated as such—*heavens, no!*—but the two dozen players knew their appointed roles for the evening and came prepared to present a seven-figure check for a worthy cause.

Aidan had earned his money by investing other people's resources, and now the couple was poised for their ascent into the rarefied air at the summit of the city's steel-girded social strata.

A million dollars. Gone with a few strokes of the pen.

The power and prestige of it left Sofia near to fainting.

She responded affirmatively the following afternoon, secretly pleased at how easily she'd handled the phone call to one of the grande dames of Pittsburgh. They would fit in. They *would;* she was certain now.

Sofia was scanning the *New York Times* later that evening, looking for some hint of an upcoming Manhattan runway show where she might find a suitable gown, when Aidan arrived home later than usual. She glanced up; then the newspaper slid to her feet, forgotten.

"Aidan?"

He was hunched over the wing chair, his skin deathly pale, his breathing erratic.

She shivered, as if a breeze had skittered through the room. "Aidan, what is it?"

It took a full minute before he could say the words. "We're...broke."

"We're *what?*" It was inconceivable. "Aidan, really!"

He yanked his tie off with a noisy sigh and tossed the length of silk in the direction of her oak secretary. "Sorry to be so direct, darling. If you spent as much time reading the business section as you do the fashion pages, you'd understand."

"Understand what?" She heard the terror in her voice, the discouragement in his. "Start at the beginning, Aidan. What has happened to all our money?"

He quickly lost her in a barrage of stock-market information that confused her further, but he clarified one thing beyond doubt: There would be no million-dollar contribution to the foundation, no dinner, and no new gown, not even from a dress rack at Kaufmanns.

"What are we going to do?" Sofia sank into the plump cushions of her pale-striped love seat, her hands dropping next to her, limp. "I can't bear to think of giving up our beautiful home."

"Now, now, my little Fia."

He hadn't called her that since they'd moved to Pittsburgh, but she was too distraught to appreciate the endearment. He squeezed next to her, slipping a comforting arm around her sagging shoulders, a bit of color returning to his face. "It's not as bad as all that. When I said we were broke, I meant our discretionary income has dried up. We won't lose our house or our cars. But mind me, wife." He shook his finger at her with mock severity. "No more shopping."

"And no more Philanthropic Society?" She knew she was whining but couldn't seem to stop herself.

Aidan slowly shook his head, his lips tightening in a frown. "Not this year."

"But they won't ask us again!" she wailed, smacking the love seat and his knee with equal fervor. "It's our only chance!"

Sighing heavily, he stood and paced in front of her. "Sofia, the only way we could manage such a donation would be to sell our property in West Palm Beach."

"Not our vacation house!" she moaned.

"It's the only thing we own that's not mortgaged to the hilt."

His confession pressed her back against the throw pillows. "Are you serious?"

"I'm always serious about money. You know that." He dropped to his haunches, the fabric of his fine suit stretched across his knees. "Look. Let me make a few calls, ask a few questions."

"They all have homes down there," she cautioned. "Remember? That's why we bought a house in West Palm, to hobnob over the winter months with the Old Guard. If we put it on the market, they'll all know where we got our million."

"But wouldn't selling that property and willingly donating all the proceeds show them how serious we are about philanthropy?"

Sofia shrugged, seeing the wisdom of it even as she saw her precious second home on the nicest street in West Palm slipping through her hands.

He patted her knee, then stood. "I promise to be beyond discreet. Besides, when our bank account is bulging once more, we'll buy another one. A bigger one." He tugged at her ear with a playful pull. "You fret too much, Fia. Let me worry about where the money comes from, all right? Your job is to find the most head-turning gown our limited resources can buy. Are we in agreement then?"

The man was utterly charming. She couldn't possibly refuse him. "I promise, husband of mine. I'll handle the cachet; you handle the cash."

Three months later she found herself slipping into a slim satin dress of deepest jade that matched the exquisite jewels dangling from her ears and draped around her neck. "This dress does things for those bewitching green eyes of yours," Aidan murmured, fastening the necklace clasp, then nibbling briefly at the back of her bare neck.

"No time for that," she scolded, slipping her brand-new faux mink coat around her shoulders. She'd sighed over the real furs but knew full well that in this social circle animal fur was frowned upon. Her imitation was the best of its kind, more expensive than many of the genuine furs. It was full length and a perfect fit. With her hair swept up in a becoming French twist, Sofia almost didn't recognize herself in the mirror, so thorough was the transformation.

She watched Aidan check his pocket for the fourth time, patting the envelope there for assurance. *One million, no more, no less.* They'd promised the Society—in writing—that they'd donate all the proceeds, then placed their Florida house on the market with a one-million-dollar price tag. Clever Aidan reminded her that if it sold for less than a million, they'd still be admitted to the society, having given more sacrificially than most.

How could they have foreseen that a developer would come along and offer them more than their asking price just to close the deal in a hurry? When Aidan confessed to Sofia that they had "a little more than expected," they agreed there was no need to add it to their contribution.

Wasn't a million dollars enough?

It was surely providential that they had pocketed a nice profit. Except it wasn't in their pockets; it was on Sofia's back and in their driveway. A mink and a Mercedes seemed quite the thing for their premiere in Pittsburgh society.

They arrived at the dinner precisely at seven, noticing how shiny and showroom-new their Mercedes looked next to the properly aged BMWs and Lincolns parked along the curb. Theirs would look used soon enough. Handing the keys to the valet, Aidan escorted Sofia up the steps to the club and steered her toward the first-floor salon where the women gathered while the men convened in the second-floor smoking room.

So it had been for a century, and so it would be tonight.

For that, Sofia was elated. She wanted everything to be exactly the same as it'd been in Carnegie's day, with one important addition: *her*. And Aidan, of course. They wouldn't be there without his keen financial mind. He'd been especially free spirited with their unexpected windfall the last few days, which had delighted her to no end.

From the doorway of the salon she admired his broad shoulders as he made his way up the carpeted staircase to the second floor. He turned to give her a confident wink, and she felt the heat rise to her cheeks. How handsome he looked this evening! His formal attire fit him like the proverbial glove, and his expensive haircut from Philip Pelusi was clearly worth the investment. The man looked every inch a millionaire. For a brief moment he would be one, before their check purchased their entrée into a whole new world.

Feeling giddy, she pursed her lips in a swift, invisible kiss, which he returned before disappearing at the curve of the landing.

Sofia spun around and floated into the salon, the corners of her mouth turned upward—*not too much!*—and her hands empty, prepared to receive a glass, a handshake, or whatever might be offered. A matronly sort approached her, slipped her arm through the crook of Sofia's elbow, and guided her along a bank of seated women as if they were flowers in a formal garden being identified by genus and species.

"This is Mrs. Randolph McCormick." Her tone was starched lace. "And Mrs. Daniel Stevenson."

Pittsburgh Steel. Sofia nodded politely. *Pittsburgh Plate Glass.* She smiled and bobbed her head past the dozen women with whom she would be sharing not only an evening but—the fates willing—the rest of her life. She and Aidan had produced no children, just money. Their immortality, then, could come only from using those dollars to make a name for themselves.

She couldn't help but notice how plainly the women were dressed. Their gowns were of a good cut but simple and hardly the latest styles. Jewelry was limited to pearls or a tiny diamond necklace. *Well!* Her striking green gown and glistening emeralds felt ever so slightly out of place, though Sofia assured herself that she'd dressed properly. It was they who were out of step with fashion, not her.

Grandmother had taught her to hold her tongue whenever she found herself in an unfamiliar setting, so she merely listened at the matron's elbow as the women discussed their various charity projects. *How odd.* No mention of trips abroad or shopping excursions. None of the usual subtle games of one-upmanship she'd seen in her own, lesser circles of influence.

These wives were genuine. Nice, even. And so generous with their time for community efforts, which could hardly have earned them much praise, let alone money.

When a strange *thump* sounded above them, as if a heavy object had been dropped on the floor, the women jumped, then stared at the ceiling. After several seconds of awkward silence, the Stevenson woman quipped, "Daniel must have dropped his wallet," which started a nervous titter of relief around the parlor.

Moments later a balding man in a bad toupee charged through the parlor doorway, his desperate gaze immediately landing on Sofia. "Are you Aidan's wife?"

She nodded, her lips suddenly glued shut, and stepped toward him, feeling slightly dizzy. Grabbing her elbow, he practically dragged her toward the staircase. "If you would, please, join us upstairs."

The gasps from the women behind her told her all she cared to know: This was not done, not ever. Something was very wrong.

Before she could take one good breath, Sofia and her escort reached the second floor, where a pair of opulent mahogany doors hung open and a circle of men stood waiting, ringed by cigar smoke and a shared expression of distress.

Aidan was nowhere to be seen.

"Aidan?" She started forward, but the balding man pulled her back with a gentle tug. "What's happened?" She snatched her elbow from his grasp. "Where is my husband?"

The circle of men parted to reveal Aidan's inert body in a heap on the thick carpet.

"Aidan!" Her hands turned to ice, and her knees felt wobbly.

There was no doubt. Aidan was dead. His color, the odd position of his limbs, the absolute stillness of his chest told her more than she could absorb. Had it been a heart attack? Some terrible accident? She had no answers, only questions spinning through her shattered mind like broken glass.

Dead. Oh Aidan…

An ancient man stepped into her line of vision. He looked vaguely familiar, perhaps from decades of having his photo in the newspaper. "We're truly sorry, my dear. It seems the shock of our confrontation was too much for your husband."

Somewhere in the distance an ambulance siren wailed.

The octogenarian spoke again. "Randolph here called 9-1-1."

It was then she noticed the envelope in the man's hands, the same envelope Aidan had carried in his pocket. "Is that…our money?"

His laugh was humorless. "Ah…well, it *was* your money. Your…er, late husband agreed, in writing, to contribute to the Society the entire proceeds from the sale of your property in West Palm Beach. Is that correct?"

She tried to swallow, but her mouth was as dry as Florida sand. "Ah… yes, that's right."

He held out the envelope for her inspection. For a fleeting moment she wished she had her priceless brass letter opener to use, if only to bolster her confidence. Instead, she accepted the envelope with a shaking hand and, realizing it was already open, slipped out the check.

Forcing a smile to her face, she said brightly, "One million dollars. That *was* the asking price for our property."

His voice was low but firm. "Yes, but not the *selling* price, was it, Mrs.—?"

She cut him off with a frustrated groan. "It most certainly was! What does this have to do with my…my…husband? Oh, Aidan!" She stared at her beloved's body, shaking her head in denial. *No, Aidan. Not this!*

The ambulance was out front now. She heard doors slamming and muffled voices shouting, neither of which offered the slightest bit of comfort. Dazed, she murmured to no one in particular, "What were you saying about the selling price?"

"This is hardly the time, Mrs.…er…well. If you must know, James here owns the Florida real-estate agency involved. We knew the precise selling price and made our charitable commitments to various recipients based on that complete figure. But your husband's check was only…" He cleared his throat with an awkward *harrumph.*

"I see." She saw almost nothing, so hazy were the lights circling her head. *They know.* She was motionless, numb to her fingertips. *It's over. All over.* All she'd waited for, hoped for. Her life with Aidan. Her future in society. *Over. Over. Over.*

Her head fell back with a sickening snap. The medallions on the ceiling began to spin, followed by the corners of the room, as she felt her legs give way. The plush carpet beside her husband's body rose to catch her in its velvet embrace…

Greedy for a Moment, Dead Forever: Sapphira

Sapphira was very generous with her monetary giving.

Alas, she was also very generous with her momentary fibbing.

Generosity was the hallmark of the first-century church. New converts by the thousands pooled their resources and shared the whole shebang with one another, regardless of station.

Mi casa, su casa.

> All the believers were together and had everything in common.
> Selling their possessions and goods, they gave to anyone as he had
> need. *Acts 2:44-45*

The communes of the 1960s had their roots here. Imagine one big, happy family of five thousand or so. It was a unique experience in the history of the church, an outpouring of the Holy Spirit, a "jump-start" if you will, for the body of Christ.

No one was more philanthropic than a certain fella from Cyprus:

> Joseph, a Levite from Cyprus, whom the apostles called Barnabas
> (which means Son of Encouragement), sold a field he owned and
> brought the money and put it at the apostles' feet. *Acts 4:36-37*

Way to go, Joe (better known as Barney to his friends). Barnabas was magnanimous in his giving. Without being required to do so, he sold his field and donated his money—all of it, we presume—so the apostles might divvy up the proceeds among the deserving.

Other landowners in the brand-new congregation couldn't have missed the praise and respect showered on Barnabas for his selfless act. Barnabas was hailed as a hero and the epitome of encouragement, a trailblazer for others to follow.

Even in the most egalitarian of economies, when someone is lauded above his brothers and sisters, the jade-eyed joker is bound to make an appearance. One couple in particular decided to play that ancient game of the Holy Land: "Me, too!"

> Now a man named Ananias, together with his wife Sapphira, also
> sold a piece of property. *Acts 5:1*

The "also" in this passage is a dead giveaway—pun intended.

Ananias and Sapphira were clearly well-known among the believers. These two weren't no-names or low-profilers. My sense is, they made sure of that. Perhaps they served in some leadership capacity for the young church, side by side as husband and wife, or had a thriving business that provided plenty of disposable income to support the cause.

Whatever the scenario, two truths stand out: (1) They were followers of Christ, and (2) they had the means to further his kingdom in a significant way. At first blush Sapphira was a Good Girl, not a Bad one.

But while others were filled with the Holy Spirit, these two were drained of the Spirit's power, emptied by their own jealousy and need for prestige and recognition. By selling their land exactly as Barnabas had, they hoped to get the spotlight off him and on them.

Two thousand years later we foster such poorly motivated giving in the church when we offer brass plaques mounted on favorite pews or names leaded into stained glass windows or hymnals with the donor's name printed on the flyleaf. The sales pitch is obvious: Give in a big way so all will know how generous you are.

It reminds me of a church I once visited that for years tolerated a sanctuary decorated with screaming green carpet. It was donated by one person under one condition: The donor got to pick the color. (Why be cleansed by the Spirit when you can be awash in limeade?) The carpet has since been replaced with a lovely shade more conducive to worship, and I imagine if such an offer is made in years to come, the building committee will wisely raise a red flag…not a green one.

In the last verse and this one, it's clear that the twosome were working in tandem.

> With his wife's full knowledge… *Acts 5:2*

Other translations shed more light on the fullness of her knowledge: "His wife had agreed to this deception" (NLT), and "they agreed to cheat" (CEV). Unlike Adam and Eve, who took turns pinning the blame elsewhere for their deception, these two worked on a full-disclosure basis—but only with each other. As one writer phrased it, "They were agreed with each other, but not with God."[1]

The good news is, Sapphira wasn't painted as subservient in any way. The bad news is, she didn't prove to be very responsible either, as we'll see shortly.

> …he kept back part of the money for himself, but brought the rest
> and put it at the apostles' feet. *Acts 5:2*

Wait a minute. What's so bad about keeping some of the money? Wasn't it their money? If I sell a set of tires through Bargain Mart, am I supposed to put every dime in the offering plate?

The issue was honesty, not money. If I sell my tires for a hundred dollars but say I got eighty dollars for them and put that in the plate as if it were the whole amount, quietly pocketing the twenty-dollar difference and taking a bow for being completely altruistic…well, even with my limited math skills, I know that adds up to 100 percent deceit.

The apostle Peter knew it too.

> Then Peter said, "Ananias, how is it that Satan has so filled your
> heart that you have lied to the Holy Spirit and have kept for
> yourself some of the money you received for the land?" *Acts 5:3*

Wait *another* minute. How did Peter know Ananias had held some of the proceeds back? In today's real-estate world, the selling price is a matter of public record, printed in the newspaper after closing. But in those days, unless the buyer bandied his purchase price about, how could Peter have found out? One commentator surmised, "Through the coming of the Spirit at Pentecost, Peter received a prophetic insight enabling him to read the thoughts and intents of Ananias and Sapphira."[2]

That's certainly within the realm of possibility. Maybe Ananias wore a guilty expression, had clammy hands, or couldn't look Peter in the eye when he handed over the money. Maybe the selling price *did* get around, such that Peter was expecting to receive a particular sum and was shocked when he didn't.

In this story it isn't the *how* but the *what* that matters most, and it's not Peter's actions that are in question but those of our ill-fated couple. What Ananias and Sapphira did was "the first open venture of deliberate wickedness" in the infant church.[3] In that sense they were very much like the first couple of the Old Testament, deceived—as Peter pointed out—by the wily serpent once again and quick to lie to cover their sins.

Greed was not their only sin. Nor was it just the ugly fruit of that greed—a false witness. They lacked sufficient faith that God would provide for their needs and so hoarded some "just in case." They lacked trust in their brothers and sisters to share fairly and so kept a portion "just in case." They lacked the willingness to live with less and place their hope in a spiritually rich future rather than a financially rich present, so they put some wealth aside "just in case."

(And just in case you haven't noticed, I'm stepping on toes here. They are attached to my own feet. Felt any pressure on yours yet?)

Peter made sure their claim to the land was free and clear, with no mortgage to swallow up the proceeds and no moneylender waiting for his due.

> "Didn't it belong to you before it was sold? And after it was sold, wasn't the money at your disposal?" *Acts 5:4*

Ananias's response had to be "yes" and "yes." How low his head must have drooped!

> "What made you think of doing such a thing? You have not lied to
> men but to God." *Acts 5:4*

A thousand years earlier David confessed before the Lord, "Against you, you only, have I sinned."[4] If Ananias had made such an admission, even at this late hour, he might have been spared.

We'll never know.

> When Ananias heard this, he fell down and died. *Acts 5:5*

Splat! That was that. Notice that Peter didn't strike him dead. We're not even told that God smote him. Perhaps his own guilt took him out. Whatever the case, Ananias wasn't *mostly* dead. He was history.

> And great fear seized all who heard what had happened. *Acts 5:5*

The bad news got around fast, as it always does, followed closely by a wave of fear. One writer summed up the reaction of the witnesses to this tragedy perfectly: "They knew God was not to be trifled with."[5]

> Then the young men came forward, wrapped up his body, and
> carried him out and buried him. *Acts 5:6*

I'm amazed they were willing to touch the body, so great was their apprehension surrounding the man's swift demise. It's certain they wasted no time in putting him in the ground, because the day was still young when the little woman showed up.

> About three hours later his wife came in, not knowing what had
> happened. *Acts 5:7*

Where had she *been?* we wonder. Shopping? Getting her nails done? How had she missed the news? Wouldn't somebody—a friend, an enemy—have tracked her down to tell her what had happened? Perhaps Peter asked them not to, intending to give her a chance to clear her own name. Or perhaps their fear kept them from seeking her out.

For God's purposes it was important that she come alone and without forewarning. Just as these two were judged for their sins separately, so will we stand alone before God someday. No amount of "My husband made me do this" will cut the mustard, dear ones.

When it comes to sin and judgment, God is exceedingly fair. And frighteningly just, which Sapphira soon discovered.

> Peter asked her, "Tell me, is this the price you and Ananias got for the land?" *Acts 5:8*

Peter offered her a chance to be saved from certain death. He was neither accusing nor judging her here. Her choice was clear: Tell the truth or tell a lie. He wasn't sealing her doom; he was giving her the freedom to come clean. In the words of one writer, "Repentance was not yet too late—return to reason was not even now impossible."[6]

As with Eve, all hinged on her answer to one question.

> "Yes," she said, "that is the price." *Acts 5:8*

"Ohhh…!" we groan, knowing the inevitable outcome.

Ananias held the money back as well, but we're not told he lied to Peter outright, as Sapphira did. Why did she sin even more grievously?

"Sapphira's lie began with fear," suggested one writer.[7] Maybe it was the fear of not having enough—enough money, enough recognition, or enough of what she might have hoped those things would buy her: love. We hoard when we fear loss. We can all live without stuff. None of us can live without love. When we see someone demanding attention, as Sapphira did, it's a sure bet that what's needed isn't wealth, fame, or applause. It's love.

But she knew what she was doing, that she was flirting with disaster. "For the wages of sin is death"[8] was not a foreign concept to her. Sapphira chose to sin and flaunted her sin before Peter, before her fellow Christians, and before God.

> Peter said to her, "How could you agree to test the Spirit of the Lord?" *Acts 5:9*

She and Ananias had not only agreed to keep some of the money, they must have also agreed that the Holy Spirit, newly abroad in the land, was not powerful enough to know of their deception. As such, they tested God's strength against their own…and lost. If only they had written this truth on the tablet of their hearts: "Do not be deceived: God cannot be mocked."[9]

Sapphira's name was as beautiful as a jewel, but her heart was as hard as a stone. Before long, the rest of her would follow suit. In that, she reminds us of Lot's wife, who also made one wrong move and paid for it with her life.

Peter delivered her sentence like the bang of a gavel.

> "Look! The feet of the men who buried your husband are at the
> door, and they will carry you out also." *Acts 5:9*

Even without an electric chair, her punishment was swift. And terrible.

> At that moment she fell down at his feet and died. *Acts 5:10*

One might chalk up such a death as a heart attack if it happened once in a blue moon. This occurred twice in one spot, in one day. Two such divine judgments tell the tale. When Peter said it would happen, and "at that moment" it did, a promise from Proverbs must have run through the minds of the onlookers: "the lamp of the wicked will be snuffed out."[10]

> Then the young men came in and, finding her dead, carried her out
> and buried her beside her husband. *Acts 5:10*

Were there any heirs? Did they use the balance of funds from the land sale to buy a dual grave marker? Did anyone mourn them?

They certainly were remembered, as "partners in business, partners in crime, partners in death."[11] Their sad story was recorded in Scripture as a lesson and as a warning.

> Great fear seized the whole church and all who heard about these
> events. *Acts 5:11*

This is the earliest use of the word "church" in the book of Acts. Note the other key word of the sentence: "fear." How I wish that the whole church had been seized with great *grace* or *love* or *joy*. Those things come with the Spirit of the Lord, to be sure. But "the fear of the LORD is the beginning of knowledge."[12] During that season of signs and wonders and miracles, it was necessary for the Lord to strike fear in their hearts, the sort of fear that would ultimately keep them safely in the kingdom.

Fear, when it is justified, is healthy. Fear keeps a toddler from running into the street—the second time. The first time, it's a parent's wrath and promises of hasty punishment if the action is repeated that gets his or her attention.

This toddler of a church in Jerusalem literally had the wrath of God presented to them through Ananias and Sapphira. We can sympathize with her naiveté, identify with her unnecessary hoarding, and mourn her death. But let's not follow in her footsteps.

Interesting how Sapphira's story still has the power to teach us. I was in the middle of working on this chapter when I stopped at an airport bookstore and spotted a lovely book of quotes. It was a small but splendidly illustrated hardcover gift book, which I snapped up with glee. I didn't even look at the price, expecting something in the range of $10. When the clerk rang it up as $5.95, I silently marveled at the bargain and flipped open the cover to see if it was on sale.

No. It was 5.95 in British pounds, but 8.95 in American dollars. Since the British price was in larger type, it was obvious why the clerk had rung it up wrong. Since I'd already paid for it and put away my wallet, our transaction was complete as far as the busy employee was concerned.

Okay, girls. What would *you* have done?

I opened my mouth, then closed it.

I checked my watch and reminded myself I had only twenty minutes until takeoff.

I reached for my wallet and put it back, remembering I didn't have any more one-dollar bills. And besides, it would involve voiding the previous receipt and starting all over. It could take hours. Well, precious minutes at any rate.

Was I within my rights as a consumer to smile and leave with my accidental bargain?

Yup. Which is exactly what I did, still ticking off perfectly valid reasons why my choice was fair and acceptable.

An old memory verse ran through my head and stopped my heart cold: *"Anyone, then, who knows the good he ought to do and doesn't do it, sins."*[13]

I was not struck dead at the airport. But to think that, knowing and loving Christ as I do, I'd still withhold money, acting as though it's mine to do with as I please when everything I own belongs to him, leaves me shaking my head in disgust.

Instead of a simple bit of business at the register that would have left the clerk grateful for my honesty and me three dollars poorer in cash but much richer in spirit, I carried my shame around with me all weekend. Even the joy of reading the pretty book was diminished every time I opened it and saw the correct price boldly printed inside the slipcover.

Never fear, sisters. I asked God's forgiveness. Found the receipt. And sent off a check for the difference plus state tax. But how like Sapphira I was, to sidestep the truth and pay for it later.

I did not pay with my life. But to the extent that the Spirit was quenched, an opportunity for demonstrating grace was lost, and the Adversary claimed a small victory—to that degree a tiny bit of my life in Christ was dealt a deathblow. And for that, I mourn.

What Lessons Can We Learn from Sapphira?

Pride and generosity don't mix.
God delights in seeing us share our time, money, and resources for no reason other than the joy of giving. When our motives are pure, then giving is not only easy, it's downright fun. When we give with an expectation of receiving accolades or seeing our names carved in stone, though, the joy is gone, chased away by fear and a hunger for approval that can never be satisfied.

> Each man should give what he has decided in his heart to give, not reluctantly or under compulsion, for God loves a cheerful giver.
> *2 Corinthians 9:7*

Learn to give when nobody's looking.
I have a dear friend who loves to slip a hundred-dollar bill in an envelope and tuck it in someone's Bible when he or she isn't looking, someone for whom it means another week with a roof over the family's head or milk for the children. This is pure giving, without anyone knowing the source, not even the recipient. She just writes, "A gift for you from Jesus" on the envelope. I would never have known if I hadn't caught her in the act and been sworn to silence! Your secret's safe with me, friend.

But when you give to the needy, do not let your left hand know
what your right hand is doing, so that your giving may be in secret.
Matthew 6:3-4

Honesty isn't the best policy; it's the only policy.
Sapphira could have saved her life *and* learned her lesson, if she'd only
reconsidered and told the truth. There might have been a penalty to pay,
and she'd still have been a widow—but a living, breathing one. When we
have a choice (and we always do), let's tell the whole truth and nothing but
the truth. In the long run it's easier—nothing ugly to cover up or worry
about. In the short run it's the right thing to do. Always.

Keep your tongue from evil and your lips from speaking lies.
Psalm 34:13

You pays your money, you makes your choice.
Sapphira made the wrong choice because she was pursuing temporal riches
instead of eternal ones. Before we donate our resources, let's figure out
what's in it for us. If the answer is *nothing,* then we can proceed with joy!
The wise woman makes giving a priority, knowing that when she goes to
glory, it's all left behind anyway. Let's choose carefully those recipients for
whom our gifts could mean the difference between a meaningless death
versus a meaningful life in Christ.

The truly righteous man attains life, but he who pursues evil goes
to his death. *Proverbs 11:19*

Good Girl Thoughts Worth Considering

1. How does the idea of believers pooling their resources for the common good strike you? Any instances where you've seen it work? How
could we as a church be more generous with one another? What steps
do you need to take in your own life to move toward a more generous
spirit?

2. What are some reasons we donate money, other than a pure desire to do so? Do you see weaknesses in your own life in this area of motivation? How could your heart needs be met in a more godly fashion, rather than through public recognition of giving? Is there a place for such accolades?

3. Part of Sapphira's problem was a case of "keeping up with the (Barnabas) Joneses." How can we help one another combat that natural-but-not-nice drive to play "me, too" and allow our greed to overcome our desire to do what is right?

4. What excuses do you suppose they gave themselves for their subterfuge? Any of them sound familiar? What are some practical ways you can prevent yourself from falling into an excuse-making mode when the temptation to lie strikes?

5. If they truly needed the money they held back, what options did Ananias and Sapphira have instead of hiding it? Is investing money in a portfolio the same as hoarding it? Does doing so indicate prudent planning or a lack of faith?

6. Did my story of the price sticker at the airport bring to mind any similar experiences of your own? How did you handle it…or *wish* you'd handled it? Is something this seemingly insignificant important to God?

7. Where is grace in this story? Should Sapphira have been given another chance or been told what had happened to her husband *before* she was asked the fateful question? How do you reconcile Sapphira's story with your understanding of a God who forgives?

8. What's the most important lesson you've learned from the sad but sinful Sapphira?

KNOCKIN' ON HEAVEN'S DOOR

7

*He who has courage and faith
will never perish in misery!*

ANNE FRANK

The angry fist banging on Rae's front door matched the accelerated rhythm of her heart. *Trou-ble. Trou-ble. Trou-ble.*

She took a deep breath, then shook her mahogany curtain of hair, filling the air with the scent of musk, quickly bolstering her confidence. After all, she was used to men knocking at her door, wasn't she? *Lawmen, firemen, councilmen, chiefs.* A throaty laugh slipped out as she turned the latch then opened the door only far enough to slide out one silk-stockinged leg.

"How can I help you, Officers?"

The four plain-clothes cops looked nonplussed for a heartbeat before the one in front assumed a practiced sneer. "Two men ducked in your doorway. Where are they now?"

"Two men?" She forced her voice to remain steady. "Perhaps you mean my brothers, who stopped by earlier today. Surely they haven't broken the law?"

"No games, Rae. We have everything we need to haul you downtown. Do I make my point?"

She shrugged and swallowed a smile. His Sergeant Friday growl was a lousy imitation. "You win. Yes, two men were here earlier."

"Uh-huh." He tightened his tie, obviously proud of himself for getting a confession out of her, not realizing it was all she planned to give him.

A bone thrown to a snarling dog. He ran an appraising eye over her, taking much too long about it. "Did they tell you why they've come to San Francisco?"

She shook her head, swinging her dark hair around her face. "Not a word. They got out pronto when they…ah…uncovered my…line of business."

His leer was predatory. "Scared them away, did you?"

"Something like that." She glanced at her watch, then up Kearny Street toward Vallejo. "Look, I'm expecting someone, okay?"

His eyes became slits. "My guess is, a woman like you is always expecting someone."

A woman like you. How many times had she heard that in her lifetime? She wanted to tell him she was different now, that inside her something had clicked, something good for a change. Something like hope.

But he'd never believe her.

No one would.

Except maybe the two strangers she'd sent scurrying up to her roof mere minutes earlier.

"Which direction did they head?" The cop was persistent, she'd give him credit for that. "South, toward Broadway?"

She fought a growing smile. *No. North, toward heaven!* Biting her lips into a narrow red line, she shook her head. "Wish I could help you. The sooner you start looking the better, don't you think?"

He backed down her weed-infested sidewalk, his buddies following in silence, his eyes boring into hers as if searching for the truth.

The truth? Hadn't she been looking for that most of her life? She eased the door shut, then collapsed against it, tasting her lies like sour candy in her mouth.

Forgive me, Lord.

She straightened suddenly, her heart in her throat. What was she doing, talking to God as if he had time for the prayers of a prostitute? She knew better. Surely the pair upstairs would agree.

They'd come knocking on her door. Desperate men, but clearly not dangerous, with their conservative clothes and earnest faces and talk of being on a holy mission of some sort.

Despite her misgivings, she couldn't bring herself to turn them away, not after they'd introduced themselves the minute their eyes met.

"I'm Stan, this is John," the taller one had offered between gulps of air. "Praise God you answered the door, miss."

Miss? She'd pinched off a smile. "The name's Rae. Keep talking."

The one called John had stammered, "We...we're from Caltech." He'd looked over his shoulder, his eyes wary. "Could we...would you mind if we stepped inside?"

Strangers had been stumbling over her threshold for years, Rae had reminded herself as she swung the door open wider and waved them inside. Besides, they'd looked harmless enough. "Are you...teachers?"

"Seismologists," they'd chimed in unison.

"Size what?"

"Scientists who study earthquakes." Stan's explanation had kicked her heart into overdrive. People who lived near a fault line didn't take shakers lightly. Before John or Stan could speak another word, the cops had come a-knockin', and she'd shoved her two visitors in the direction of the roof, precisely where she was headed now, determined to get some information. And not just about earthquakes.

An oppressive blanket of unseasonably warm air pressed down on her as she reached the top step and pushed open the heavy steel door. The midafternoon sun blinded her for a moment. When her eyes began to focus again, she scanned the flat rooftop for her two unexpected visitors.

There. Under a pile of rags and debris, a telltale man's dress shoe gave away their hiding spot. "John? Stanley? It's safe now. They're gone."

Two men wearing wrinkled suits and sheepish grins rose from the refuse and brushed themselves off, their eyes fixed on hers. "We owe you one," the taller one said with a wink. "And please call me Stan, will ya? Otherwise, I'll think you're my mother."

In the shadowy hallway downstairs she hadn't noticed how handsome the man was, his thick, wavy hair like a mane, tamed by a narrow bit of leather at the nape of his neck. Not much older than she was. Definitely not son material.

Rae winked and tossed her head. "Yes, you do owe me, Stan, and I intend to collect." She marveled at the playfulness in her voice. What was she doing, letting her guard down like this? In a minute she'd be spilling everything—all her fears, all her questions. Could she trust them, these two strangers from the other side of the California desert?

"Why'd you help us?" John didn't waste time getting to the point.

She had no idea why. It wasn't rational, wasn't smart. Was downright idiotic even.

"Sit." She waved at a circle of discarded porch chairs facing northwest toward the Golden Gate. When all three were seated, their knees almost touching, Rae offered them a tentative smile. "I'm not sure why, but I trust you."

John exhaled in obvious relief. "All I can say is, thank God."

"You're on the right track there." She took a shaky breath and pressed forward. "You two...know God, don't you?"

They nodded, exchanging some bit of information with their eyes. She couldn't guess what. Stan's gaze then settled on her, doing a slow sweep, from head to toe. Not degrading, just...looking.

Her throat tightened. *What does he see?* A small, dark-haired woman older than her two dozen years? A tattered soul in search of mending? Or merely a Kearny Street hooker wearing too much makeup and not enough clothes?

Only one way to find out, Rae. She'd start at the beginning, tell them her story, hope they'd understand. "God was always real to me, but never...good. He was all about fear and judgment and being ashamed." Despite her best efforts, her voice was starting to tremble. So were her hands.

She clasped them together and plunged forward. "For the last couple of months, a woman who works at the grocery store on Montgomery has been slipping little pamphlets about God in my grocery sack."

John looked startled. "Tracts?"

"If you say so." She shrugged, embarrassed she hadn't known what they were called. "Anyway, I usually toss them in the trash the minute I get home, but last Tuesday the woman looked right into my eyes and said, 'Young lady, do you know that God loves you?'" Rae's throat tightened, squeezing her voice to a raspy whisper. "That was news to me."

Stan's expression quickly softened. "Good news, I hope?"

"You could say that." She swallowed hard. "Anyway, I read the... tract...and it mentioned some verses from the Bible, so I found a thick red one at a used bookstore and started reading."

"And?" Stan's dark eyes, lit as if from the inside, told her what she needed to know: that he understood, that he was with her.

"And..." She blinked when one stubborn tear threatened to spill out. "I found out God *does* hate sin, but he loves people."

The men shared a quick smile, then Stan added, "Wise woman."

She lowered her gaze, suddenly uncomfortable with their easy acceptance of her. Didn't they see who she was, how she'd spent her days... and nights?

Stan slipped one rough knuckle under her trembling chin and lifted it, forcing her to look at him. "Rae, God sent us to San Francisco to save lives. It seems he's already started with yours." The sincerity in his eyes was unmistakable. "Is that the way you see it?"

She tried to look away, but Stan's grip on her chin was too firm. "I... I want...I mean..." She made herself say it. "Y-yes."

His grip on her heart was tighter still. She felt it breaking open without a word, only a warm gaze that told her what she longed to hear. *You are loved, Rae. You are forgiven.*

Hot tears stung her eyes until they slipped down her cheeks, burning a path toward the very center of her soul. How many years had it been since she'd cried? Five? Ten, maybe?

It felt awful. It felt wonderful. The voices in her head were shouting a long-forgotten refrain that sounded like joy.

She gulped a much-needed breath of air. "Why...?" It was all she could do to keep herself from falling utterly apart. These men didn't know her, couldn't grasp what she'd been through. Better to focus on their needs, not hers. Not now.

She started again. "Why are you two here in the city? I mean, other than chatting the time away on a prostitute's roof?"

The men looked at each other, then back at her, reluctance plainly stamped on their features.

She waited, patting her cheeks dry while thoughts of her family—her mother and father, her younger brothers and sisters—swirled through her mind. If trouble was coming, she wanted them safe. "Earthquake scientists on a mission can mean only one thing, fellas."

John shifted in his chair. "If you mean the Big One, we've lived with that possibility since 1906."

"No. You know something more than history." Rae leaned forward. "You know God. Did he tell you when and where it will hit?"

"Yes."

"*No!*"

The two men glared at each other. Clearly they hadn't agreed on how to explain themselves.

Stan broke the lengthy silence first. "For your sake and ours, Rae, you can't breathe a word of this to anyone. Not until we find a way to safely break the news publicly. Promise?"

She arched one carefully drawn eyebrow. "I saved your hides, didn't I?"

"And we're grateful for that, believe me." John's hand dragged through his wiry, short hair. "It's like this: Stan and I have been working on an experimental piece of equipment that measures seismic activity with greater precision than anything we've used to date. Our calculations predict that a significant earthquake—7.0 or better on the Richter scale—will hit the Bay Area in the next four hours."

"What?" She collapsed against the back of the chair. "Are you sure about this?"

"No."

"*Yes!*"

Stan elbowed his partner. "C'mon, John. Truth is truth. Numbers and equations are predictable. The earth is not. When we prayed about what we should do with this information, God said, 'Tell them!'"

"So?"

"So, we did." John shrugged. "They dismissed us as a couple of Caltech kooks. Told us to keep our mouths shut. Ranted and raved about the World Series going on this week and how such an announcement would create a major-league panic."

Stan added, "We threatened to go to the media with our findings, then stomped out the door. Ten minutes later we were being chased by a quartet of plain-clothes cops. Without your help, well…" He slipped his hands lightly around hers. "Some people would rather risk death than admit they're wrong, Rae. I'm glad you're not one of them."

Heat rose in her cheeks. *Blushing,* of all things! *What's happening to you, girl?* Her words came out in a rush. "Look, you two should head for the hills, pronto. Those cops will be back, and they won't take my word for it next time." She ducked her head, willing away the warmth in her face, wondering if she dare ask for their help. When she looked up, Stan's eyes were filled with empathy, as if he knew what she was going to say. "Will you…will you come back for me? Before the quake comes, I mean? I haven't got a car, and anyway the streets…"

He squeezed her hands, then gently released them. "You bet. We'll be monitoring the seismic activity every second. I promise, we'll get here in time to get you out."

Her grin was wobbly but genuine. "Better bring a big vehicle. I want my family spared too."

"How many people are we talking about?" John was obviously the numbers man.

She counted on two hands and flashed him the total.

John groaned. "It'll be a tight fit. Where do they live?"

"The Marina district."

He groaned even louder. "The soil is so water-saturated there, it could be the hardest-hit place. Yeah, bring 'em here and we'll manage. And for heaven's sake, keep everyone inside. The street is the worst place to run in an earthquake."

"Gotcha." Rae exhaled in relief. "We'll be waiting. Anything else I can do?"

John stood and rolled his shoulders. "Is there a fire escape we can borrow?"

"Sure." She angled her head toward the rear of the building. "What else?"

Stan was staring at the sun, a hazy globe above the urban skyline. "Paint a big, red *X* on your roof."

"A wh-wha—"

He turned to her, his face filled with concern. "No more questions; just do it. And be ready, woman." He rose to his feet and looked down at her, compassion and conviction mirrored in his eyes. "It's hard to say precisely when we'll be back for you this afternoon, but know this: It won't be long."

"There it is!" Stan shouted above the whir of the blades. "Can you land there?"

"Legally?" the pilot hollered back.

"Look, when this thing hits, no one will remember seeing a Jet Ranger in North Beach, got that? Just put it down." He glanced at his watch. *Almost five.*

"She'll be ready. I know she will." Stan's voice cut through the deafening sound. "This shouldn't take two minutes."

The pilot circled the rooftop bearing a large *X,* then hovered into position and dropped down on the flat surface. Hunched over to avoid the lethal blades, Stan followed John in a straight path toward the metal exit. Two steps short of the threshold, they were nearly knocked over when the door flew open with a thunderous bang.

Raven-haired Rae stood in the doorway, a small knot of people behind her, their faces full of apprehension. Her own face was triumphant. "See, everybody? I told you they'd come!"

Stan reached for her hand, pulling her toward him. "Of course we came." Despite the hammering in his chest, he managed a slight smile. "Who could ever forget a woman like you?"

The faintest tremor beneath their feet sent the little band scurrying toward the helicopter, heads low, eyes on the ground. He gripped Rae's hand, guiding her across the roof to safety, realizing he had no intention of letting her go, now or ever.

He lifted her into the last passenger seat as the ground began to shift, throwing his lengthy frame forward onto the copter's floor. "Go, go!" he shouted above the ominous rumbling, dragging his legs in as the Ranger lifted off the rooftop with a sudden lurch.

A quick check of his watch confirmed the time: Tuesday, October 17, 5:04 P.M. The accuracy of their prediction offered little comfort. Stan watched in resignation as the first walls began to crumble...

Rising like a Phoenix from the Ashes of Jericho: Rahab

> Then Joshua son of Nun secretly sent two spies from Shittim. "Go, look over the land," he said, "especially Jericho." So they went and entered the house of a prostitute named Rahab and stayed there.
>
> *Joshua 2:1*

Some folks are defined by their occupations, and that's clearly the case with Rahab. Truth is, her job was practically her last name.

Rahab-the-Harlot. Rahab-the-Harlot.

There were two kinds of prostitutes in her day—the religious ones who worked at the Canaanite temple and the run-of-the-mill harlots who worked for cash.

Rahab was the second kind. The Hebrew word was *zoonah;* the Greek word was *porne.* But any way you spell it, Rahab was a whore.

Ugly word. Sounds like a curse, and often is.

She may have been "bad, like the rest, and smart and resolute,"[1] but she wasn't called "Rahab the *Brain.*" She was the sort of woman everyone talked *about* but not *to,* especially not in public. Prostitutes were social outcasts—ostracized moral lepers, tolerated but in no way honored. Even the men who beat a path to her door at night turned their backs on her by the light of day, as did the rest of Jericho.

Older commentaries insist Rahab was more of an "innkeeper." Well… Her establishment, situated as it was by the city gates of Jericho, undoubtedly served many a weary traveler. The difference was, for the price of clean sheets, a guest found a woman waiting between them.

Innkeepers usually *were* women, offering food, lodging, and…amenities. "Call the front desk if you left anything at home." By any label, Rahab's vocation was a lowly one, with no husband to provide for her or protect her worldly goods or her worldly self.

She was on her own but not alone in life. Her family—father and mother, sisters and brothers, no mention of children—lived in another part of town. No surprise there. Rahab's house was hardly a home, and besides, having family members around would've cooled the ardor of her clientele.

Two things not discussed in Scripture are worth remembering: First, this was a woman who knew how to handle men. Knew how they thought, how they behaved, and what they needed. Second, according to rabbinical tradition, Rahab was one of the four most beautiful women in the ancient world. Business was undoubtedly brisk.

Even given these truths, one still might ask why our two righteous Israelite spies landed at a harlot's doorstep. Didn't the wisdom of the ages warn against it, as Solomon, Rahab's own descendant, would caution men four centuries later?

> Keep to a path far from her,
>
> do not go near the door of her house. *Proverbs 5:8*

Problem was, Rahab's house was hard to miss, nestled as it was against the town wall at the gate, her high roof level with the ramparts. Archaeologists say the double walls of Jericho were built twelve to fifteen feet apart—plenty of room to squeeze in a cozy house, supported between two walls by stout timbers.[2]

Besides, these two guys didn't call ahead for reservations. Spies can't be choosy. The king of Jericho knew they had come and had his men combing the streets for two foreigners. Where better to lie low than in a place with lots of traffic, where questions weren't asked, and strangers came and went at all hours? *Perfect.*

> The king of Jericho was told, "Look! Some of the Israelites have
> come here tonight to spy out the land." *Joshua 2:2*

One commentator suggested that the two men probably partook of Rahab's services while there. Say *what?* They were on a dangerous spy mission, being chased by the king's seek-and-destroy team, and were obviously honorable, zealous Israelites. Take time for a dishy detour? *Humph.* Clearly the commentator *partook* of too many James Bond movies. In real (Hebrew) life the two men simply needed a place to hide and providentially found their way to the door of this woman—Rahab-the-Harlot—whose high roof offered the ideal vantage point for a spy on assignment.

The men arrived, their clothes still damp from the waters of the turbulent Jordan River, which they'd navigated a few miles back. They were not only anticipated—rumors had been flying for years about the Exodus from Egypt and the miraculous crossing of the Red Sea—they'd already been spotted.

> So the king of Jericho sent this message to Rahab: "Bring out the
> men who came to you and entered your house, because they have
> come to spy out the whole land." *Joshua 2:3*

This wasn't a suggestion; it was a command, with an appeal to her supposedly patriotic soul since spies were enemies of the state. The messengers didn't need to specify which men. Everyone in town would have identified the duo as Israelites by their accent and appearance.

Rahab was faced with a difficult choice, much more challenging than the one Delilah was given when a handsome stranger darkened her door. In Delilah's case the authorities offered her money for information on the stranger. In Rahab's case they not only didn't offer a reward, they implied a threat on her life if she didn't cooperate.

In every life story, including our own, decisions are made in haste that determine the course of eternity. Delilah was "Bad to the Bone" and chose accordingly. Rahab was only "Bad for a Season, but Not Forever." Indeed, the winds of change were blowing across her doorstep at that very moment.

> But the woman had taken the two men and hidden them. *Joshua 2:4*

You go, girl! Brave, fearless Rahab risked life and limb to hide two men she'd barely met. And not only hide them—she lied for them.

> She said, "Yes, the men came to me, but I did not know where they
> had come from." *Joshua 2:4*

Clever woman. She couldn't deny the obvious—the men had already been seen entering her door—but who was to say they signed the guest register? When the oil lamps go out, all men look alike, right?

> "At dusk, when it was time to close the city gate, the men left. I
> don't know which way they went." *Joshua 2:5*

Quick thinking again. Lots of folks squeezed through the gate before nightfall. Who bothered to notice where they went after that?

> "Go after them quickly. You may catch up with them." *Joshua 2:5*

Rahab probably bit the inside of her cheek to keep from laughing when she dished out the oldest line in the book: "They went thataway!"

To those who might see her subterfuge as sin, I'll point out that if a gang of thugs appeared at my door, weapons in hand, and demanded the whereabouts of my loved ones, I would lie.

A big, juicy fib. "They left the country." Whatever.

Rahab's actions were even more courageous because these men were *not* family; they were strangers. What possessed her to protect them, to hide them under the four-foot stalks of wet flax she'd spread out to dry in neat rows on her roof?

Obviously, this wise woman sensed an upheaval—spiritual and otherwise—about to sweep through Jericho. She reasoned things through and made the most important decision of her life.

> Before the spies lay down for the night, she went up on the roof
> and said to them, "I know that the LORD has given this land to you
> and that..." *Joshua 2:8-9*

Hold it, honey. *The Lord?* Would that be Baal or some other, lesser god? Do you mean *the* God, the one true God, the God of the Israelites, revealed his holiness to you? You, of all people—a woman, a hooker, unmarried and unworthy, the lovely but unloved Rahab?

My, my, will wonders never cease?

(No, thank the Lord, they won't!)

> "…a great fear of you has fallen on us, so that all who live in this
> country are melting in fear because of you." *Joshua 2:9*

Finally she spoke the unvarnished truth: "You scare us silly!" Maybe she was more afraid of these two than all the king's men. But not too afraid to save them or to speak to them plainly. How they must have admired her valor. Rahab the lionhearted!

She went on to explain how the citizens of Jericho had trembled at the news of the parting of the Red Sea and of the Israelites' utter destruction of two neighboring kingdoms ruled by Sihon and Og.

> "When we heard of it, our hearts melted and everyone's courage
> failed because of you…" *Joshua 2:11*

Well, not *everyone's* courage, Rahab. Not yours.

> "…for the LORD your God is God in heaven above and on the
> earth below." *Joshua 2:11*

Sister, the angels rejoiced at the sound of those words! Rahab, the harlot, the Canaanite, the worshiper of Baal and worse, had come to her senses. "God is God!" She'd seen the power of Jehovah God at work, accepted the reality of his existence, and confessed with her mouth to these witnesses that the One they called God *was* God, the almighty God.

One author described it succinctly: "First she heard the Word, then she believed. This belief led to faith, which then led to works. In the process, she was saved."[3] What a familiar progression to readers of the New Testament! Rahab was thirty-four centuries ahead of many of us as she made her profession of faith beneath a Passover moon on a night full of fear and wonder in old Jericho.

So much for Baal, Molech, and Ashtoreth.

This soiled dove found peace and bright hope for the future with one God, not myriad gods. She probably saw the duo's arrival at her doorstep as divinely ordained, saving her from certain death, not only physical but also spiritual. Talk about your "aha!" moment.

Generous Rahab was even more concerned about the lives of others.

> "Now then, please swear to me by the LORD that you will show kindness to my family, because I have shown kindness to you."
> *Joshua 2:12*

If we didn't already know so much about this woman, her words might have sounded self-serving or manipulative. "Give to get" goes the modern business philosophy. But Rahab's selfless actions to this point suggest that she's merely a determined overseer of her family's welfare, and bless her for that. What family wouldn't want a warrior princess like Rahab fighting for its safety?

> "Give me a sure sign that you will spare the lives of my father and mother, my brothers and sisters, and all who belong to them, and that you will save us from death." *Joshua 2:12-13*

Rahab wanted her family saved too. (Don't we all?) The men were quick to agree, probably out of relief and gratitude and more than a little respect.

> "Our lives for your lives!" the men assured her. "If you don't tell what we are doing, we will treat you kindly and faithfully when the LORD gives us the land." *Joshua 2:14*

This "sure sign" that Rahab requested was a binding pledge with the terms carefully stated. True, it was spoken, not written—but so are marriage vows, and they're plenty binding. Note that trust flowed in both directions. Her newfound faith empowered her to trust these complete strangers—and a strange, new God—to save her life. Their seasoned faith enabled them to trust a harlot wearing her changed heart on her sleeve to save them from death.

We're talking a God-size miracle here.

With her belief in God stated and her trust in his messengers confirmed, Rahab acted on her faith, posthaste:

> So she let them down by a rope through the window, for the house
> she lived in was part of the city wall. *Joshua 2:15*

Why do I get the feeling this escape route had been used before? Most of us don't keep a rope strong enough to support a man tucked away in our bedroom closets, just in case. But Rahab did. Husbands escaping jealous wives? Politicians escaping angry citizens? Rahab dwelled on the outskirts of polite society in more ways than one.

She told them to run for the hills and hide for three days until the king's henchmen gave up searching for them. The spies had some parting instructions for her, too.

> The men said to her, "This oath you made us swear will not be
> binding on us unless, when we enter the land, you have tied this
> scarlet cord in the window through which you let us down."
> *Joshua 2:17-18*

Scarlet. Now there's a color that makes a statement. *The Scarlet Letter.* A scarlet woman. "Though your sins are like scarlet…"[4] Scarlet reeks of fallen women, of red-light districts, of Scarlett O'Hara sauntering into Miss Melanie's party in a shocking red gown that launched all of Atlanta into a social tailspin.

If you were playing the part of a shameless hussy, what color nail polish would you wear? Of course.

Rahab's sins were as scarlet as the thread that draped from her window, and every bit as obvious. Oh, can I identify with that! That's why God's grace is so amazing. When we confess our sins—literally let them all hang out like Rahab's red thread—and repent, leaving the old life behind as Rahab did, we are forgiven and washed clean, without a spot or blemish left.

We no longer look like scarlet sinners; we look like grateful grace-bearers. On Rahab—on all of us—red is a very becoming color when it signifies a confession of our sins and our desire to trust God.

Red is also the symbol of blood, of life flowing into death. Or, more accurately, death flowing into life, like the red blood of a sacrificial lamb smeared over the doorpost of a house so that all who lived there might be spared when the Lord passed over. Or like the doubly thick scarlet cloth that kept a woman's family safe and warm: "When it snows, she has no fear for her household; for all of them are clothed in scarlet."[5]

And hey, let's be practical. A bright red cord would show up against the mud and stone around Rahab's window, even in twilight. Otherwise, things might've gone haywire when the men came back with their armies to wreak havoc on Jericho.

"I think it's this house."

"No way, buddy. Her place was on the other side of the gate."

"Huh-uh. Don't you remember the crooked steps? Trust me, it's this one."

The red cord was necessary. Practicalities matter, then and now. As a prostitute, Rahab had nothing to lose reputation-wise. Hang a red cord in her window? No problem.

The men explained that she must bring her loved ones into her house and keep them there or the men wouldn't be responsible for their safety. And if Rahab spilled the beans on their plans, then all bets were off.

> "But if you tell what we are doing, we will be released from the oath you made us swear."
>
> "Agreed," she replied. "Let it be as you say." So she sent them away and they departed. And she tied the scarlet cord in the window. *Joshua 2:20-21*

The Hebrew terms used here for "rope" and "cord" are different words, so it wasn't the dangling escape rope that was scarlet but a smaller cord—a mere ribbon, some translations say. Notice she tied it in the window the minute their feet hit the ground. A regular Girl Scout, this one. *Be prepared.* It was a foreshadowing of the New Testament as well: "Keep watch, because you do not know the day or the hour."[6]

When Joshua and the gang showed up, Jericho prepared for the worst.

> Now Jericho was tightly shut up because of the Israelites. No one went out and no one came in. *Joshua 6:1*

Imagine the tension in Rahab's house, filled with children and grand-parents and every extended family member they could squeeze in. No doubt desperate fists pounded on her door day and night, demanding more information about the spies who'd disappeared without a trace.

The siege lasted seven long days, during which the citizens of Jericho heard the Israelites marching around the city. Not storming the walls, just marching. How a sense of dread must have filled the lost souls inside those walls! Under Rahab's roof, hope still lived, though it surely was put to the test on the seventh day.

> They got up at daybreak and marched around the city seven times
> in the same manner. *Joshua 6:15*

Nothing new there. Maybe the Israelites were too scared to use force? Sketching out a battle plan while they marched? Breaking in their new sandals? You can be sure all that marching had the citizens of Jericho trembling in their own sandals.

> The seventh time around, when the priests sounded the trumpet
> blast, Joshua commanded the people, "Shout! For the LORD has
> given you the city!" *Joshua 6:16*

"Shout?" I've heard of "Twist and Shout," but shout and destroy? Joshua's command was to decimate everything, take nothing for them-selves, and kill everyone in sight. Well, almost everyone.

> "Only Rahab the prostitute and all who are with her in her house
> shall be spared, because she hid the spies we sent." *Joshua 6:17*

Rahab and her family waited, holding their breath inside their sanctu-ary, while outside their whole world fell apart.

> At the sound of the trumpet, when the people gave a loud shout,
> the wall collapsed; so every man charged straight in, and they took
> the city. They devoted the city to the LORD and destroyed with the
> sword every living thing in it—men and women, young and old,
> cattle, sheep and donkeys. *Joshua 6:20-21*

After seven days of relative silence, the horrible sounds of death and destruction outside her door must have tested Rahab's new faith to the core. Did she feel like Noah with his family in the ark, hearing the cries for help as the rains fell and swept away their friends and neighbors? When we choose to acknowledge God but others around us don't, suffering is sure to come on both sides of the wall.

Speaking of walls, if Rahab's house was attached to the walls of Jericho, and they all fell down, how could her house have been spared? The miraculous strikes again. It wasn't Joshua and his army that spared her house—it was God.

> Joshua said to the two men who had spied out the land, "Go into the prostitute's house and bring her out and all who belong to her, in accordance with your oath to her." *Joshua 6:22*

And look who went in to lead her out to safety—the only two Israelites she knew and trusted. Perhaps even at that late hour she feared for the lives of her family at the hands of the Israelites and their powerful God. No need to worry, woman.

> But Joshua spared Rahab the prostitute, with her family and all who belonged to her, because she hid the men Joshua had sent as spies to Jericho—and she lives among the Israelites to this day.
> *Joshua 6:25*

When Rahab walked out of that house for the last time and out of Jericho forever, she left everything behind. Whatever furnishings, gold, or other valuables she owned were left in the rubble. Unlike Lot's wife, Rahab did not look back with longing at her city or her possessions. She became part of the Israelite community and lived among them "to this day," not in the flesh but through her descendants.

She was a beautiful woman, inside and out. It's only natural that Salmon, perhaps one of the two unnamed spies who saw her embrace his God with passionate abandon, would embrace her himself. As his wife. From the ashes of Jericho, romance bloomed.[7]

Check out these opening lines from the New Testament:

> Salmon the father of Boaz, whose mother was Rahab, Boaz the father of Obed, whose mother was Ruth, Obed the father of Jesse, and Jesse the father of King David. *Matthew 1:5-6*

Wait. Rahab the harlot an ancestress of the royal line of David? Girl, don't tell me the Lord doesn't have a sense of humor! One commentator wrote, "Thus poor Rahab, the muddy, the defiled, became the fountainhead of the River of the Water of Life."[8]

Sigh. I love happy endings. With God, it isn't who you *were* that matters; it's who you *are becoming.* Rahab's courageous act earned her a spot in the Hebrews honor roll:

> By faith the prostitute Rahab, because she welcomed the spies, was
> not killed with those who were disobedient. *Hebrews 11:31*

Only one other woman in biblical history—Sarah—appears in that lengthy passage. James also referenced Rahab as an example in his teaching on living faith:

> You see that a person is justified by what he does and not by
> faith alone. In the same way, was not even Rahab the prostitute
> considered righteous for what she did when she gave lodging
> to the spies and sent them off in a different direction?
> *James 2:24-25*

It's grand to see our heroine Rahab so touted, but I have a question: Why did the New Testament writers still insist on calling her a prostitute? Can't she lose the old label? Must those of us with a hairy history wear our past around our necks like a scarlet thread for the rest of our lives?

Yes. And no.

Paul and James mentioned Rahab's past for the same reason people share their testimonies today—to demonstrate the "before and after" power of knowing the Lord. Stories of how God has changed lives aren't intended to glorify sin; they are meant to glorify God's *grace.*

Even so, some people have a hard time getting past our past. When I share my story—candidly, not trying to make it pretty because it wasn't— I watch some of the dear women in my audience emotionally, even physically, pull back. The room grows very quiet, and their eyes reveal their thoughts: "Oh, you were *that* kind of woman."

It's not judgment so much as it is a foreign concept. Women who've grown up in the church don't always know what to do with a Rahab.

Especially in a smaller fellowship, Rahabs may feel they don't fit in, that no one "gets it."

Beloved, if that's you, listen to Lizzie: There are thousands of us. After I share my own story, women track me down and pour their hearts out. "No one in my church knows." "I can't tell a soul." "I always thought I was the only one."

Take heart, my sisters. We're not the only ones.

Thank the Lord we're finding our way back to the cross, nailing our sinful pasts to the foot of it, and pressing on. The apostle Paul was an "other" too. Different? Ooh baby, he *persecuted* the Christians—and then became one! He called himself "chief among sinners" yet proclaimed himself made new in Christ.

> I am not ashamed of the gospel, because it is the power of God for
> the salvation of everyone who believes: first for the Jew, then for the
> Gentile. *Romans 1:16*

If God can turn a harlot into a holy vessel, entrusting her with the very genes that would one day produce the King of kings, surely those of us with a past can leave our shame in the rubble and walk away, fixing our eyes on the One who washes us white as snow.

What Lessons Can We Learn from Rahab?

Our past does not determine our future.

Rahab is remembered not for her harlotry but for her bravery. Not for loving men but for trusting God. She was blessed with a good husband in Salmon, an honorable son in Boaz, and a useful place in God's kingdom— not because she "deserved it" but because God was faithful and extended grace to her. In the same way, we need to get past our past and stop telling ourselves we don't "deserve" forgiveness. *No one does.* It's a gift...with our names on the tag!

> Therefore, there is now no condemnation for those who are in
> Christ Jesus. *Romans 8:1*

Rahab cared about her family's safety, not merely her own pretty neck.

When it came to being spared from certain death, Rahab's family was even less "deserving" than she was. We're not told that they recognized the God of Israel or humbled themselves or kept their mouths shut or even thanked her when it was all over. Yet she loved them, provided for them in her home, and saved them. No wonder Salmon the Spy wanted such a generous, unselfish woman for the mother of his children. I wonder…if tragedy struck, would I think of my family first at my own peril?

> If anyone does not provide for his relatives, and especially for his immediate family, he has denied the faith and is worse than an unbeliever. *1 Timothy 5:8*

Obedience often requires public confession.

When Rahab hung the scarlet cord out her window, exactly as the spies commanded her, she marked herself as a prostitute, not only for the two who'd come for her, but for all the Israelites, including Joshua himself. She didn't "blend in" with her new people—she stood out. To their credit, they embraced her. To her credit, she was not afraid to wave her red flag and say, "Here I am, that harlot! Somebody save me!" Sharing with others your shameful past and God's glorious grace doesn't bind you to your past—it frees you from its power to hurt you any longer. Tell your story, dear heart!

> Let the redeemed of the LORD say this….
> Let them give thanks to the LORD for his unfailing love
> and his wonderful deeds for men. *Psalm 107:2,8*

Faith that's demonstrated is remembered.

James chose Rahab as a good example of someone who walked her talk, who put feet to her spoken faith. We can go to Bible studies, sing praise songs, and warm the pews of a church six times a week, but if no one ever says of us, "You would not believe what this woman did because of her love for God!" then it's time for us to open the doors of our hearts and see what brave thing God might be asking us to do.

As the body without the spirit is dead, so faith without deeds is dead. *James 2:26*

Good Girl Thoughts Worth Considering

1. Are there any Rahabs in your life, women with a past who need to know they are loved by God no matter what their history? Do you believe they *are* forgiven, completely? How might you communicate that to them?

2. Do you ever find yourself judging such women, avoiding their company, or viewing them as distasteful? What are some ways you can push past your prejudice?

3. If you identify with Rahab in some way, what names have you been called—or have you called yourself—because of your past? Do those labels still have the power to wound you? What steps do you need to take to be set free from your past? How might you "hang out your red cord" and let others know the truth about your past—and your hope for the future?

4. Is it possible that Rahab didn't truly acknowledge God but instead told these men what they wanted to hear so they would spare her life? What clues in her behavior point to true faith—not falsehood—in action?

5. Why did the Lord destroy Jericho? And why, of the thousands of people who lived there, was Rahab the only one who heard the Lord's voice calling her out of sin?

6. One of the themes of this story in Joshua is obedience. Point out all the ways various people were obedient...and disobedient.

7. Of Rahab's many good qualities, which one impresses you most? Who in your circle of friends demonstrates that same virtue, and how has she done so?

8. What's the most important lesson you've learned from the ultimately redemptive story of Rahab the harlot?

FRIENDS IN LOW PLACES

8

The rooster may crow,
but the hen delivers the goods.

ANN RICHARDS

Not again, Abe! Jasmine rolled her eyes for no one's benefit but her own. Her husband was up to his usual tricks, staring across Dumaine Street as if the pale blue stucco building, festooned in ironwork, would suddenly sprout letters spelling his name—instead of his neighbor's—over the arched doorway.

Booth, the carved tiles declared. Not *Kingsbury,* as Abe so fervently desired.

Jasmine snapped her magazine open to another page, then another, barely scanning the headlines. How long had her husband pined over that decrepit house and its overgrown courtyard garden anyway? As if it mattered whether he owned that particular property or not. As if he needed more real estate.

Abe Kingsbury already held the deeds to dozens of buildings in the *Vieux Carre,* including most of the historic houses on this block. Not to mention garden houses on Royal, Toulouse, Chartres, and the Bourbon Street properties, her personal favorites. Business was booming at every location—readings, herbs and oils, candles, gris-gris bags.

Why Nate's house? Jasmine tossed her head, sending her long earrings on a spirited jig. Did they really need another project?

She knew the truth of it: Every man has a weakness. For Abe, it was buildings, land developments, deals. For her father, it'd been power, control, and growing his empire to the glory of the *Loa,* the spirits of Vodun.

"Do whatever it takes," her father had drilled into her. What it took was a wedding where love was incidental to the bargain. When she and Abe tied the knot years ago, it wasn't a marriage—it was a merger.

Jasmine rose from her perch on the desk chair and tossed her magazine aside to stretch her cramped arms. Her bracelets jangled toward her wrists as she studied her husband's inert form, his body draped in an awkward pose across the divan, his sullen expression wiping away any memories of his handsome youth. A once-luscious plate of sliced fruit sat near him, untouched, already starting to decay in the sultry August heat.

"Eat something, Abe." Honestly, the man could be so childish. "Why don't you tell me what the problem is?" She already knew; it was merely a habit they'd fallen into over the years. Abe found something to complain about; she found some way to fix it.

His words were a low-pitched whine. "Nate Booth won't sell me his property."

"Oh, Abe!" She couldn't keep the irritation out of her voice. Instead of the strong, decisive leader she longed for in a husband, she'd settled for pleasing her father and marrying the man of *his* dreams—a landowner with connections but no backbone. "Why don't you march over there and make him an offer he wouldn't think of turning down?"

"Already did." Abe rolled over to face her, propping his head on a meaty fist, his eyes full of misery. "Offered him one of my nicest houses. Or a market basket full of cash. His choice."

To think the man fancies himself a real-estate magnate! She pointed her eyebrows toward the ceiling. "And what did Nate say?"

"He said no deal, not for any amount of money." Abe's head collapsed on a pile of faded silk pillows. "He insists the house has been in his family for generations. Nate won't budge."

Jasmine felt the heat rising to her cheeks, felt her stomach knotting as she struggled to keep her anger in check instead of verbally slapping her weak-willed husband silly.

When had Abe become such a wimp?

When did you become such a witch?

The truth only sharpened her tongue and dulled her conscience further. "I'll handle things from here, Abe." Her strident tone filled the small study, dimly lit by a scattering of scented candles. "You'll have your stucco house and vine-choked garden; I can promise you that."

Nate Booth's place on Dumaine was just another ornate relic from another era. *Except...except a new temple closer to home would be nice. Yes.* A handy spot for greeting her adoring public, the ones who'd crowned her Queen of the Quarter two decades ago. A new *hounfour,* a place for worship and ritual, mere feet from her doorstep. *Yes!*

Some of the less enlightened thought Vodun was all her idea, a religion of her own making, instead of an ancient practice she'd imported from her father's people. Who could have imagined how entertaining it would turn out to be, watching Hollywood fill the screen with scary images of voodoo dolls and stickpins and heads on stakes? All of which missed the point.

Gaining her father's approval, making him proud of her—that had been the point long ago. Gaining the favor of the spirits, the *Loa*—that was the point now. Her religion gave her power—over Abe, over everyone. Ceremonies, sacrifices, whatever was required, Mambo Jasmine knew how to manipulate the *Loa* and get what she wanted.

Once upon a time she'd tried to convince herself she wanted Abe Kingsbury. And she'd gotten him too, for better or for worse.

At the moment it was definitely worse.

She stepped through the doorway, her patterned gown swirling around her ankles, then turned to fix a pointed gaze on the man who'd neither moved nor responded. "Our neighbor doesn't understand the sort of force he's up against here, husband of mine." *But he will. Oh, he will!* Her days of pleasing and appeasing were over. She'd finally learned that whatever she wanted she had to get for herself.

Jasmine was on the phone moments later. "You still have the ear of that parish official who oversees real estate, do you not?" She heard the man at the other end of the line grunt his affirmative answer. "Good. Here's what I need you and Henri to do for me." She outlined her simple but foolproof plan—when Abe was involved, it had to be foolproof.

"I need the deed to Nate Booth's house and a duplicate set of papers prepared for me to sign." With Abe's forged signature, naturally. The less the man knew, the faster things went. "Once the new deed is back in the proper file drawer at the courthouse, we'll put a title search in motion, and the rest is…ah, beignets and café au lait, no?" She laughed, imagining the look on her neighbor's face when he sat in the street, evicted from his own home. "Very good then," she sang out. "Keep me informed, as always."

Dropping the receiver in place, she breathed a sigh of satisfaction. Mambo Jasmine might not be welcome among any of the social clubs of New Orleans, but she had connections of her own that served her well. Her circle of friends didn't organize fancy balls with royal courts like the *krewes* did, but her people had push, pull, and a dagger or two well-hidden in their vests.

Within days the papers were in her hands, perfect duplicates of the originals, requiring only Abe's signature to seal the fate of the blue stucco house and its current occupant. She tested her fountain pen on scrap paper first, perfecting the scrawl that would spell out *Abe Kingsbury*—and Nate's doom.

Her hand moved across the paper in swift strokes. *There.* Only those with a trained eye would notice a difference. And if they did, nothing would be said. They'd be too afraid to challenge the Queen of the Quarter over something as trivial as a man's inheritance.

Capping the pen with an exaggerated sweep of her hands, Jasmine gazed out the balcony window and imagined the tropical beauties she would soon press into the fertile soil of their newly acquired garden. "She's her father's daughter," people in the Quarter often said. Jasmine rewarded herself with a broad smile. *High praise indeed.*

Abe took one step through the stucco archway and smiled until his sun-baked face ached. *What a woman!* He didn't know how Jasmine had managed it—didn't want to know, really—but the house was his, every square foot of it. He moved quickly through the rooms, his eyes scanning the walls that needed painting, the floors that begged for sanding before the *veve*—

a pattern of cornmeal for the *Loa*—could be spread on the floor to prepare for the rituals.

Plenty of time for that later. Right now it was the garden he wanted to see. He strolled out of the darkened house and into the late afternoon sun which bathed the courtyard in a golden haze of light and shadows. Jasmine was right, as always—the plantings were in a sorry state. But, with a little fertilizer, a little coaxing, the garden had potential.

He settled on a stone bench, avoiding a damp patch of moss, and surveyed the enclosed space: a mosaic of brick wrapped around kidney-shaped garden plots, surrounded by four stucco walls two stories high. Jasmine would want exotic flowers and herbs; he'd want greenery and vegetables. He ran his hands through his thinning hair and sighed. *It'll be flowers then.* Hadn't he accepted his role in their marriage years ago?

"What did you do to Nate Booth, Mr. Kingsbury?"

Abe abruptly rose to his feet, startled not only by an unexpected visitor but by the man's disturbing question, whoever he was. His eyes searched the dim corners of the courtyard as his words came out in a croak. "Who's there?"

"Didn't you hear? Nate killed himself." The voice came from the entrance to the house.

Abe swung that direction in time to see a man he knew only as Eddie sauntering toward him. Abe relaxed, the tension in his shoulders already gone. Eddie was a loose cannon but hardly a serious threat. He was a street preacher, routinely dressed in drab clothes and toting a Bible. The *Vieux Carre* was his parish, a vendor's cart his pulpit, as he preached to the shuffling crowds of tourists and locals. "Worship the one true God!" Eddie called out endlessly to all who would listen. The list was short.

The man was not only crazy, Abe decided; he was uninformed. There were hundreds of spirits, not one. *Agwe,* the spirit of the sea, and *Erinle,* the spirit of the forests, and *Dambala,* the serpent spirit. One god, one spirit? *Ludicrous.*

Abe regarded him with thinly veiled contempt. "What are you babbling about today, preacher man?"

Eddie stood before him, a small fellow with a wiry build and piercing blue eyes. "Nate Booth was found swinging from a short rope attached to one of your balconies over on Toulouse."

"What has that to do with me?" Abe maintained a calm expression but felt his stomach tightening. Jasmine had never mentioned murder. "You say he killed himself? That's hardly my affair then, is it?"

Eddie's eyes narrowed. "This is what the Lord says: 'Have you not murdered a man and seized his property?'"

"No, I have not." Abe's protest sounded meager, even to him. True, he hadn't killed Nate, but however Jasmine had acquired the property, it had clearly put the former homeowner over the edge. "Suicide isn't murder, not in any court of law."

"In the eyes of God you've sinned, Abe."

"*Your* god, Eddie."

Eddie's expression softened. "He was your God once, Abe. Before you sold yourself to that daughter of the devil."

Abe knew he should strike the man down for such blasphemy, but his hands stayed by his side. Maybe it was cowardice, but Abe feared it was worse than that. It could be the man spoke the truth.

Clearing his throat, Abe did his best to sound threatening. "I'll not have you speak ill of my wife, preacher."

"The Word of the Lord has already spoken concerning her. 'Dogs will devour her.' Prepare yourself, man, for you will not be spared either."

Abe felt as if a knife had plunged into his chest, so pierced was he by the prophecy of the man of God. Yes, his own God once, before Jasmine became Queen of the Quarter and dragged him into her sacred voodoo-hoodoo nonsense.

No. That wasn't true. He wasn't dragged. He went willingly, eagerly, abandoning all-powerful Jehovah God for a powerful woman and her plethora of spirits. The truth forced the knife in further, twisting it until Abe found himself slumped over the stone bench, hot tears stinging his eyes. He tore at his shirt, as if to relieve the pain in his chest. "Forgive me, God. Please…forgive me!"

He looked up, hoping to find compassion, even absolution, in Eddie's eyes. But the man was gone, the courtyard silent except for his own tortured groaning.

Mambo Jasmine had the best seat in the house.

Within minutes the first of many Mardi Gras parades would flow beneath her balcony, where she'd carefully positioned herself on the brick corner support.

"Jean-Paul, a fresh glass of mint tea. Quickly." She heard her servant's footsteps echoing through the house and smiled. *Born to give orders, Abe had always said. Poor Abe.* Gone years ago. Killed when his carriage ride through the Quarter turned into a deadly encounter with a vanload of sightseers. Her sons had filled their father's shoes, with mixed results. She still held the purse strings, still called the shots. Abe's dying words about watching her back had almost faded from memory, haunting her only in the predawn darkness of their lonely bedroom.

Jasmine straightened at the wail of a saxophone and a muffled drumbeat. The musicians were warming up mere blocks away. She offered a regal nod to the familiar faces strolling the street below, their admiring eyes turned upward, obviously pleased with her attire. She'd dressed for public display in her finest silks of vibrant hues, had taken special care with her makeup, and piled her hair on her head with jeweled combs that sparkled in the evening twilight.

The life of a queen brought with it certain expectations, did it not?

Jean-Paul appeared on the balcony, a tall glass of iced tea in hand. His brief nod as he handed it to her was servile enough, but she caught a flicker of disdain in his eyes as he took his place behind her. Something would have to be done about him. Servants with attitude problems simply would not do.

Jasmine craned her neck as the parade rounded the corner, filling the narrow street with a cacophony of music, colorful costumes, and exuberant dancing. Out of the corner of her eye, she watched two more servants join Jean-Paul on the balcony. No point fussing at them for laziness when they surely wouldn't hear her. The drums were deafening, their rhythm primitive, sending the masked dancers swirling like dervishes. A small pack of dogs nipped at the mummers' heels, snarling and barking in the noise and confusion below.

Suddenly a familiar face appeared among the revelers—a city official, and not a friendly one. Jasmine fixed a chilly stare on him, knowing her heavily lined eyes would emphasize her displeasure. He looked up at her, his own gaze filled with scorn, as she leaned forward to offer him a caustic greeting, raising her voice so the words would drown out the incessant barking beneath her...

She's Got Big, Bad, Bette Davis Eyes: Jezebel

You knew we'd eventually come up against the baddest Bad Girl of the bunch, the one scholars have called "the wickedest woman in all the world."[1]

Jezebel. Even her name tells a story. It's a term unto itself, part of our vocabulary, a word that's seldom capitalized when it refers to a morally corrupt woman—with or without heavy eye makeup.

Her husband, Ahab, the king of Israel, was equally evil, but you never hear someone sputter at a man, "Oh, you...you...*Ahab!*" His name is more likely to conjure up images of Ray Stevens singing about "Ahab, the A-rab" with his funky singing monkey and a camel named Clyde.

On the other hand, "You...you...*Jezebel!*" constitutes what my Kentucky hubby calls "fightin' words," thrown down like a gauntlet. In the 1938 movie *Jezebel,* set in antebellum New Orleans (fancy that), Bette Davis plays a headstrong, willful, hot-tempered miss (sounds familiar . . .) who manipulates a man into defending her honor. When she gets the brave buck killed in the process, Bette's screen mother gazes at her, eyebrows arched, and drawls, "I'm thinking of a woman called Jezebel who did evil in the sight of God."

Bette could chew up scenery with the best of them, but she couldn't hold a candle to her ninth-century B.C. foremother.

The Phoenician princess Jezebel was born rich and in charge. She was the daughter of Ethbaal, king of the Sidonians. Her marriage to Ahab was strictly a political alliance between two nations. *Yawn.* We've seen those before. But it was her personality and her past—not her position alone— that made her dangerous.

She grew up as a worshiper of Baal and was determined to drive Jehovah God out of Israel and to usher in Baal and Asherah, a fertility god and goddess of love—eros, not agape, unfortunately. Jezebel filled her palace and surrounding worship centers with 450 priests and 400 priestesses of her foreign gods.

Sexual immorality, temple prostitution, even the sacrifice of children were the order of the day. Oh, lovely. "Viewer Discretion Advised." If it took murdering a few hundred holy men of Israel to promote her religious beliefs, so be it, it seemed.

> Jezebel was killing off the LORD's prophets. *1 Kings 18:4*

Notice it was Jezebel, not Ahab, who gave the orders to wipe out the prophets. Called "the Lady Macbeth of the Bible" by various scholars, she was a woman who urged her weak husband into a life of crime. Ahab, however, was the one who took the heat from Elijah, one of God's favored prophets.

> "I have not made trouble for Israel," Elijah replied. "But you and
> your father's family have. You have abandoned the LORD's
> commands and have followed the Baals." *1 Kings 18:18*

After all, Jezebel never claimed allegiance to the Hebrew God. But Ahab, as king of Israel, turned his back on the Lord and embraced his wife's religion. Major no-no. As such, the greater blame fell on his shoulders.

Next came a big, splashy scene, filled with casting extras and pyrotechnics. Elijah demonstrated the power of the God of Israel by inviting the 450 prophets of Baal to prepare a bull for sacrifice and collectively to call on Baal to set fire to their altar.

The pretend priests called on Baal all day. No show.

That evening Elijah built an altar of twelve stones, one for each tribe, poured water on it three times, and called upon the Lord God. *Whoosh!* The fire of the Lord fell down from heaven, burning up the sacrifice, the wood, the stones, the soil, *and* the water. Talk about your attention grabber! The people fell prostrate before the Lord and did the bidding of Elijah by killing all 450 of Jezebel's prophets.

Back at the palace, the fan blades started spinning...

> Now Ahab told Jezebel everything Elijah had done and how he had killed all the prophets with the sword. *1 Kings 19:1*

There was Ahab, wringing his hands and sweating spear points, while Jezebel listened in heated silence, anger sending a jolt of adrenaline coursing through her veins.

> So Jezebel sent a messenger to Elijah to say, "May the gods deal with me, be it ever so severely, if by this time tomorrow I do not make your life like that of one of them." *1 Kings 19:2*

Wouldn't it have been easier to say, "Back atcha, bro"?

Even wrapped in flowery language, Jezebel's words weren't pretty. In fact, all of her pronouncements are contained in five verses. When it came to speech making, this Bad Girl packed a brief but vicious punch. Her first statement was a threat. The second was a complaint. The third was sarcastic. The fourth was an audacious order. The fifth was an insult. Two of them referred to murder; the other three were direct hits at Ahab's dubious leadership abilities.

When Jezebel spoke, it paid to wear flame-resistant long johns.

She was one of those women you might admire for their courage but never invite over for lunch. She had almost none of the qualities we associate with biblical women. We're never told she was beautiful or alluring, though she certainly knew how to make the most of her appearance with cosmetics and costumes. Such would have been part of Queen Bee 101. We're never told that Ahab loved her—though he was certainly under her spell—nor are we told that she loved him or anyone else.

Potiphar's wife loved men. Delilah loved money. Jezebel loved power. Not the kind conferred by God, like Samson's. This was power she created herself, the hard way, one dead prophet at a time.

Was there *anything* to recommend her? Oh, sure:

1. She had a finely tuned mind.
2. She had boldness and courage.
3. She had strong leadership abilities.
4. She had an assertive personality.
5. She had a royal lineage.

Sounds like Elizabeth I or Victoria, with a little kohl eyeliner tossed in for good measure. Except Jezebel twisted that queenly list of traits for the glory of Baal:

1. She used her bright mind to devise evil schemes.
2. She used her courage to commit murder.
3. She used her leadership skills to take over the throne.
4. She used her assertiveness to draw people away from God.
5. She used her queenship to manipulate her subjects.

Queen with Attitude, in other words. A century ago one writer observed that Jezebel was "very proud of her pride."[2] Never was that pride more on display than in scene 2, set in A & J's private chambers.

Ahab looked out his window with longing, his eyes transfixed—not on the lush body of a Bathsheba but on his neighbor Naboth's small, verdant vineyard. King Ahab had a thing about land, it seems, and wanted the property for a vegetable garden, so he offered Naboth a choice: a bigger vineyard or a big check. The man turned him down, insisting the land was his inheritance. Didn't Ahab of all people know that such a real-estate transaction was prohibited by Mosaic law?

Oops. Forgot that one.

Ahab acted in a regal manner, worthy of his calling. That is to say, he pouted.

> So Ahab went home, sullen and angry because Naboth the
> Jezreelite had said, "I will not give you the inheritance of my
> fathers." He lay on his bed sulking and refused to eat. *1 Kings 21:4*

King with Attitude. Granted, Jezebel was a handful, but Ahab was hardly a prize, described as "uncouth, crabby, and often cowardly."[3] Jezebel's opinion might have included words like "wimpy," "whiny," and a "world-class wuss."

Moments later Ahab developed a queen-size headache.

> His wife Jezebel came in and asked him, "Why are you so sullen?
> Why won't you eat?" *1 Kings 21:5*

A caring wife, concerned about her hubby's welfare and diet?

Not on your life. This was Jezebel, delivering her words in a taunting singsong, no doubt. How easy it is to picture her, hands on hips, dark eyes glaring, her crimson-stained lips curled in a contemptuous sneer.

Chances are she'd seen this act before, and it was getting old.

> He answered her, "Because I said to Naboth the Jezreelite, 'Sell
> me your vineyard; or if you prefer, I will give you another vine-
> yard in its place.' But he said, 'I will not give you my vineyard.'"
> *1 Kings 21:6*

To his credit, Ahab told her the truth. It did not, however, earn him any brownie points with Jez. Two liters of chilled whine, coming up.

> Jezebel his wife said, "Is this how you act as king over Israel?"
> *1 Kings 21:7*

I could so easily condemn her for these cruel, belittling, manhood-robbing words...if I hadn't said some sadly similar things to my own dear husband early in our marriage. Bill had just finished a one-year teaching position and was looking for a new job. I vividly remember stomping in the door after work—yes, hands on hips, eyes glaring, red lips pouting and whining, "Have you made any calls? Gone on any appointments? Is this what being the head of our household means to you?"

Heavenly Father, forgive me for being an insensitive ignoramus.

Earthly husband, forgive me for...well, the same thing.

None of us has killed a prophet, but more than one woman among us is guilty of slaughtering her spouse's self-confidence with a verbal blow. Bette Davis in *Jezebel* challenged her fiancé with the words "It couldn't be you're afraid someone might call you out and you'd have to defend me?" Said with hands on hips, eyes glaring...

Our pastor, Bob Russell, has counseled many a modern Ahab who has been run over by a domineering wife. In a discussion about A & J, he commented, "A man's sins in this circumstance are fear of rejection and insecurity. His wife's verbal agility and aggressive personality make it difficult for him to feel in charge, and his sense of self-worth plummets."

Bring on Jezebel in her new role as a motivational speaker.

"Get up and eat! Cheer up." *1 Kings 21:7*

Oh, that's rich. "Don't worry about it," reads the *New Living Translation*. "Let your heart be happy," says *The Amplified Bible*. And 2800 years later it became a hit song: "Don't Worry, Be Happy."

"I'll get you the vineyard of Naboth the Jezreelite." *1 Kings 21:7*

She didn't offer advice or seek it—she simply took control. That's what jezebels do best. "Wicked women are often excessively fond of power,"[4] and Jez was nothing if not wicked and excessive.

(Lest any feathers get ruffled, the truth is, we don't like *men* who behave like this either.)

> So she wrote letters in Ahab's name, placed his seal on them, and sent them to the elders and nobles who lived in Naboth's city with him. *1 Kings 21:8*

In most states, forgery nets you ten years without parole. But first you have to get caught. And who would have been brave enough to blow the whistle on a murdering schemer like her? The letters would have been written in columns on a scroll, sealed with clay or wax, and posted by Priority Male.

> In those letters she wrote: "Proclaim a day of fasting and seat Naboth in a prominent place among the people." *1 Kings 21:9*

Oh, a day of fasting? How religious of her. A place of honor. Lots of witnesses. Jez thought of everything.

> "But seat two scoundrels opposite him and have them testify that he has cursed both God and the king." *1 Kings 21:10*

She knew the Mosaic Law inside and out. Two witnesses, as required, both of whom would insist that Naboth cursed God *and* king. Jez made sure all her bases were covered so the crowd would have no choice but to give innocent Naboth the sentence he seemingly deserved.

> "Then take him out and stone him to death." *1 Kings 21:10*

In the story of David and Bathsheba, King David had a neighbor killed because he lusted after the man's wife. Queen Jezebel had a neighbor killed because her husband lusted after the man's *land*. Even more, she loved asserting her husband's power.

The verses that follow are a verbatim retelling of the previous ones, meaning the elders and nobles executed her commands to the letter—"as Jezebel directed." Forget Ahab's sealing wax; they knew who wore the loincloth in that household, and they acted more out of fear, perhaps, than respect.

After all, didn't Jezebel sip her morning java from a mug emblazoned with the phrase "She Who Must Be Obeyed"?

> Then they sent word to Jezebel: "Naboth has been stoned and is
> dead." *1 Kings 21:14*

She immediately sent hubby down to claim what was (un)rightfully his. While Ahab was walking in his new garden, he had a visitor. The words of the Lord came to Ahab through his prophetic mouthpiece, Elijah:

> "This is what the LORD says: Have you not murdered a man and
> seized his property?... This is what the LORD says: In the place
> where dogs licked up Naboth's blood, dogs will lick up your
> blood—yes, yours!" *1 Kings 21:19*

Ahab had been taking lessons from his evil wife. He didn't acknowledge the prophet's dire words but instead called him his enemy. Elijah laid down one perilous prediction after another, concluding with a zinger:

> "And also concerning Jezebel the LORD says: 'Dogs will devour
> Jezebel by the wall of Jezreel.'" *1 Kings 21:23*

Now *that* got Ahab's attention. He tore his clothes and fasted and acted like his old self.

> He lay in sackcloth and went around meekly. *1 Kings 21:27*

Ahab repented, however temporarily. Jezebel did not. Ain't that a shocker?

Bette *Jezebel* Davis repented. After making a public spectacle of herself wearing a red dress to the Olympus Ball where every other unmarried woman was wearing virginal white, she hid in seclusion for a year, then saw the error of her ways. "I was vicious and mean and selfish. I'll humble myself before him."

Jezebel of the Bible did no such thing. She remained the proud queen, even when an arrow neatly landed between the sections of her husband's armor and he died by nightfall. Even when her son Ahaziah succeeded his father as king, she ruled. A commentator of generations past made the politically incorrect observation that "where a woman rules, the order of nature is inverted."[5]

It's not the natural world that concerns us here; it's the divine leadership of God that was put aside by Mrs. Bad to the Bone. Her rejection of Jehovah God continued through the death of Ahaziah and the anointing of Jehu as king of Israel. The new king sought out Joram, another of the sons of Jezebel.

> When Joram saw Jehu he asked, "Have you come in peace, Jehu?"
>
> "How can there be peace," Jehu replied, "as long as all the idolatry and witchcraft of your mother Jezebel abound?" *2 Kings 9:22*

She practiced witchcraft in the sense of being under the influence of a spirit—Baal—other than God Almighty. Even when she was no longer on the throne, her nefarious influence prevailed.

Jehu knew it was time to put an end to it.

> Then Jehu went to Jezreel. When Jezebel heard about it, she painted her eyes, arranged her hair and looked out of a window.
> *2 Kings 9:30*

In the manner of a later statesman, Sir Winston Churchill, Jezebel ascribed to the theory "Never give in, never give in, never, never, never, never..." She took the time to paint her eyes and adorn her hair, no doubt with a crown or jewels. It was her public face. No longer a young woman, Jezebel—like most of us—had to work harder to look good.

At the last minute Ahab repented once more. Did Jezebel? Alas, we know better. She was beyond repentance, by her own choice.

Nonetheless, she was a bright woman. She saw the signs, heard the news. Death was knocking at her window—no doubt the very one that looked upon the vineyard of poor, dead Naboth—yet her steady hand lined her eyes and styled her tresses. Proud, vain, and defiant to the end, she intended to go out looking her best, prepared for burial if necessary.

It wouldn't be necessary.

> As Jehu entered the gate, she asked, "Have you come in peace,
> Zimri, you murderer of your master?" *2 Kings 9:31*

"Have you come in peace?" mocked three similar statements made to Jehu. As I said, she did her homework. Calling him Zimri was like calling someone Jezebel today—an insult—since Zimri was a traitor who only lived a week after overthrowing his master.

None of that slowed down our man Jehu. He didn't even address Jezebel—what, and get more of the same grief? Instead, he shouted to the servants standing next to her.

> He looked up at the window and called out, "Who is on my side?
> Who?" Two or three eunuchs looked down at him. *2 Kings 9:32*

We can only imagine being ordered around for thirty years by witchy Jezebel. Wonder how long those fellas thought through Jehu's question?

About two seconds.

> "Throw her down!" Jehu said. So they threw her down...
> *2 Kings 9:33*

She was in an upper chamber, so it was a l-o-n-g way down. I don't think they took the time to pick her up bodily and throw her, or she'd have cleared the wall. One good shove was more like it.

Symbolically and literally, the evil queen fell to her death.

> ...and some of her blood spattered the wall and the horses as they
> trampled her underfoot. *2 Kings 9:33*

Ugh.

In her own final scene, Bette Davis rolled off in a wagon, headed for an island full of yellow-fever victims, her beloved Preston's head cradled in her lap as she begged his wife, "Help me make myself clean again." But the real Jezebel's final words weren't recorded, nor were they likely so sweet. Whether she cursed or screamed or called on Baal, we'll never know.

Justice was sudden and final. And messy.

Ugh.

Jehu's appetite, however, wasn't a bit ruined by the gore.

> Jehu went in and ate and drank. "Take care of that cursed woman,"
> he said, "and bury her, for she was a king's daughter." *2 Kings 9:34*

A backhanded compliment, that. She was the daughter of a king, yes, but *not* the queen of Israel. Her love affair with Baal made sure of that.

As I said, the eye makeup and hairdo weren't really necessary.

> But when they went out to bury her, they found nothing except her
> skull, her feet and her hands. *2 Kings 9:35*

Why those specific body parts? I wonder. No commentator offered an opinion, so I will. Her wicked heart was history. Ditto with her evil smirk. Everything that made her female was destroyed. The only parts that remained were unidentifiable as belonging to Jez. Sure, today we could check fingerprints or dental records. But back then, hands, feet, and skulls were a dime a dozen. It was God's prophecy fulfilled, nothing more. And nothing less.

> "Jezebel's body will be like refuse on the ground in the plot at Jezreel,
> so that no one will be able to say, 'This is Jezebel.'" *2 Kings 9:37*

Torn asunder by her fall, trampled by horses, eaten by dogs, left as garbage, the woman called Jezebel was summarily wiped off the face of the earth, along with all her seed and offspring.

Read this horrid conclusion for what it is: *Warning! Warning!*

You can't mock God and get away with it. He gives grace to the humble, but as for the haughty—watch out!

Our politically incorrect commentator declared that a genuinely wicked woman "is capable of a refinement in depravity to which the meanest man that ever lived could never attain."[6] Oh, I don't know, fella. Hitler and Caligula were plenty depraved.

Jezebel stands out because she was a gifted woman who had every opportunity for greatness. Instead, she threw her chances out the window to embrace a foreign god who—when push came to shove—couldn't save one of his most devoted followers from a terrible end.

(There was never a man like Ahab, who sold himself to do evil in the eyes of the LORD, urged on by Jezebel his wife.) *1 Kings 21:25*

What Lessons Can We Learn from Jezebel?

Like father, (not necessarily) like daughter.
Jezebel chose to follow in her evil father's footsteps. We can choose otherwise. Don't have godly parents? Break the tradition, and resolve to establish a new inheritance for your family. Even our own past doesn't have to hold us back. History provides a great example but a terrible excuse. Ultimately, God is our Father. Let's look forward, not backward!

> A father to the fatherless…is God in his holy dwelling. *Psalm 68:5*

Ruling your country is one thing; ruling your husband is another.
We can all think of situations in which a woman has done a fine job of serving her country as its political leader—Margaret Thatcher comes to mind. For marriage, though, God offers a different model of leadership. Though we are equal in God's eyes and colaborers in the kingdom, in the home the husband is head of the wife—providing he's willing to die for her. His leadership comes only via sacrifice. With such a servant-leader in the family, biblical submission is an act of worship…and is a whole lot easier.

> Wives, submit to your husbands as to the Lord…. Husbands, love your wives, just as Christ loved the church and gave himself up for her. *Ephesians 5:22,25*

No one wants to work for a witch.
Even when we have a legitimate leadership role, there's no reason to make our employees miserable. Judging by the hasty way they shoved her out the window, Jezebel's servants were happy to get rid of her. Might those who serve beside us at work or at church feel the same way? If we've been given the skills and talents to lead, let's do so with grace and compassion. We never know when the CEO may show up for a staff meeting!

Masters, provide your slaves with what is right and fair, because you know that you also have a Master in heaven. *Colossians 4:1*

The only person who saw Ahab as weak was Jezebel.
Jezebel's cosmetics couldn't make up for her ugly attitude toward her husband. Some of our men may be viewed as competent and capable in every setting but their own home. It may be our strong-willed nature—and not their weak-willed one—that makes them appear "less than." Let's pray for a gentler, more supportive spirit. Even when we are right, does it necessarily make our men wrong? If we want warrior-poets for husbands, let's treat our men as if they're already toting mighty shields and sharpened quills.

> Your beauty should not come from outward adornment....
> Instead, it should be that of your inner self, the unfading beauty
> of a gentle and quiet spirit, which is of great worth in God's
> sight. *1 Peter 3:3-4*

Good Girl Thoughts Worth Considering

1. Do any of Jezebel's personality traits match your own? Are you ever strong-willed, domineering, quick to criticize, eager to take charge, slow to relinquish control, sharp-tongued, stubborn, impatient, or unwilling to admit you're wrong...ever? Which one(s) do you identify with most, and why?

2. Jezebel didn't even try to curb her nature. What proactive steps could you take to keep the above traits from dominating your own life? If this isn't you at all, is it someone you know? How could you lovingly help him or her without resorting to the same tactics yourself?

3. How can the positive aspects of a more aggressive personality—leadership, courage, boldness—be used for the cause of Christ as effectively as Jezebel used them for the cause of Baal?

4. Jezebel followed in her father's footsteps in worshiping a false god. Are there children in your circle of influence whose parents have a highly negative spiritual influence on them? What is your responsibility in such cases?

5. Was Jezebel truly "beyond repentance"? Why or why not? At what point would a woman sin so grievously that she would be beyond forgiveness? Can you find biblical support for your answers?

6. Scripture says Ahab "sold himself to do evil." How did Jezebel "buy him" away from his God? Why did Ahab allow Jezebel to rule over him? Did he contribute to his wife's wicked ways? If so, how? What could he have done to prevent his kingship from turning into the most evil one recorded in Scripture?

7. Think of a woman you know—publicly or personally—who is opposed to your faith, who has her heart set on tearing down Christianity. Would you be willing to pray for her heart to be changed? What would it take to change her attitude? What would it take to change your feelings toward her?

8. What's the most important lesson you've learned from the utterly unlovely story of Ahab and Jezebel?

OUT OF STEP

9

Will you, won't you, will you, won't you,
will you join the dance?

LEWIS CARROLL

One look at her father's beet-colored face told Michele all she needed to know. She gritted her teeth and prepared for the tirade.

"Young lady, you are *not* going out on a date with that...that..." The reverend's voice shook with intensity.

"That friend of the family? That talented musician?" Michele kept her voice steady and her tears at bay, smoothing her hands across her jeans to calm herself. "You always said Dave was the most gifted worship leader you'd ever met, Daddy. You haven't changed your mind, have you?"

Dumb question. Her father *had* changed his mind about Dave, their youthful minister of music, for one reason: Dave was good. Too good.

After years of being known as the biggest congregation in Oklahoma City, then suffering a steady decline in membership, Rockstone Community Church had suddenly started increasing in numbers...and in spirit. Something bordering on enthusiasm had tiptoed into the worship services.

The reason was obvious: Dave. They called him "The Music Man." Week after week the time allotted for worship grew from two hymns and a special number to four hymns, then six. Some weren't even in the hymnal. Because Michele's father was adamant—church was to last one hour and not a minute longer—that time was borrowed from his sermon.

The congregation was thrilled. The reverend was not.

Michele loved her father, despite his stubborn pride, his ties to tradition, and his refusal even to consider updating their worship services. "You don't have to come all the way into the twenty-first century, Daddy," she'd teased him gently one morning. "Even the 1970s would be good."

He wouldn't hear of it. Worship to him meant singing all eight verses of a hymn written by a long-dead composer, followed by the offering, an organ interlude, his forty-minute sermon, and a prayer of dismissal.

Eleven to noon, then off to Sunday brunch. See you next week.

Dave, however, put a wrinkle in her father's smooth style.

After an especially moving choral number one Sunday, the church accidentally broke into applause. When Mrs. Magruder shouted out a hearty "Amen!" in the middle of one of Dave's impassioned solos, Michele knew the music minister's days were numbered.

She eyed the door, anxious to escape her father's angry countenance. "Daddy, I gotta go. Dave is expecting me to meet him for a movie. I'll…see you later." A tinge of guilt pierced her heart as she grabbed her jacket and slipped out the front door. She couldn't bear watching her father's bitterness and jealousy harden his heart to granite.

When she got home that night, another stern lecture awaited her. She was not to see Dave. Period.

She *had* to see Dave. Often.

The tug of war took its toll on her heart.

Michele stopped talking about Dave, stopped trying to convince her father to change, stopped pretending she wasn't falling in love with her Music Man.

It all came to a head one stormy Sunday afternoon.

The wide Oklahoma sky was packed with steel-colored clouds heavy with rain as she and Dave scurried across the parking lot of the Sooner or Later Grill, far across town from Rockstone's after-church crowd. Thunder rumbled ominously overhead. The storm was a heartbeat away.

Seconds later, squeezed into the same side of the booth, their backs to the entrance, they didn't hear the door crash open like a clap of thunder, didn't see the reverend come barreling through with his trench coat flapping, didn't know he was pointed like an Apache arrow straight at them.

By the time Michele spotted him, it was too late.

"Isn't this a pretty picture?" Her father was visibly trembling, his rage was so acute. "After I forbade you to see him, Michele, you deliberately disobeyed me—"

"Daddy, I...I..." She felt as though a pipe organ had landed on her chest.

Dave leaped to her rescue. "Reverend, this—"

"Enough!" The older man banged his fist on the table for emphasis, sending their water glasses dancing. "My daughter may be eighteen, but she still lives under my roof. Your relationship—or whatever you call it— is over, effective immediately." He pointed toward the door with a shaking finger. "Michele, my car is in the parking lot. I expect you in the front seat within thirty seconds."

She caught a glimpse of Dave's anguished expression as her father dragged her out of the booth and shoved her toward the door. "No, Daddy!" Her sobbing pleas were ignored. Stumbling toward the door, her cheeks on fire, she rehearsed the things she would say in apology when Dave called later.

He will call, won't he? Surely he would.

Dave braced himself against the corner of the booth, a dozen emotions vying for his attention. It took every ounce of self-control that God could provide to keep from punching the man's lights out.

It seemed the sentiment was mutual.

The reverend's voice dropped to a menacing pitch. "And you, Dave. You can sing your tune for some other man's daughter. Mine is spoken for."

Dave gulped and prayed for strength. "That's right, sir. Michele is mine."

The older man's laugh was a derisive snicker, devoid of humor. "I beg to differ. Phil Trimble has asked me for her hand in marriage. She's going to be thrilled when I tell her the answer is yes."

"Phil who?" Dave was stunned to silence. Michele had mentioned a friend named Phil in her adult Bible class but not with any hint of feelings for the guy, romantic or otherwise. He slid to the edge of the booth. "Sir, I'd like to talk with Michele about this, if you don't mind."

"I do mind." The reverend planted his hands on the table, his face the exact color of his blood-red tie. "If you call our house, I'll have the number changed. If you darken the door of our home again, I'll have you arrested. If you even think about interfering with my daughter's marriage plans, I'll make very certain you're never on the staff of any church in this state." The man leaned forward, lowering his voice to a growl. "Don't think I can't do it, Son. I carry a big stick in our state association. I'll run your sorry self out of town faster than you can play two notes on that baby grand at Rockstone."

Dave knew all about the man's formidable sway. Truth be told, it was why he'd shown an interest in Michele in the first place, until his guilty conscience had forced him to back away just in time for Michele to throw herself at him. He'd caught her with open arms.

Michele. His heart tightened in a knot. How could she even consider a proposal from another man and never have given him the slightest hint he wasn't the only one? Obviously her true colors had remained under wraps. Until now.

Dave slid against the back of the booth, defeated. On top of everything else, the thought of the most powerful senior pastor in Oklahoma City making his life miserable was more than he could bear. "Have no fear, sir." His voice was low but steady. "I won't be calling Michele again. You can count on it."

Michele tossed her car keys and choral folder on the kitchen counter. "Phil, I'm home!" No answer. *There's a nice surprise.* In a dozen years of marriage, he'd seldom given her much breathing space. An empty house would be a blessing for a change.

She dropped onto the couch in an exhausted heap, her head pounding from a grueling Wednesday night at church. They were doing an eighteenth-century cantata for Easter—her father's favorite and a Rockstone tradition. Except for the year Dave had led Easter worship with the choir stretched around the sanctuary, waving palm branches and singing some upbeat version of "Hosanna in the Highest" with a full-throttle brass section.

Michele shuddered at the memory, then chuckled as she grabbed the remote control for the television. Why she'd fallen for his boyish charm so long ago was anybody's guess. Must've been the curly hair and soft brown eyes. *Or your soft brain, silly!*

When her father explained why he'd been forced to make such a scene at the Sooner or Later Grill that afternoon long ago, it had all made sense. He described in painful detail how Dave had tried to use her to earn brownie points with him and the other denominational leaders. How Dave had undermined her own father's ministry, with plans for more of the same in the years to come. How Dave had no intentions of ever marrying Michele. In fact, he'd been seen with a certain girl named Abby several Sunday nights running.

The saddest truth of all: Dave never called her again. Never. He'd tendered his resignation, claiming "doctrinal differences," and left town to start his own ministry.

It all added up to good riddance, she'd decided. When her father introduced her to Phil Trimble, it seemed like a match made in…well, if not heaven, at least Oklahoma City. He was safe, he was attentive, and he never tried to rock the boat at her father's church. Just the opposite—he was an active deacon and faithful tither. Though their marriage had little passion, it also had little pain.

Her husband worshiped her almost to the point of embarrassment. But after Dave's dishonesty, then desertion, Phil was blessedly dependable.

Michele slipped off her too-tight shoes and surfed through the channels, barely pausing at each program, until a familiar face suddenly flashed across her screen. *Speak of the devil!* There was Dave—dressed in black, banging on an electronic keyboard for all it was worth while a gaggle of shapely females with headset microphones crooned in the background, flashing hundred-watt smiles at the camera.

So Dave is on tour again. His ministry had exploded to the national level a few years back. Sold-out concerts, chart-topping CDs, custom T-shirts, the works. She found it all a little excessive. Distasteful, even. Good thing she hadn't ended up with *him.*

Liar.

Michele groaned and flopped over on a pile of pillows. No use pretending she didn't think about him, dream about him, wonder how he was doing. Despite her predictable life with Phil, hardly a day went by that didn't include some small memory of Dave.

She turned the volume up a little, then soon found herself leaning forward to get a better look at him. The years had been exceedingly kind to the man. His hair was still a curly mane; his eyes glowed with intensity. She felt something inside her begin to uncurl—a knot of bitterness being released—and a spark of interest take its place.

Oh, Dave...

The shrill ring of the phone launched Michele to her feet with a breathless start. She answered it, certain it was Phil telling her he'd be home at precisely 9:25.

"Hi, Michele," a male voice purred. "It's your old Music Man."

Her knees started to buckle under her. "*Dave?* But...! I was just watching you!"

"On TV, huh? We taped that service last week in Dallas." The warmth in his voice stirred her heart like a silver spoon swirling honey into hot tea. "I'm in town, Michele. Hope it's okay...I...just wanted to give you a call."

"Dave, I can't believe...after so many years." She sat down with an ungraceful thump, looking at the handsome man on screen and realizing the same man was on the other end of her phone line. "You look...great!" *Stupid, stupid!*

"Uh...thanks." He cleared his throat, obviously embarrassed by her outburst. "The reason I called is, I'm leading a citywide worship service at the Myriad Convention Center downtown tomorrow night. I thought... well, I thought you might like a ticket."

Her heart was beating so loudly she was sure he could hear it. Go to the Myriad for church? Alone? Downtown? The idea was absurd. And absolutely wonderful. She found herself agreeing to go, taking down directions, hanging on every word as he caught her up on the last dozen years of his ministry.

She bided her time, working up her confidence, until she finally asked him. "Dave, I gotta know. Why now? Why…me?"

Silence sang across the phone line.

"Michele, don't you know? You were always my first girl. Nothing can change that." His sincerity was obvious. His voice, his charisma, and the good-looking man staring back at her from the television screen managed to turn Michele into a stammering teenager all over again.

"Tomorrow night, then." She was so happy she could cry. When she hung up a few minutes later, she did cry. That's how Phil found her when he came rushing in the door at 9:25.

"Honey, I tried to call you, but the line was busy." He slipped off his coat, then joined her on the couch. "Michele? Are you okay?"

She shook her head and sniffed. How in the world was she going to explain herself? She decided not to try. "Phil, it's like this. I'm going to a…concert tomorrow night downtown. A…a friend got a ticket for me. I'm meeting…my friend there."

His eyes, always so open, narrowed slightly. "The only concert I know about is Dave what's-his-name, that guy you used to date. Is that the one?"

There was no getting around it, so she nodded with a slight shrug, hoping he'd let it drop.

He didn't. "Who are you meeting there, Michele?"

Before she could stop herself, before she could think and reason and sort out her feelings, they came spilling out in a great gush. How she'd never stopped thinking about Dave. How she'd missed his music, his creativity, his zeal for God. And his gently insistent kisses—yes, she even told Phil *that*.

You're a fool, Michele! But she couldn't seem to stop herself. Phil didn't speak, didn't move, only grew paler by the minute until she finished.

"Go, then." His sigh was filled with anguish. "I can't promise I'll be here when you get back."

However softly spoken his words were, Michele felt as if he'd slapped her.

"Oh, Phil! I'm...sorry." She could barely bring herself to look him in the eye. "It's just something I have to do to...uh, get him out of my system. Don't you see? I'll be home no later than ten o'clock with the whole thing behind us."

Who was she fooling? After a dozen years Dave was still very much in her system.

She spent the next day behaving like a nervous schoolgirl preparing for her first date. A fresh manicure, a facial, a zippy new outfit that didn't make her look thirty. She scrutinized every wrinkle and suspicious gray hair. After seeing him on television, would he look as good close up? Would she?

She hoped to get out the door before Phil got home from work, but he stumbled into their bedroom an hour earlier than usual, tears rolling down his cheeks. "Don't do this, Michele. Please stay home."

His sentimental slobbering made it easier to go, not harder. She'd never noticed what a truly weak man he was. Anger, like her father's, she could handle. But Phil's tears were just plain embarrassing. She left early, kissing him on the cheek and reminding him she'd be home by ten.

The spring air welcomed her with a fragrant embrace. On her solo drive downtown, windows rolled down, she listened to an old tape of Dave's, gearing herself up for the service. *And for Dave.* She hadn't told him she was married. He'd never have let her come if he'd known. *Good old righteous Dave.* Nothing would come of the evening, right? Just friends. Just music. Just a stroll down memory lane.

Before she was truly ready, she was turning into the Myriad's parking lot, picking up her ticket at the box office, finding her seat in the first balcony, high up but front and center. The perfect vantage point with a huge screen in front to magnify everything that happened on stage.

A twenty-foot-tall Dave. *Works for me!* Michele shivered in anticipation, especially when the houselights blinked off and a hush fell over the audience.

Colored lights began swirling, and the crowd started clapping as the spotlight illuminated one corner of the arena where an enormous wooden cross was lifted up with a deafening cheer. A dozen trumpeters in white and gold stood behind it, heralding the start of the worship service, followed by elaborately dressed girls with tambourines, then more young men with brass cymbals. The procession moved toward center stage and began to fan out, no doubt making room for the headliner.

For Dave. *Her Dave!* How could she have convinced herself all these years that she didn't love him, when it was clear they were meant for each other?

Michele found herself standing, straining to see, before she remembered to look at the screen above her, where every detail was magnified. *There!* She was certain it must be Dave since the crowd was screaming.

He suddenly came into view, chin lifted, arms raised, wearing an ear-to-ear smile and...a...loincloth?

Michele gasped. Where did he think he was...Jerusalem?

His skin was bronzed, which made his teeth flash their whitest, his eyes sparkle even in the dark arena. She felt almost sick to her stomach as she watched him parade toward the stage in little more than a bathing suit, his movements nothing short of erotic.

Well, not erotic exactly. But he *was* dancing. Nothing else one could call it. The man was prancing like a...like a *heathen!* Behind him some two dozen young women were dancing as well, leaping and singing. "Joy to the Lord!" it sounded like.

She dropped into her seat, her hopes sinking just as quickly. *Dave, how could you?*

On the screen above her, Dave swirled, he swayed, he rocked, he rolled, following the cross up onto the stage. After a final flourish from the trumpets, Dave stepped to the microphone and shouted, "Let everything that has breath praise the Lord!" The audience roared its approval.

That was enough for Michele.

While the enthusiastic crowd settled in for a long night of music, she elbowed her way toward the exit sign, fighting tears and nausea. She hadn't known. *Hadn't known!* He'd been more reserved years ago, but *this*... It was unseemly and uncivilized and everything her father hated. She hated it too. Thank God she hadn't married him after all.

Phil! The man she had married, her beloved husband, was waiting for her at home. She had to apologize, beg him to forgive her, do something. She'd lost her mind, that's all. Dave was nothing more than an old flame that had been snuffed out in an instant.

Phil, please! Please forgive me! She said it over and over the whole drive home, preparing to kiss his feet if necessary—whatever it would take for him to welcome her back and forget the whole foolish incident.

The house was dark when she walked in. An eerie silence filled the air. When she flicked on the kitchen light, a large note on the fridge caught her attention immediately.

> Michele—
>
> *You will never know how much you've hurt me tonight. I want to forgive you, but I'm not sure I can. If Dave has thought about you all these years the same way you've thought of him, then I hope you two will be very happy.*
>
> Phil

Michele crumpled to the floor, even as the letter crumpled in her freshly manicured hands...

From Bold Heroine to Bitter Has-Been: Michal

Everybody loved David.

Only one person (on record) loved Michal, bless her heart.

The women of Israel in particular thought David was hot stuff, literally singing his praises: "Saul has slain his thousands, and David his tens of thousands."[1]

Everybody loved David *except* King Saul, who feared the young lad's popularity. "And from that time on Saul kept a jealous eye on David."[2] Honey, Saul did more than eyeball the guy. He threw a spear at David while the young man was playing the harp—hey, don't shoot the piano player!—but the agile David eluded him twice.

Then Saul offered David the hand of his older daughter Merab in marriage with the understanding that David would continue to fight on his behalf (and thinking that David would fall to his death at the hand of a Philistine).

No go.

David's humility wouldn't allow him to marry the daughter of a king. (On the other hand, maybe Merab was as ugly as a mud fence.)

Meanwhile, Merab's younger sister, Michal, was standing in the wings, watching the handsome young warrior-poet as he played his harp for the royal court. In no time David stole her maiden's heart.

> Now Saul's daughter Michal was in love with David...
>
> *1 Samuel 18:20*

Her name, like the male counterpart *Michael,* means "Who is like God?" It's pronounced "MEE-kal," with a soft *k* sound. (You're right; it *does* sound like you're clearing your throat.)

What was it about David that made him so irresistible to men and women alike, and especially to Michal?

To begin with, like Joseph of chapters past, David was a looker. "He was ruddy, with a fine appearance and handsome features."[3] Other translations are more specific: "David had a healthy reddish complexion and beautiful eyes, and was fine-looking" (AMP); "a healthy, good-looking boy with a sparkle in his eyes" (CEV); "a fine boy, tanned and handsome"(ICB).

In other words, ooh-ooh, child.

Not that his good looks had anything to do with David's being chosen as God's anointed one. Not hardly. "Man looks at the outward appearance, but the LORD looks at the heart."[4] David had a heart for God, and that alone made him attractive, not only to his Creator but to earthly types as well.

He also had talent; as a musician and a songwriter, David was without parallel. More than seventy of the psalms came from his musical pen. What woman wouldn't love a man who could sing her to sleep with an original lullaby written only for her?

But there's more. He was a shepherd, tanned and muscular from working outdoors. He was young and innocent, not yet hardened by life. He was crowned a hero for killing the giant Goliath. And he was humble, always an admirable trait in a man. (I'd even say *rare,* but that's tacky.)

Imagine combining the fighting ability of a Navy Seal, the godly talent of a Michael W. Smith, and the rugged good looks of a young Mel Gibson.

Are you getting the picture, girls?

Can we blame Michal for hiding behind a pillar at court and sighing as this shepherd boy plucked the strings of her heart? How the girl's hopes must have soared when David humbly refused the hand of Princess Merab, her older sister. Michal didn't even have to dip her sister's tresses in ink or tie the girl's pantyhose in a knot. Without any effort on her part, Michal watched as the bridal baton was passed down to her.

Thanks to some court gossip, the word soon traveled to her father's chambers that Michal had a thing for David.

> …and when they told Saul about it, he was pleased. *1 Samuel 18:20*

My, what a loving, supportive father!

Not.

Saul saw this as the perfect opportunity to let someone else kill David without a spot of blood hitting his royal sandals.

> "I will give her to him," he thought, "so that she may be a snare to
> him and so that the hand of the Philistines may be against him."
> *1 Samuel 18:21*

The word "snare"—in Hebrew, *moqesh*—suggests something that would bait or lure David into a net and lead to his destruction. "Snare," as defined in English, means "something deceptively attractive." If King Saul wanted to keep tabs on David's whereabouts, what better way than to marry him to his lovely young daughter?

> So Saul said to David, "Now you have a second opportunity to
> become my son-in-law." *1 Samuel 18:21*

It's all I can do not to jump up and down here, waving my arms, frantically trying to get young David's attention. "No, Dave, no! Bad move, handsome!" But the humble musician had his own reasons for nobly refusing to marry her: As a lowly shepherd from an impoverished family, he didn't have the money—the necessary bride price—to seek Michal's hand in marriage.

> But David said, "Do you think it is a small matter to become
> the king's son-in-law? I'm only a poor man and little known."
> *1 Samuel 18:23*

Saul no doubt anticipated such a reaction, since David had made the same argument when offered Merab's hand. The king suggested a different price tag, one that suited his own taste for blood—both that of this young upstart and of the hated Philistines. However, that's not how he phrased it for his attendants.

> Saul replied, "Say to David, 'The king wants no other price for the
> bride than a hundred Philistine foreskins, to take revenge on his
> enemies.'" *1 Samuel 18:25*

Ugh. Foreskins? Couldn't David just bring home their dog tags?

> Saul's plan was to have David fall by the hands of the Philistines.
> *1 Samuel 18:25*

For Saul, it was a two-for-one deal. He'd get rid of both enemies in one bloody swoop.

For David, it was the perfect solution. The young warrior wasn't worried about dying on the battlefield, not when he had God on his side. To his way of thinking, the price for his bride was a bargain.

> When the attendants told David these things, he was pleased to
> become the king's son-in-law. *1 Samuel 18:26*

One thing bothers me, on Michal's behalf. It does not say David was "pleased to become Michal's husband"; rather, he was "pleased to become the king's son-in-law." The whole thing was politically motivated. We're told that Michal loved David but never that David loved Michal.

It grieves my woman's heart to think of it.

Eager to be welcomed into the king's household, David wasted no time earning his right to claim Michal.

> So before the allotted time elapsed, David and his men went out
> and killed two hundred Philistines. *1 Samuel 18:26-27*

Double or nothing for this guy! Why stop at one hundred when two hundred was just as easy? Did he count every last foreskin in a grisly ceremony or simply hand the ashen-faced Saul a sack?

Remember, this wasn't the outcome the king had hoped for at all. He was forced to keep his promise. Like it or not—*not*—his daughter now belonged to his sworn enemy.

> Then Saul gave him his daughter Michal in marriage. *1 Samuel 18:27*

Saul was expecting to go to a funeral, not a wedding! But he'd stated the price, in front of witnesses, and David had delivered, twofold.

And so the two became one. One flesh, without question, but one heart? One spirit? Despite her godly name, Michal showed no evidence of being a woman who yearned to please God the way her husband did. David was called a man after God's own heart;[5] Michal was a young woman who was after *David's* heart.

David loved God more than he loved Michal. That was good.

Michal may have loved David more than she loved God. That was bad.

A poor pairing. Saul would have agreed, but for an entirely different reason.

> When Saul realized that the LORD was with David and that his daughter Michal loved David… *1 Samuel 18:28*

Double whammy! Saul had neither the Lord's allegiance nor his daughter's loyalty.

> …Saul became still more afraid of him, and he remained his enemy the rest of his days. *1 Samuel 18:29*

Plenty of husbands have trouble with their in-laws, but fathom being the mortal enemy of your wife's father. Never-Give-Up Saul told Jonathan to kill David, but instead the levelheaded son warned David, then convinced his father that David was their friend, not their foe.

It didn't work for long. Once again, while David was playing the harp, Saul threw a spear at him. (Maybe the king simply didn't like the *song*.)

> Saul sent men to David's house to watch it and to kill him in the morning. *1 Samuel 19:11*

Apparently David and Michal lived in their own separate quarters yet near enough that Saul could send over henchmen to do the dirty deed by daybreak.

> But Michal, David's wife, warned him, "If you don't run for your life tonight, tomorrow you'll be killed." *1 Samuel 19:11*

As a new bride, Michal wasn't about to lose her dearly beloved merely because Daddy said so. How courageous she was in this scene, not only in warning her husband but in sending him away, knowing she might never see him again. Putting his needs above her own, Michal helped hubby make his getaway by the dark of night.

> So Michal let David down through a window, and he fled and escaped. *1 Samuel 19:12*

Clever Michal knew the ruse wasn't over yet, so she carried out a bit of subterfuge.

> Then Michal took an idol and laid it on the bed, covering it with a garment and putting some goats' hair at the head. *1 Samuel 19:13*

The Hebrew word for idol—*teraphim*—indicates a household idol. God had clearly forbidden such graven images, which means the house of Saul had not completely embraced Jehovah God, no matter what sort of public posturing they did. Inside their own walls they had idols. Big ones, if they looked even remotely like a sleeping David. What Michal wouldn't have given for the male version of one of those blow-up party dolls! Alas, she had to make do with the materials at hand, which worked at least temporarily.

> When Saul sent the men to capture David, Michal said, "He is ill." *1 Samuel 19:14*

I'll bet *that* was hard to say with a straight face.

We must resist the urge to judge Michal for her deception. Like Rahab, Michal lied to evil-minded men to protect a good one.

But King Saul didn't take "ill" for an answer.

> Then Saul sent the men back to see David and told them, "Bring him up to me in his bed so that I may kill him." *1 Samuel 19:15*

Can we talk *determined* here? Saul's approaching madness was dotting the horizon. Whether he was sane or not, Saul's men did his bidding.

But when the men entered, there was the idol in the bed.
1 Samuel 19:16

Sounds like they picked up the bed and the thing rolled out and went *clunk* on the floor. A dead giveaway. Word quickly got back to the king, who was not amused.

Saul said to Michal, "Why did you deceive me like this and send my enemy away so that he escaped?" *1 Samuel 19:17*

Saul wanted to know why. He may not have understood her motives, but we do.

Michal risked her future, her very life, for any number of reasons, including her boundless love for David, her delight in acting as the heroine, even her long-awaited chance to tick off her father.

When we look at those possible explanations, one problem surfaces. What initially appeared as the selfless act of a loving wife might turn out to be the selfish game-playing of an immature, infatuated girl.

Desperate to avoid her father's unpredictable temper, Michal lied again—this time not to protect David but to save her own pretty neck.

Michal told him, "He said to me, 'Let me get away. Why should I kill you?'" *1 Samuel 19:17*

Michal suggested her own life was at stake. Few things would soften a father's heart like seeing his daughter's life threatened. Her accusation didn't paint David in a very good light, though. Was she sorry he hadn't taken her along on his midnight ride?

We don't hear of Michal again for several chapters while David hid in the hills and Saul sentenced priests to death by the dozens. David chose a second wife—the beautiful and wise Abigail—and a third, Ahinoam of Jezreel. What happened to poor, neglected Michal?

But Saul had given his daughter Michal, David's wife, to Paltiel, son of Laish, who was from Gallim. *1 Samuel 25:44*

Notice how Saul got around the fact that David was still alive and Michal's marriage to another husband was illegal. Men could marry many women simultaneously; women could marry only one man at a time. Perhaps Saul was punishing Michal for her deceit. Maybe he couldn't bear to look at her anymore. Or Saul's intent may have been to thumb his nose at David and cut off any claim David would have to the royal family.

And what was Michal's opinion of being handed off to another man? We're not told, because (gulp) it didn't matter what she thought. As was so often the case with biblical women, "Michal the princess becomes Michal the slave."[6]

She had no voice. She had no choice.

And her love for David? A nonissue for father and son-in-law alike. Welcome to womanhood, 1000 B.C. style.

After the death of Saul, David was anointed king of Judah, but war continued between the house of Saul and the house of David for a long time, long enough for David to father six sons by multiple wives.

> David grew stronger and stronger, while the house of Saul grew
> weaker and weaker. *2 Samuel 3:1*

Abner, the commander of Saul's army, was no fool. He saw which way the wind was blowing and so sent a messenger to David, saying "Let's make a deal."

> "Make an agreement with me, and I will help you bring all Israel
> over to you." *2 Samuel 3:12*

David liked the idea, but he countered with a surprising stipulation.

> "Good," said David. "I will make an agreement with you. But I
> demand one thing of you: Do not come into my presence unless
> you bring Michal daughter of Saul when you come to see me."
> *2 Samuel 3:13*

My, David, it's only been *fourteen years*. We thought you'd forgotten your first wife. She was young then, fresh as a primrose in June. By now, the bloom has faded from her cheeks. Her tears are long dried. Another man has loved her for lo these many seasons.

Get ready, big guy. You may not like what strolls through your gates.

> Then David sent messengers to Ish-Bosheth son of Saul,
> demanding, "Give me my wife Michal, whom I betrothed to myself
> for the price of a hundred Philistine foreskins." *2 Samuel 3:14*

He remembered the price but not the princess all those years. As one scholar noted, "Even though she is a princess, she is traded like a trophy."[7] Why was she the pivotal point of this exchange? Politics. Her father was dead, and the kingdoms were being united. Suddenly Michal had value to David. But not as a woman. As a trading card in a biblical game of winner-takes-all.

> So Ish-Bosheth gave orders and had her taken away from her
> husband Paltiel son of Laish. *2 Samuel 3:15*

One can only guess how this must have torn Michal's heart. We can imagine her snarling, "Pish-posh, Ish-Bosheth! Thanks for nothing, brother of mine." Though Michal had no children, she'd lived with Paltiel as her husband, legally or not, for all of her adult life and had spent only a brief time with David.

Any woman would understand if Michal were angry, bitter, resentful, or despondent. Paltiel, also a victim of the king's whim, was devastated.

> Her husband, however, went with her, weeping behind her all the
> way to Bahurim. *2 Samuel 3:16*

Interesting. He wept all the way, but she did not. Was she numb with grief? Hurt but resigned? Or was Michal eager to return to David's side, even though he'd left her high and dry fourteen years earlier without so much as a note, let alone a child in her womb.

It was lame duck Paltiel's turn to walk away empty-handed.

> Then Abner said to him, "Go back home!" So he went back.
>
> *2 Samuel 3:16*

More battles, more bloodshed as David conquered Jerusalem, was anointed king of Israel, then defeated the Philistines. Once again, there's no mention of Michal. What *was* she doing?

We know what David was doing. He was busy collecting more concubines and more wives—at least twenty in all. David was a busy man, since eleven more children were born to him in Jerusalem.

But what he wanted more than anything was to bring the ark of the covenant into the City of David. When he did so, it was a serious party.

> David and the whole house of Israel were celebrating with all their
> might before the LORD, with songs and with harps, lyres,
> tambourines, sistrums and cymbals. *2 Samuel 6:5*

As a composer, David orchestrated a spectacular musical entrance for the slow-moving ark. Thousands marched, instruments in hand, creating a cacophony that surely was heard for miles. It was only natural that ecstatic dancing would accompany all that music.

> David, wearing a linen ephod, danced before the LORD with all his
> might... *2 Samuel 6:14*

Ditching his robe, his tunic, and all other symbols of class and wealth, David sported only a simple ephod—a ceremonial apron or loincloth that probably covered very little of his...uh...manhood. David wasn't an exhibitionist. On the contrary, he wanted to humble himself and identify with his people as their priest, not as their king.

How it must have delighted the thousands of participants who saw the mighty David celebrating his Lord with such enthusiastic abandon! All along the route the generous king offered sacrifices, blessed his people, handed out cakes with raisins and dates, and in general partied like it was 1999.

> ...while he and the entire house of Israel brought up the ark of the
> LORD with shouts and the sound of trumpets. *2 Samuel 6:15*

Shouting? Trumpets? This was one loud procession, easily heard even from high in the palace.

> As the ark of the LORD was entering the City of David, Michal
> daughter of Saul watched from a window. *2 Samuel 6:16*

Is it significant that both of Michal's big scenes took place in windows—first, when she helped him escape, and here, as she watched him dance before the Lord? In the movie *King David,* starring Richard Gere, David criticizes Michal for not being part of the fun. But custom did not permit the wife of the king to participate in the festivities surrounding the ark. Instead, she gazed down from on high, distanced from David by more than a few cubits.

It wasn't her *altitude* that was the problem.

It was her *attitude.*

> And when she saw King David leaping and dancing before the
> LORD, she despised him in her heart. *2 Samuel 6:16*

His leaping was the last straw, but the haystack had been building for a very long time. David had deserted her, ignored her, married other wives, fathered other children, and neglected even to include her in his life until it was politically expedient.

I know that David has always been painted as a prince among men and a hero's hero, but his treatment of Michal was a smeary inkblot on his résumé, don't you think?

Underneath the queenly gowns of Michal beat the heart of a hurting young girl, abandoned practically at the altar, then years later forced to share her handsome husband with other women. Imagine competing with the wise and competent Abigail and, later, the comely Bathsheba—two among many who provided David with strapping sons.

We identify with Michal's jealousy and shattered emotions.

But when it came to godly obedience, Michal was off the mark.

Even if she no longer loved the man, she should have joined him in worshiping God. But perhaps Michal never fully understood David's God, never openly embraced Jehovah as her own, never grasped the value of worship.

David's dancing didn't turn her heart; it turned her stomach. Various translations tell us she was "filled with contempt" (NLT), "disgusted" (CEV), and that she just plain "hated him" (ICB).

The exultant David didn't have a clue what awaited him back at the palace.

> When David returned home to bless his household, Michal
> daughter of Saul came out to meet him... *2 Samuel 6:20*

She went out to *meet* him? Ooh, the woman was hot! She'd been building up steam since the *Flash Dance* number. The minute she saw him approach the house, Michal made her move.

One minor note: She's called "daughter of Saul" here, not "wife of David." Was that a clue to her allegiance? Was blood thicker than her seethrough sham of a marriage?

...and [she] said, "How the king of Israel has distinguished himself today..." *2 Samuel 6:20*

Even on paper, her biting sarcasm drips from every word.

"...disrobing in the sight of the slave girls of his servants as any vulgar fellow would!" *2 Samuel 6:20*

Michal had three problems with David's dance: (1) He removed most of his clothes, (2) the lowest women in the kingdom saw portions of David that were supposed to be the queen's territory alone, and (3) he looked like a common jerk (that's the Lizzie Revised Version), or as more scholarly types have phrased it, "foolish" (ICB), "base" (NKJV), "indecent" (NLT), "worthless" (AMP), and my favorite, "a dirty old man" (CEV)!

The truth is, Michal missed the point. She didn't comprehend the purpose of David's dancing. She saw it as a passion of the flesh, when David knew it was a spiritual passion for God that set his feet in motion.

David said to Michal, "It was before the LORD, who chose me rather than your father or anyone from his house when he appointed me ruler over the LORD's people Israel—" *2 Samuel 6:21*

Ouch, David! Obviously his temper was heating up as well. He reminded her, none too gently, that the Lord had chosen him instead of selecting someone from Saul's household.

"I will celebrate before the LORD." *2 Samuel 6:21*

He made his purpose—and his future plans—clear.

"I will become even more undignified than this, and I will be humiliated in my own eyes." *2 Samuel 6:22*

In other words, "You thought *that* was bad, Michal? Baby, you ain't seen nothin' yet! I intend to make a bloomin' fool of myself."

"But by these slave girls you spoke of, I will be held in honor."
2 Samuel 6:22

David had spotted the green-eyed monster lurking in Michal's eyes when she mentioned the slave girls, and he used her jealousy as a sharp knife, severing their relationship for good. As one writer put it, "he cut her from his heart."[8]

We are never told that David divorced Michal.

Nor is she ever spoken of again, except for one sad closing verse.

> And Michal daughter of Saul had no children to the day of her
> death. *2 Samuel 6:23*

Still called the "daughter of Saul." To me, that was the whole problem in a nutshell. Michal never left her father and mother and cleaved to her husband. To his grave—and hers—she was Daddy's girl.

In the same way, she never reached out to her heavenly Father, never gave her heart to God. Though her caustic words to David made Michal *Bad for a Moment,* in truth she never depended on the goodness of God to make her whole.

That last verse is a telling one. To die with no children was the ultimate disgrace for a Hebrew woman. Some commentators suggested that God closed her womb. I beg to differ, only because that isn't so stated. A more likely scenario? David never brought her to his bed again. She never knew him as a wife knows a husband, nor was she allowed to bed with another man...and live. Hence, no children.

Not that she didn't have the chance to care for little ones. When her sister Merab died at an early age, Michal raised her sister's five sons, only to suffer a mother's anguish when all five were literally hung out to dry on a hill at Gibeah.[9]

As King David's first wife, Michal had the opportunity to learn true worship from a flawed but passionate man after God's own heart. Instead, she threw away such blessings with both hands, then shoved her manicured fists inside the folds of her costly tunic, determined to be miserable forever.

And so she was.

What Lessons Can We Learn from Michal?

When God says dance, strap on your tap shoes!
Sometimes we don't know what to do around Christians whose exuberance for the Lord includes lifting hands, clapping, or dancing. If we join in strictly to please men, our motives are wrong, and the Lord won't be glorified, no matter how fancy our footwork. But if we dance unto the Lord, as

David did, even in the privacy of our own homes, we just might experience the same attitude adjustment that David discovered, including a whole new wardrobe of joy!

> You turned my wailing into dancing;
>> you removed my sackcloth and clothed me with joy.
>> *Psalm 30:11*

Nothing stops worship like unconfessed sin.

Michal wouldn't have seen her unsupportive, critical words as sin—but we would. She didn't merely reject David; she ridiculed his God. When the appeal of worship eludes us—when we find ourselves judging the soloist, the choir, the robes, the flowers on the altar, whatever—that's a sure sign that sin has hardened our hearts. As one writer phrased it, "Michal was proud and cold of heart—toward God, toward her people, toward her husband."[10] Before we fall into the same trap, sisters, let's confess, repent, and start singing with a lighter heart!

> An evil man is snared by his own sin,
>> but a righteous one can sing and be glad. *Proverbs 29:6*

Words spoken in the heat of anger are sure to burn.

Michal has been called "a divine looking-glass for all angry and outspoken wives."[11] Yes, I see myself in her, and I don't like the view. If only I could take back every angry word I've ever spoken! When our tempers flare and words follow, they scorch the listener, but the flames lick at our own souls, too. How many times do you suppose Michal eyed other wives with their arms full of babies and regretted her angry diatribe? Hot words may eventually cool, but the burn scars last forever.

> Everyone should be quick to listen, slow to speak and slow to
> become angry, for man's anger does not bring about the righteous
> life that God desires. *James 1:19-20*

Wise is the woman who rises above her circumstances.

Michal had a right to feel hurt, to feel abandoned, to resent how the men in her life—her father, her brothers, her husbands—passed her around like a moldy fruitcake at Christmas: "Here, you take her this year!" Yet other women in Scripture were similarly misused and still managed to transcend such situations to honor God. It isn't circumstances that should determine our actions; it's a desire to please God above all things. So easy to say, so hard to do, and don't I know it! Let's keep reminding ourselves: Bad Girls blame their situations. Good Girls rise above them.

> When times are good, be happy;
>> but when times are bad, consider:
> God has made the one
>> as well as the other. *Ecclesiastes 7:14*

Good Girl Thoughts Worth Considering

1. Have you ever dated, or been married to, a man who was popular or very talented? What sort of feelings did that bring out in you? Did you find some constructive ways to turn any potential jealousy into joyful support? How might Michal have done that?

2. We get to know Michal's father, Saul, quite well; we never even meet her mother in these stories. Why do you suppose that is? Do you see any "like father, like daughter" tendencies in Michal's actions or personality? If so, which ones?

3. List any good traits Michal had that we might emulate. Make a list of negative ones as well. Do any of her personality traits match your own? Of those you might long to change, which one has the most potential for improvement, and how might you go about that, practically speaking?

4. Why do you think Michal helped David escape? Did she realize she might never see him again? Were her lies to her father justified? To whom was her first allegiance—her husband or her father? Psalm 59 was David's version of the same scene. Did the Lord use Michal's bravery, then, for his good purpose?

5. When Michal's father gave her to Paltiel, she had no choice in the matter. Again, how might a godly woman have managed to honor her marriage vows, even when her father didn't? Should she have run away and thrown herself at David's mercy? Opposed her father? Enlisted Paltiel's help in finding David? Think through the possible ramifications of those choices, or others.

6. Have there been times you were told to do something you *knew* was wrong? How did you handle it? How would you handle it today? Can you find a biblical basis for your actions then or for your twenty-twenty hindsight now?

7. Considering the evidence we're given in Scripture, did David love his wife Michal? Why or why not? How did his love for her (or lack of it) affect her responsibility to honor God? If David did not show her sufficient love, what other resources might Michal have looked to? And where else may we turn for love and affection if we're unmarried or have an unresponsive mate?

8. What's the most important lesson you learned from the story of Michal, a woman ultimately *not* seeking after God's own heart or her husband's either?

I BEG YOUR PARDON

10

Bliss like thine is bought by years
Dark with torment and with tears.

EMILY BRONTË

The boldface headline covered the front page of the *Post and Courier* like a ladle of steaming she-crab soup covers a bone-china soup plate: "Mayor Hosts Gala Public Reception at White Point Gardens."

Brushing a wayward strand of hair out of her eyes, Anita scanned the news story for more details. *Well.* The mayor wouldn't be too "gala" about seeing *her* there tonight. It wasn't His Honor she'd be seeking out though.

She tossed the newspaper on her narrow bed, thankful for clean sheets and a firm mattress, and let out a lengthy sigh. The article said the public was invited. No problem. She was as public as it got. Probably half the men there could claim they knew her once—in the biblical sense. For the rest of them, her reputation preceded her. In her heyday she'd been, if not Charleston's finest, at least its busiest.

Leaning forward, she brushed her hair in long, slow strokes from scalp to feathery black ends that almost touched the floor. The stiff bristles tingled against her skin, tugging at her roots as she swept her arm downward in one fluid stroke after another. Anita marveled at the simple pleasure of it, grateful no one was watching in frank approval, eyes glazed with lust, with greedy hands reaching out to touch the soft, dark strands.

It seemed like decades ago. It seemed like yesterday.

A whisper of a breeze stirred the bedroom curtains, ushering in the faint scent of lilacs blooming in her landlord's garden one story below.

Spring. A time for new beginnings, her parole officer had insisted. A good season for starting from scratch.

She could hear Cal Jackson's words, see his stern face as he handed over the keys to her spotless new apartment on Tradd Street. "Lord knows why, girl, but the governor of South Carolina saw fit to give you a last chance. Once-in-a-lifetime stuff, you got that? Don't blow it, Anita."

Blow it? *Not blinking likely, Cal.*

Straightening up, she shook her hair back over her shoulders, then gathered the silky mass into a neat French twist and plunged a wooden hair clasp into the center to hold it in place. She reached for her cologne, then thought better of it and slipped it into her purse. *For later maybe.* She didn't want to risk offending the governor with her perfume, however much it cost her, however long she'd waited to own such a luxury again.

Without bothering to look in the mirror, she yanked open the closet door and surveyed her meager choices. *Not the navy blue dress. Definitely not the white one either.* She didn't care what the mayor thought of her, let alone the crowd, but she cared very much what Governor Sheppard might think if he saw her.

Didn't she owe him? For her life. Her freedom. Her soul. *For everything.* The honored guest at tonight's reception was the man who'd unlocked her prison cell door. One way or another she intended to show her gratitude for his eleventh-hour pardon.

Her hands dropped to her side, suddenly limp, as the truth crushed against her chest once more. *Pardoned!* After all the things she'd done wrong, after all the investigations, all the court proceedings, all the years on death row—pardoned, for no reason other than sheer mercy.

How could she possibly tell him what this release from prison meant to her? She'd never been good with words, always spoke too softly to please the warden. What would she say if she met Governor Sheppard face to face—a no-account, murdering prostitute speaking to the highest authority in the state?

Shaking her head to silence a nagging conscience, she felt a slight smile move across her lips. *Worry about the words later, honey. Worry about the clothes now.* The charcoal gray dress then. Unobtrusive. Modest. She held it in front of her, sneaking a glance in the full-length mirror. The loose tunic stretched from chin to ankles, missing her generous curves completely. Made of a soft cotton fabric, it was as gray as a rainy day except for the tiny embroidered flowers that circled the hemline and wrists.

Perfect. She'd never be recognized.

Thirty minutes later she felt the warmth of the late-afternoon sun streaming across her shoulders as she hurried along Meeting Street toward the Battery. All around her, azaleas in full array shouted hosannas to the season with riotous red and pink blossoms. Creamy white magnolias nodded their cool heads in the slight breeze, bathing her senses with their sweet fragrance. The houses grew older, larger, and more ornate, with side porches facing courtyard gardens rather than front porches pointed toward the street, exactly as she'd remembered.

Anita brushed away an unexpected spate of tears. *Charleston. Home!* It'd been years since she'd walked Meeting Street as an innocent girl, glorying in her own youthful beauty. *Fool.* That was before her steep descent into a shadowy world of nightclubs and strip joints, of drugs by the gram and men by the hour. When a stubborn john refused to pay, her weak protest earned her a battery of bruises and the first of many trips to jail for disturbing the peace.

What about *her* peace? Hadn't that been disturbed too?

There wasn't a soul alive who had cared one way or the other.

If that miserable customer of hers hadn't come back, if he hadn't tried to beat her senseless again, she never would've hit him with a weighted doorstop. She'd stopped him, all right. Cold.

Stopped her own life, too. No one noticed if a whore went to prison for murder. It wasn't self-defense, the judge reasoned. She'd asked for trouble and gotten nothing more than what she deserved.

It was hard to argue with the law. No, *impossible.*

Determined to put such memories behind her, Anita lengthened her stride. White Point Gardens, a landscaped oasis of palmettos along the

Cooper River, waited less than a block ahead. The streets were overrun with people of every age and hue, happy to help themselves to free food and entertainment. That was good news for her—the more people, the less likely anyone would take notice of a quiet woman in a gray dress.

She scanned the staging area where a knot of official-looking men stood talking among themselves. Governor Sheppard wasn't with them, nor could she spot his silvery head of hair in the crowded reception line. *Wait!* There he was, sitting with the mayor in a semisecluded corner of the gardens, balancing a plateful of food in his right hand.

Anita knew she'd never have a chance like this again. *Go, go!*

Slipping past the crush of shoulders and elbows, she made her way toward him, a flush of anticipation making her skin tingle. His face was so kind, so open. Would he even know who she was without the layers of makeup and the thigh-high dress? She looked nothing like her mug shot, nothing like the photo they'd run in the paper a zillion times. *Nothing like the woman you used to be.*

Maybe that was good, or the security guys who were eyeing her now might have already clapped her in handcuffs and directed her toward the nearest squad car.

The sight of the uniformed men made her spirits sink to the hem of her gray tunic. What was she thinking, showing up like this? That she could stroll right up and meet Governor Sheppard, shake his hand, pat his cheek? Her, of all people?

With her heart pounding in a slow rhythm of despair, she surveyed the governor's entourage, desperate for a friendly face, someone she might convince to help her. There was the lieutenant governor, who—along with the mayor—opposed her pardon to begin with. *No hope there.* Several others she didn't recognize were standing behind him, plates in hand.

Then she saw him. The governor's son, stretched out in the grass, off to the side by himself. His jacket, shoes, and socks were cast aside, as if he were a college student cutting classes on a warm spring day. Or a hospital patient taking his daily constitutional.

Of course! She remembered the stories from the evening news. How he'd contracted some mysterious, life-threatening disease. Had open wounds that refused to heal and suffered from various painful symptoms, not the least of which was suspicion and grossly unfair judgment on the part of John Q. Public.

She'd forgotten his name. Wait...*Jess*. Yes, that was it. Thanks to his health problems, Jess—Governor Sheppard's only child—faced an uncertain future. A tragedy, everyone said. Even her cellmates thought it was a sad story. Gazing at him now, she saw little evidence of his illness, though his skin was drawn and his hands displayed more than one ugly scar.

His eyes were bright though.

And he was looking straight at her.

What am I supposed to do? Something, apparently. She offered him a tentative smile, waiting. His eyes beckoned her forward. Almost against her will she found herself moving in his direction, past the governor, who surely hadn't noticed her, and past his handlers, who seemed unconcerned about a stranger approaching the famous man's son.

She wanted to talk to his father—oh so much!—but maybe, just maybe, this son could get a message to him.

Reaching the bare spot of grass at his feet, she paused, close enough to gaze fully into his eyes and read his expression. What she saw there was surprising. No, *shocking*. It was forgiveness.

His father's pardon was one thing. A legal exercise. But this was something else again, something more profound, more permanent. It was as if—*but this is ridiculous!*—as if the son knew her, knew her story, all of it.

And forgave her. For all of it.

The first tear surprised her, running down her cheek, then down her neck, staining the collar of her gray tunic. *He sees me!* It was the only thought that would take shape in her addled brain, whirling with conflicting emotions.

But that was the whole of it: *He saw her.* Saw her for who she truly was. *Anita.* Not a whore, not a murderer, not a once-pretty girl who'd lost her way, not a punching bag for a parade of losers. He saw the *now* of her, the *essence* of her. And found her worthy as is.

Miraculous wasn't the half of it.

More tears followed, cascading down her face until she couldn't bear to hold up her head any longer. Her chin dropped to her chest, sending her tears dripping downward, onto the ground around his ankles, landing at last on his bruised heel.

He never said a word. Neither did she. Not even when she found herself on her knees with her wet cheek pressed against his bare feet. In the fragile silence she felt Jess's hand rest lightly on the disheveled mass of hair falling around her shoulders like a bridal veil.

She thinks I don't see her. Governor Sheppard smiled to himself, nodding as the mayor droned on and on about his plans for cleaning up the criminal element of Charleston. How could he miss those eyes full of sorrow, that face full of fear and longing? Even before he saw her, he'd sensed her presence, felt her moving toward him, reticent but determined. She was gutsy, he'd give her that. After what she'd been through, the woman held herself together well.

When the mayor paused, obviously waiting for some sign of approval, the governor presented him with a brief nod and an affirming murmur, launching the man on another laundry list of accomplishments.

The governor watched her out of the corner of his eye. She was on her knees now. *Good, good.* Humility became her, like a fine velvet cloak. She had an inner strength and beauty few bothered to notice. His son had seen it immediately. Jess had studied her case at length and had offered his always-wise counsel: *Pardon her.* As a father, he could hardly dispute his son's compassionate directive. Yes, the decision had ruffled a few feathers. *So be it.* He'd done that plenty of times and planned to do it plenty more.

When he finally shifted his gaze back to the mayor, he realized with chagrin that he'd unintentionally drawn the mayor's attention to Anita.

"Who is that slobbering all over your son, Governor?" The mayor peered at her, then leaned back, clearly appalled. "Don't tell me it's that prostitute you pardoned last week!"

He shrugged. *No getting around this one.* "I believe she's the same woman, Mayor."

"I'll call my chief of police!"

"No need." He squeezed the man's shoulder, hoping to calm him, but above all to stop him. "She's not breaking the law, is she? Perhaps she simply wants to express her gratitude in some way."

The mayor snorted. "What does crying all over Jess's feet have to do with saying thank you?"

The governor fixed the man with a steady gaze. "Not everyone is willing to touch my son."

"I see." The mayor shifted in his chair, a guilty look crossing his features. "But…aren't you worried about his…health?"

Governor Sheppard knew his smile wouldn't soften the blow of his words. "My son has only a short time to live. Believe me, she can do him no harm." He turned back to watch her as she slowly dried Jess's feet with her hair. *Incredible!* The woman's complete lack of pride was astounding. "Look how it delights her to do this." He shook his head in amazement. "Do you see her?"

The mayor exploded. "Of course I see her!"

"No, I mean do you see how grateful she is to be forgiven?"

"What I see is a woman making an utter fool of herself in public. Look at that! She's…she's…"

"Kissing his feet," the governor whispered. "Splendid!"

"Are you mad, sir?" The mayor was sputtering now, his face the color of beets in a June garden. "Do you expect your constituents to worship you?"

"I'm honored when they're grateful, yes." Reluctantly turning away from the tender scene nearby, the governor trained his eyes on the red-faced mayor. "Unlike you, for example."

"Me?"

"When I arrived for this event, supposedly held in my honor, you didn't even offer my son something to drink. Yet this woman has showered his feet with her tears."

"Well...I'm..."

"And when someone splashed lemonade all over his hand, you laughed and left him dripping. Yet she dried his wet feet with her own precious hair."

"Oh! Surely you don't..."

"And while you required me to listen to all your good deeds, she spoke not a word to my son, only kissed his feet with gratitude."

"Sir, I'm truly...I'm..."

The governor suddenly rose to his feet, catching the eye of everyone within a hundred yards. The whole corner of the garden grew silent, waiting for him to speak, as the scent of some rare perfume wafted through the air, bathing the unsuspecting crowd with its invisible glory...

Winning the Lord's Favor Without a Word: The Sinful Woman

She's our final Bad Girl—and my far-and-away favorite. Suppose we join her for dinner.

> Now one of the Pharisees invited Jesus to have dinner with him, so
> he went to the Pharisee's house and reclined at the table. *Luke 7:36*

Don't you know everybody must have wanted Jesus over for chicken 'n' dumplings? The man was the talk of the town—healing the leper, giving sight to the blind, raising the widow's son right out of his coffin. Honey, his dance card had to be full of invitations to one social occasion after another, Simon the Pharisee's dinner among them.

Although this party wasn't his idea, Jesus attended nonetheless, willing to be used by his Father in the home of this pious (and, let's be honest, pompous) Jew. It was quite a feast, with the guests stretched out on their left sides, as was the Greek custom, propped up on their elbows while eating with their right hands. It beats trying to eat standing up— something I can never manage without wearing half my meal—but it still sounds awkward. On the plus side, even if half the town showed up for dinner, the host wouldn't have to worry about tracking down more chairs.

Some attendees, though, were more interested in the guest of honor than in the menu, including one soul who would've been counted among the least of these.

> When a woman who had lived a sinful life in that town...*Luke 7:37*

Sigh... Another Bad Girl without a name. At least the woman at the well had a consistent label. This shady lady is variously referred to as "the sinful woman," "the woman who anointed Jesus," or "the woman with the alabaster jar." Considering the whole town knew her reputation, it's odd they didn't also know her name.

In my radio days I once prefaced an on-air story about Henry VIII by asking the newsman on the microphone that morning, "How's your history?"

"Sordid," was his cheeky reply.

That exchange describes our soon-to-be-heroine perfectly. Her sins aren't detailed, but we can surmise she was a woman of the streets—a prostitute—with a long history of sin. *The Amplified Bible* calls her "an especially wicked sinner" and, in verse 39, "a notorious sinner" and "a social outcast, devoted to sin." The *New Living Translation* describes her as "a certain immoral woman."

Okay, okay, we've seen that movie.

Whatever her shortcomings, she stayed well-informed about the late-breaking news of the day.

> ...[she] learned that Jesus was eating at the Pharisee's house...
> *Luke 7:37*

That's odd. What would a woman of the street want with a man of the cloth?

Lucky for her, a personal invitation to Simon's dinner wasn't necessary. The less fortunate were allowed to visit such public banquets in order to snatch up the leftovers. (Some things never change. I've seen folks visit restaurant buffets after church, line their purses with napkins, and stuff in everything short of mashed potatoes and gravy.)

Since women weren't permitted to serve the food at fancy meals like this one, let alone recline at the table as invited guests, the best Miss No-Name could do was hang around the periphery, hoping for a few table scraps and an occasional glimpse of the grand Pooh-Bahs lounging around the head table.

The minute she heard about the banquet in progress, our Bad Girl quickly located the one item most precious to her and made tracks for Simon's place.

>...she brought an alabaster jar of perfume... *Luke 7:37*

Alabaster was a soft stone, imported from Egypt into Palestine, especially popular for storing perfume and ointments. It was light and creamy in color, usually faintly lined with veins. We're talking a small flask here, something she could easily have slipped inside her tunic. (So much for the mental image I always had of a small, dark woman carrying on her shoulder a marble vase of perfume the size of the giant display bottle at the Estée Lauder counter.)

Wrong.

Think pint-size. Palm-size. Purse-size.

Alabaster jars were common—it was the substance hidden inside that was valuable. Her jar undoubtedly contained all the perfume she owned. Pure nard, all essence, no alcohol, very expensive. The tiniest dab on the appropriate pulse points lasted well into the dark desert night.

But she wasn't wearing the perfume, drawing attention to herself with its luscious scent. She was carrying it in a small alabaster vial, her attention fixed on finding one particular dinner guest who might appreciate the fragrant aroma of her sacrifice.

She knew what the townsfolk thought of her. Their whispered words and rude stares made that painfully clear. But this Jesus was different. His words were kind, not cruel. His gaze reflected compassion, not judgment. The thought of such a man looking at her surely had her trembling with expectation.

Miss seeing the man from Galilee? Not this girl.

Perhaps she only meant to catch a glimpse of him from afar, but seeing his gentle countenance, she was drawn toward him, closer and closer, until she stood right behind him.

That's when the tears came unbidden.

> ...and as she stood behind him at his feet weeping, she began to wet his feet with her tears. *Luke 7:38*

Oh, my sister! Don't hurry over those words. Read them again.

Do you see this woman?

She could not move, could not speak for all her anguished weeping. From a well so deep inside her that the murky waters had never seen the light of day, tears poured out in an endless flow, streaming over her cheeks, slipping down her neck.

His utter sinlessness undid her.

Every impure thought, word, and deed of her past welled up in her heart and flowed down her face. Darkest shame mixed with a strange sense of lightness. The tears of a harlot, held back in anger from years on the street, were suddenly released and spilled out like perfume, leaving her vulnerable, exposed, repentant, not caring who saw her or what they thought of her.

She didn't try to stop herself from weeping. Couldn't, in fact. Not in the presence of Holy God. The turbulent waters of her soul had found release and refused to be contained.

Were they tears of sorrow or tears of joy?

Yes.

Unlike the woman at the well, this thirsty soul brought her water with her. Standing so close to him, she knew—*knew!*—that Jesus alone understood her, forgave her, loved her.

He hadn't sent her away, had he? Hadn't brushed off her tears in disgust. Instead, he'd allowed her to baptize his feet with her salty flow. More than allowed, he'd *accepted* her worship. His grace only increased her devotion.

With her head bowed in reverence, her body soon followed as she dropped to her knees only inches from the feet of her beloved Savior.

> Then she wiped them with her hair... *Luke 7:38*

Her hair would have been bound up, according to social custom. Let down her hair in public? Oh, honey. That was considered so bold, so provocative, so abhorrent it was grounds for divorce.

But she was already an outcast. Untouchable. Unchosen. She belonged to no one. Except perhaps this man Jesus. If he would have her.

Loosening her long hair, she let it fall around her shoulders, then bent over farther still, until his tear-drenched feet were all that her eyes could encompass. Using the dark strands like a silken hand towel, patting and wiping and caressing, she rubbed his heels, arches, and toes until they were dry once more.

She didn't dare speak, but her thoughts were surely spinning. This Jesus did not rebuke her for touching him! He'd received her adoration, not once drawing back.

Overcome with emotion, with gratitude, with devotion, she let her mouth follow the same path her fingers had taken and lightly touched his feet with her lips.

...[she] kissed them... *Luke 7:38*

In the most public of places, she performed one of the most intimate, yet innocent of acts. *She pressed her mouth to his feet.*

How easily we do this with babies, whose feet are as soft and sweet as their chubby fists. Kissing the feet of an infant, even of a toddler, is a delicious treat. Those tiny tootsies taste yummy until...well, until they're not soft little tootsies anymore but *feet.* Sneaker-scented, dirt-encrusted, who-knows-where-they've-been-lately *feet.* Ahem. Different story. Head for the tub, please.

Which is why her unabashed affection and total humility were breathtaking. To kiss an adult man's cheek or his hand or the edge of his garment was one thing, but his bare, stone-bruised *feet?* Scandalous.

But physical affection was how she made her living. It was all she knew to offer him. Men paid her money to touch them with her hands, her hair, her lips. That she lavished such attention on this man for free was her ultimate gift to him.

Nor was she finished. She had one more expression of love, quite literally up her sleeve.

> …and [she] poured perfume on them. *Luke 7:38*

Her initial intent may have been merely to touch a drop of the perfumed ointment to his head, as was common. Ah, but that was an hour ago, before she'd seen him, touched him, kissed him. It was too late for such restraint. Extravagantly, yet with purpose, she poured the contents of her precious alabaster jar over his feet.

The same perfume she'd used to seduce men was poured out—every priceless drop—to honor the one man who would never use her. The heady scent of it must have permeated the room, sending necks craning to see what woman had dared invade their male-only gathering with her frankly feminine fragrance.

No doubt their guttural whispers swirled around her, even as her ministrations required every ounce of concentration, rendering her immune to their cruel commentary…

"It's the town whore!"

"What's *she* doing here?"

"Has Simon seen her yet?"

"He won't appreciate this, I can tell you!"

You'll find similar stories in the other three Gospels—tales of a woman who spilled out her costly perfume from an alabaster jar, twice on his head, once on his feet. The other three versions, however, shift to the disciples whining about how the perfume should have been sold and the money given to the poor.

In this version, the woman and her worship are the focus of the story, not the perfume. Check out the reaction from the Lord and those around him:

> When the Pharisee who had invited him saw this, he said to
> himself… *Luke 7:39*

Good old Simon the Pharisee didn't miss a trick. As host and self-appointed spiritual watchdog, he kept an eye on everything that was said and done in the company of Jesus. One could hardly miss the woman on her knees at the teacher's feet—making a complete idiot of herself, to his way of thinking.

All that crying and kissing. Female foolishness!

"Said to himself" means Simon was thinking, not speaking out loud. Unless he was mumbling under his breath in a stage whisper meant to be heard by the audience. Then, too, maybe Simon was so peeved over this woman's actions that he needed to voice his displeasure, if only for his own satisfaction.

> "If this man were a prophet, he would know who is touching him and what kind of woman she is—that she is a sinner." *Luke 7:39*

Doubt was setting in. "If…" Prophets were supposed to know everything, the seen and the unseen. *Could be Jesus isn't much of a prophet after all. The healings this week were impressive, but who knows? Maybe it was all smoke and polished bronze.*

Simon's disgust at the situation was surely written all over his face. *Look at her! Touching him like that.* Maybe if she'd been a noblewoman, he would have overlooked her actions, but it was her station in life that upset Simon. "That kind of woman." A sinner.

Of course, for members of this legalistic sect, anyone who wasn't a Pharisee was a sinner. She was merely the worst of the worst.

The host of the party may have been sympathetic toward Jesus and his ministry, but he was completely unsympathetic toward the woman. A popular Greek proverb, later recorded in Scripture, would have suited Simon's mood well. It's easy to imagine him quoting this for Jesus' benefit, with a face devoid of compassion.

> Do not be misled: "Bad company corrupts good character."
> *1 Corinthians 15:33*

Ah, but the fact is, Simon hadn't *said* a word. He'd only *thought* these things. That's why the next verse is startling.

> Jesus answered him… *Luke 7:40*

Stop right there. "Answered"?

Does this mean the Lord interpreted the man's body language, the look of displeasure in his eyes, the frown of distaste? Or...did he literally read Simon's mind?

Fully God, remember. Jesus heard every word in the man's heart, spoken or not. These verses elsewhere in Luke confirm it:

> Jesus knew what they were thinking and asked... *Luke 5:22*

> He saw through their duplicity and said... *Luke 20:23*

And we think we can keep our sins a secret! The Lord knows about them, child. *All of them.*

Jesus immediately got his host's attention.

> "Simon, I have something to tell you." *Luke 7:40*

Polite, inviting, confidential. It drew Simon right in.

> "Tell me, teacher," he said. *Luke 7:40*

Jesus didn't teach unless there was a ready pupil. Eye to eye now with Simon, he spun out a parable—a story with a lesson—as only the Great Teacher could:

> "Two men owed money to a certain moneylender. One owed him
> five hundred denarii, and the other fifty. Neither of them had the
> money to pay him back, so he canceled the debts of both. Now
> which of them will love him more?" *Luke 7:41-42*

Some of the Lord's parables send me scrambling for a calculator or a calendar to figure them out. Not this one. Short and sweet. A banker canceled the debts of two men—one a little, one a lot.

Which one would be more grateful?

"No-brainer" would be an understatement.

Simon (proud of himself, no doubt) came up with a quick answer.

> Simon replied, "I suppose the one who had the bigger debt
> canceled." *Luke 7:43*

What's to "suppose" here? It's obvious. Ever the good teacher, Jesus acknowledged his pupil's right response.

> "You have judged correctly," Jesus said. *Luke 7:43*

He affirmed, encouraged...and lowered the boom.

> Then he turned toward the woman and said to Simon...
> *Luke 7:44*

Back at last to our fallen woman, huddled on the floor at Jesus' feet. Were you afraid he hadn't noticed her? Not a chance. The man who could sense a woman touching his cloak in a crowded marketplace definitely wouldn't miss this woman's utterly tactile tears and kisses on his bare skin.

He'd merely waited for the perfect, teachable moment.

Looking directly at her, while still speaking to Simon, Jesus said five words that changed the lives of both his listeners.

"Do you see this woman?" *Luke 7:44*

Simon had seen her, but only for *what* she was, not *who* she was. He had looked at her form but not her face. He had eyed her actions but not looked her in the eye and connected with her, human to human.

"See her," Jesus implored. "See her as I see her."

Mea culpa, Lord. I am no better than the Pharisee.

My friend Sara and I were hurrying down the streets of Edinburgh one damp, chilly December day. The Scots call such weather *dreich,* meaning "bleak, dreary, dismal, godforsaken." It was all that and then some. A thick fog had settled in, making it difficult to see more than ten feet ahead of us.

Yet Sara managed to spot the diminutive woman in ragged clothes with her back propped against the wall of an upscale department store, its windows gleaming with Christmas cheer. The contrast between the colorful decorations and this stranger's drab and wrinkled clothing was stark, unsettling.

"Do you see this woman?" Jesus said.

I didn't see her until I saw Sara bending over to slip a British pound at the woman's feet and offer her a gentle word of comfort. Sara stood and turned toward me, tears in her eyes. "She has an inhaler," she whispered.

My friend had noticed every detail and responded with her heart. I'd barely seen the woman, mentally labeling her a poor beggar and fumbling with my packages, pretending not to notice. (Please tell me you've been there. This looks so ugly on paper.)

Forced now to turn toward this silent woman in need, I was grateful for a chance to recover the eyes of the Spirit who lives in all of us who love the Christ and so added my own coin to her small pile. How much better it is, though, to see an opportunity *first* and give with joyous abandon.

That was precisely the point Jesus drove home to Simon:

> "I came into your house. You did not give me any water for my
> feet, but she wet my feet with her tears and wiped them with her
> hair." *Luke 7:44*

Barefoot or in sandals, travelers of the day arrived with their feet covered with dust and dirt. It was customary for a host to offer water and a towel for a quick foot scrub. Simon dropped the ball. The woman, however, did the right thing.

> "You did not give me a kiss, but this woman, from the time I
> entered, has not stopped kissing my feet." *Luke 7:45*

A brotherly kiss on the cheek was a common greeting, especially for the host to offer his guest of honor. Simon neglected that duty, too. Once again, Miss No-Name earned a brownie point.

> "You did not put oil on my head, but she has poured perfume on
> my feet." *Luke 7:46*

Meshiach in Hebrew, *Christos* in Greek—both mean "anointed one." If our stingy host had put a bit of oil on the head of Jesus, we might have overlooked the foot-washing blooper. Oh, but Simon missed this opportunity as well. Instead, a woman who embodied everything the Pharisee hated earned a four-star hospitality rating. In his own house.

She not only broke open her jar, she shattered the mold of how worship was to be done—passionately, personally, and with humble abandon. As Eugene Peterson observed in *The Message,* "Impressive, isn't it?"[1]

Very impressive.

By pointing out the things she did right and the things Simon *should* have done, Jesus managed to affirm her and admonish him at the same time, without stripping either one of dignity. He let the contrast of their actions speak for themselves:

No water from him versus many tears from her.

No towel from him versus gentle hair drying from her.

No kiss from him versus endless kisses from her.

No oil from him versus expensive perfume from her.

Which is especially interesting, considering that…

He was a pious man versus she was a sinful woman.

We're not told how Simon the Pharisee reacted. Was he angry? Stunned? Ashamed? Repentant? He couldn't have missed the message. This parable was anything but subtle.

Jesus took every opportunity to remind religious leaders of their hypocrisy, as in this little pronouncement to the chief priests and elders on another occasion:

> Jesus said to them, "I tell you the truth, the tax collectors and the
> prostitutes are entering the kingdom of God ahead of you."
> *Matthew 21:31*

Ouch! Politically correct? Not Jesus, no way.

And what of our dear sister, still on her knees before the Christ? Did her face remain bowed during his brief, pointed words to Simon? If so, we can imagine the blush of delight mingled with embarrassment that danced across her features while Jesus sang her praises. Or perhaps she looked up to gaze at last upon the One whom she loved and worshiped so completely.

Without question, her head would've snapped to attention on hearing this:

> "Therefore, I tell you, her many sins have been forgiven—for she
> loved much." *Luke 7:47*

True, he does acknowledge her "many sins." No getting around her former Bad Girl status. But he doesn't *condemn* her for her many sins. He doesn't even charge her to "go and sin no more," as he does a woman caught in adultery in another setting.

Since Jesus knew everything about this quiet worshiper, perhaps she'd already given up her life of sin. After all, the evidence of a changed heart was kneeling at his feet. Without a word, she expressed repentance. Without a sound, she cried out for forgiveness. Without a syllable, she spelled out the desire of her heart: to love him.

Her actions said it all.

And it was good.

In Don Francisco's haunting song based on this story, he wrote, "For the depth of God's forgiveness, it's more than you can see. / And in spite of what you think of her, she's *Beautiful to Me*."[2]

Our love and worship make us beautiful to God. And why are we surprised? When my Bill turns to me with love in his eyes and kind words on his lips, he is the most handsome man on earth. He assures me that when I speak and demonstrate love to him, I, too, am beautiful. (I usually argue with him, but he seldom listens...bless his soul!)

Every coin has two sides. Jesus turned this one over to reveal the sad corollary:

> "But he who has been forgiven little loves little." *Luke 7:47*

When I sit in church on Sunday morning feeling disconnected and out of tune with the music, the elements, the worship, it's easy to blame a bad night's sleep or a prickly discussion with Bill in the parking lot.

The truth?

I am not willing to confess my sins so that true worship can begin. I have forgotten how much I've already been forgiven so that my gratitude can flow in ceaseless praise. Quite simply, my love has grown cold.

Worship is about rekindling an ashen heart into a blazing fire. This woman was a torchbearer. Jesus surely felt the heat in her touch, her tears, her kiss. She came asking for nothing, concerned only with giving him glory, honor, and praise the only way she knew how.

On a chilly Edinburgh street or a soul-frozen Sunday morning, my only hope for fanning the flames of my faith in Christ is to do as she did two thousand years ago:

Seek him openly.

Abandon self humbly.

Worship him completely.

Embrace his forgiveness joyfully.

> Then Jesus said to her, "Your sins are forgiven." *Luke 7:48*

Finally he spoke directly to her. Simon wasn't included in this one. Forgiveness is always personal with him. He died for the sins of the whole world, but forgiveness comes to each of us, individually, when we demonstrate our readiness to accept it.

"Forgiven?" How our made-new Good Girl must have hugged *that* truth to her bosom!

The rest of the partygoers were less enthusiastic.

> The other guests began to say among themselves, "Who is this who even forgives sins?" *Luke 7:49*

Even while stuffing their faces, they'd tuned in to the drama unfolding at Jesus' feet. For once, they stopped talking about *her* and shifted their gossip to *him*.

"The nerve of this guy!"

"Who does he think he is, forgiving her sins?"

"Hope he's got all day. That hussy's racked up a ton."

"Huh. I've seen your own sandals parked outside her door more than once, Zeke…"

Jesus ignored their grumbling, keeping his focus on the woman kneeling before him as he offered her a benediction:

> Jesus said to the woman, "Your faith has saved you…" *Luke 7:50*

It was not her *love* that saved her. It was her *faith* in his power to forgive her. It was her *faith* in his steadfast love for her. And it was her *faith* expressed in actions, not words. While the story of the woman at the well was all dialogue and no action until she ran back to town, this woman teaches us without speaking one syllable. When his forgiveness flowed toward her in the sacred silence of their communion, love and gratitude filled the air with the fragrant aroma of a soul set free.

> "…go in peace." *Luke 7:50*

Peace. What everyone hopes for, prays for, longs for. *The Amplified Bible* phrases it, "go (enter) into peace [in freedom from all the distresses that are experienced as the result of sin]." Peace comes to those who are willing to move away from sin and toward the Prince of Peace, until his peace becomes their own.

"Seek peace and pursue it," wrote the psalmist.[3]

Seek and enter in, dear woman.

Hear the hearts, if not the voices, of all the nameless women through the centuries who found peace at the foot of the cross. See them beckoning you with tear-stained hands: "Come! Come meet a man who forgives sins. Even mine. Even yours, beloved."

What Lessons Can We Learn from the Sinful Woman?

People will talk, no matter what we do.
How often we get derailed by snide sidebar conversations and pointedly rude asides! When she was steeped in sin, the woman's nosy neighbors whispered about that. When she sacrificed herself in worship, they tsk-tsked about that. When Jesus forgave her sins, their tongues wagged about *that.* Let's forget trying to squelch gossips with words; they're masters of that media. The best way to zip their lips is simply to turn away from the noise and focus our eyes and ears on the One whose opinion really matters.

> We are not trying to please men but God, who tests our hearts.
> *1 Thessalonians 2:4*

The Pharisees thought they were the Good Guys.
We think of Pharisees as ancient hypocrites, religious jerks, or worse. The truth is, they were the righteous men of their day, avoiding sin and proclaiming God's Word. Simon called Jesus "teacher," invited him to supper, and sat by Jesus' side, willing to be taught. What Simon wasn't willing to do was humble himself and worship Christ as the sinful woman did. Before we're too hard on old "Simon Says She's a Sinner," we need to look in the mirror. Those of us who've been involved in church for a while may appear a tad "Simon-ized" ourselves.

> "No one is good—except God alone." *Mark 10:18*

One person's beautiful is another person's ugly.
I use my perfume, "Beautiful," very sparingly since it's potent...and pricey. Even so, one gentleman sitting next to me at an airport complained about

my "awful fragrance." Though I could—and did—change my seat to help him out, I couldn't change my cologne so easily. A scent, once released, is tough to contain. (Skunks use this to their advantage!) In the spiritual realm, since we can't change the aroma of Christ that lingers around us, even when it offends others, we might as well break open the whole bottle and let the world catch his scent.

> For we are to God the aroma of Christ among those who are being saved and those who are perishing. To the one we are the smell of death; to the other, the fragrance of life. *2 Corinthians 2:15-16*

Silence speaks volumes.

This woman didn't vocalize anything, let alone her need for forgiveness. She never even moved her lips except to kiss her Savior. Which means she couldn't have prayed what's often called "the sinner's prayer." Oh no! Was she truly forgiven? Of course. Jesus can discern our thoughts and read our intentions as if we each were a well-worn book. (Hmm…considering how often our words don't match our hearts, it's amazing the Lord listens to our lips at all.) Yes, putting words to our deepest thoughts has great value, both for us and for others. Public confession and testimony work best with words. But when we're talking to Jesus directly, as she was, we can hear better when we're listening in silence and worshiping…not talking.

> The LORD is in his holy temple;
>
> let all the earth be silent before him. *Habakkuk 2:20*

Good Girl Thoughts Worth Considering

1. Have you ever been too overwhelmed to speak and found yourself weeping instead? How did that make you feel? Weak? Embarrassed? Relieved? Cleansed? What do you imagine brought this sinful woman to tears?

2. She took down her hair as an expression of worship. What motivates people to break the bonds of convention and "let down their hair" in seeking

to worship the Lord? Think of some biblical examples of variety and creativity in worship. Have you participated in something similar? What was the result? How would we know if our worship is pleasing to God?

3. Foot kissing and perfume pouring might not be on your "To Do" list for next Sunday morning's worship service. But what could you do—privately or publicly—that would be as sacrificial and meaningful as this woman's actions? Would you be willing to try it? In public or private? How might you do it, practically speaking? What would be the benefit, spiritually speaking?

4. Considering that the woman in this story never spoke, what does that say to you? Do you identify more with the chatty woman at the well or this silent sinner at Jesus' feet? Is one personality more pleasing to God than the other? How does each personality lend itself to serving the Lord?

5. How can we know, as surely as this woman did, that our sins are forgiven? (Hint: It's in the Bible!) Find at least five verses that assure you his gifts of grace and forgiveness are the real thing.

6. The woman at the well couldn't wait to tell people about the prophet she'd met. But what do you imagine this quiet, humble woman did to spread the good news? Can you win someone without a word? Think of some ways to share your faith that don't include any words, spoken or written.

7. When people watch someone turn from an openly sinful life to an openly grace-full one, they are naturally curious, if not cautious or even downright cynical. What might we do to convince folks we're a "new creation"? To what extent is the former Bad Girl responsible for demonstrating her new status, and to what extent should Good Girls take a new believer at her word?

8. What's the most important lesson you learned from the story of this sinful-but-forgiven woman?

FROM BAD TO VERSE...

A hard beginning
maketh a good ending.

JOHN HEYWOOD

Have you found yourself among these ten women? On any given day I can identify in some way with all of them.

And did you discover the common denominator, other than our womanly roles as daughters, wives, mothers, and friends? It's simply this: Good Girls and Bad Girls both need a Savior. The goodness of your present life can't open the doors of heaven for you. The badness of your past life can't keep you out either. Not if you truly desire the forgiveness and freedom Christ offers.

Remember his promise: "He...gives grace to the humble."[1]

Lord, when we feel like the baddest of the bad, give us the humility to repent. Exchange our dirty hearts for clean ones. Fill us with fresh hope for our forever with you.

Then bring to mind one woman around us who's avoided you, feared you, rejected you, perhaps because she's afraid you've rejected her. Empower us with the courage to reach out in compassion and tell her the truth: Your arm, Lord, is not too short. Even now, you are stretching across eternity to grasp that woman's hand and draw her into your loving embrace.

Sister, if I haven't told you often enough in these pages, you are not only loved by God, you are also deeply appreciated by me. Together, let's latch on to the wisdom and knowledge found in these stories from his Word and transform our world for the Christ, who died that we might live.

Eve had a hunger that cost her a garden;
Potiphar's wife had an appetite too;
Lot lost his mate when her past swirled around her;
Delilah went bad when she snipped a new 'do.

Sapphira fell flat when it came down to money;
Jezebel ordered her husband around;
Michal missed the message in King David's worship;
To the bone, in a moment, their badness was found.

Yet…

A woman of Samaria found a thirst quencher;
A sinner, a woman, anointed Christ's feet;
Rahab, the harlot, became a believer;
Her sin, like the walls, crumbled down in defeat.

Bad for a season, but no, not forever,
Not these three role models, saved from despair.
Made new by God, their changed lives teach the lesson:
If we but ask him, grace waits for us there.

Liz Curtis Higgs

STUDY GUIDE

The questions at the end of each chapter are designed for both individual reflection and group discussion and are meant to provoke an emotional response as well as an intellectual one…and why not? We're to love the Lord with all our hearts *and* all our minds!

When all is said and done, it's important to bring our focus back to what the Scriptures teach us about the subjects being discussed, and that's the intent of the verses listed here by question number. I'd encourage group leaders to review them beforehand, then be ready to share them as needed to bring a satisfying and biblical closure to your discussion. May your efforts be richly blessed!

Eve

1. Proverbs 30:5-6; Mark 4:15; Luke 11:28
2. Proverbs 3:7; Proverbs 17:24; Proverbs 21:4
3. Isaiah 40:25; Isaiah 55:8-9; Philippians 2:5-7
4. Psalm 73:25; Romans 8:5; Romans 13:14
5. Proverbs 10:17; 2 Timothy 1:7; 2 Peter 1:5-7
6. Psalm 69:5; Hebrews 4:13; 1 Peter 2:16; Psalm 32:5; James 2:10; James 4:17
7. 1 John 1:8-9; Psalm 51:2-4; Psalm 51:10-12

Potiphar's Wife

1. Isaiah 40:26; Isaiah 43:1; Exodus 33:17
2. 1 Corinthians 12:4-5; 1 Corinthians 7:17
3. Exodus 20:14; Proverbs 2:16-18; Ephesians 4:17-20
4. Proverbs 5:18; Proverbs 20:6; Malachi 2:14-15

5. Colossians 3:5; 1 Thessalonians 4:3-7; Philippians 4:8-9

6. Proverbs 19:1; Proverbs 2:7-8; Psalm 15:1-5; Psalm 37:18

7. Psalm 4:4; Psalm 37:8; Colossians 3:8; James 1:19-20

Lot's Wife

1. Proverbs 17:1; 1 Peter 3:5-6; Psalm 39:2-4

2. Nehemiah 9:30-31; 2 Peter 3:9; 1 Timothy 1:16

3. Nehemiah 4:14; Proverbs 14:26; 2 Corinthians 6:18

4. Habakkuk 1:10-11; Psalm 123:3-4; Matthew 10:14-15

5. Deuteronomy 8:5; Hebrews 12:10-11; Proverbs 6:23

6. Exodus 4:10-15; Genesis 18:23-32; Genesis 32:24-30

7. Proverbs 13:19; Psalm 116:3; 2 Corinthians 7:10

The Woman at the Well

1. John 10:14; Jeremiah 9:23-24; Psalm 139:13-16

2. Matthew 7:1-5; Luke 6:36-37; 1 Peter 2:19; 1 Thessalonians 5:15

3. Amos 8:11-13; Isaiah 41:17; Isaiah 49:8-10; Matthew 5:6

4. Psalm 138:3; 1 Kings 10:1-3; 2 Corinthians 3:12

5. Psalm 145:19; Isaiah 54:4-5; Psalm 86:11

6. John 4:35-38; Matthew 9:37-38; Galatians 6:6-9

7. 1 Thessalonians 2:8; 2 Corinthians 9:13; Acts 20:24

Delilah

1. Proverbs 16:18; Job 24:22; Romans 7:21-23

2. Proverbs 7:21-23; Ezekiel 16:30; 2 Peter 2:14

3. Leviticus 19:18; Romans 12:19; Nahum 1:2-3

4. Proverbs 9:13; Isaiah 54:6-7; Isaiah 30:12-14

5. Matthew 27:3-5; Ezekiel 7:19; 1 Peter 1:18-19

6. Titus 3:3-5; Hebrews 12:1-2; Psalm 25:15

7. Proverbs 18:1; Philippians 2:3-4; Luke 9:25

Sapphira

1. Acts 4:32; 1 John 3:17-18; Luke 12:33-34

2. Psalm 112:5; Proverbs 11:25; 2 Corinthians 9:13

3. Luke 12:15; Proverbs 23:5; 1 Timothy 6:17-19

4. 1 Timothy 6:9-10; Ephesians 4:25; Romans 1:20-21

5. Matthew 25:14-21,29

6. Jeremiah 17:10; 1 Peter 5:6-7; Luke 12:6-7

7. Isaiah 30:15; Romans 2:4-5; Ezekiel 18:32

Rahab

1. Psalm 103:2-4; Psalm 86:5; Romans 3:22-24

2. Ephesians 4:32; Ephesians 2:8-9; Colossians 3:13-15

3. Psalm 130:3-5; Hebrews 4:15-16; Romans 6:22

4. 2 Corinthians 5:7; Romans 10:10; 2 John 1:6

5. Deuteronomy 7:1-10; Micah 4:12; Proverbs 28:5

6. Romans 16:19; 2 Corinthians 9:13; 2 John 1:6

7. Joshua 24:14; 2 Corinthians 3:12; 1 Peter 3:8

Jezebel

1. Isaiah 46:12; 2 Kings 19:22; Isaiah 57:17; Jeremiah 17:23

2. Psalm 40:4; Romans 12:16; 1 Corinthians 13:4

3. Romans 12:6-8; Isaiah 55:4; 1 Corinthians 16:13

4. Psalm 34:11; Psalm 37:25-26; Matthew 18:4-6,14

5. Acts 17:30; Proverbs 1:24-33; Romans 8:38-39

6. Proverbs 12:4; Proverbs 21:9; Proverbs 7:26

7. Luke 6:27-36

Michal

1. Proverbs 27:4; Proverbs 14:30; James 3:16-17
2. 1 Samuel 13:13-14; 1 Samuel 16:21-22; 1 Samuel 18:9
3. Proverbs 16:24; Proverbs 31:30; Romans 12:12
4. Deuteronomy 5:16; Genesis 2:24; Ephesians 5:22; Psalm 59:1-4
5. 1 Corinthians 7:10-11; 1 Corinthians 7:39; Jeremiah 2:2
6. 1 Corinthians 15:58; Galatians 5:1; Psalm 56:4; 1 Peter 3:13-14
7. Isaiah 54:5; Isaiah 62:5; Psalm 146:9; 1 John 3:1

The Sinful Woman

1. Psalm 6:6; Isaiah 25:8-9; Joel 2:12-13
2. Psalm 33:2-3; Psalm 47:5; Psalm 95:6; 1 Chronicles 29:20;
   2 Chronicles 29:11; Psalm 149:3; Psalm 150:5
3. Psalm 27:4; 1 Chronicles 16:10-11; Psalm 5:7
4. Job 6:24; Zephaniah 3:17; Psalm 71:23; Zechariah 2:10
5. 1 John 2:12; Romans 4:7; Romans 5:8; Ephesians 1:7-8;
   Psalm 103:11-12; John 8:36
6. Mark 14:8-9; 1 Peter 3:1-4; Ephesians 4:2
7. Acts 9:17-27; Jude 22; 1 Thessalonians 5:14,21

NOTES

Introduction: Define Bad

1. Elisabeth Elliot, *Let Me Be a Woman* (Wheaton, Ill.: Living Books, 1985), 52.

Chapter One: Eve

1. Gerhard von Rad, *Genesis* (Philadelphia: The Westminster Press, 1972), 77.
2. von Rad, *Genesis,* 82.
3. Genesis 2:18
4. John Milton, *Paradise Lost,* Book VIII, lines 488-489.
5. *The Broadman Bible Commentary,* vol. 1 (Nashville: Broadman Press, 1973), 128.
6. Edith Deen, *All the Women of the Bible* (New York: Harper & Row, 1955), 4.
7. E. A. Speiser, *Genesis,* vol. 1 of *The Anchor Bible* (New York: Doubleday, 1964), 21.
8. Jean Kerr, *The Snake Has All the Lines* (New York: Doubleday, 1960), 11.
9. Rose Salberg Kam, *Their Stories, Our Stories* (New York: Continuum Publishing Company, 1995), 27.
10. John 11:25-26
11. John 11:25
12. Matthew 20:33, NASB
13. "Eve," *Bartlett's Familiar Quotations* (Boston: Little, Brown, 1992), 611.
14. Kenneth C. Davis, *Don't Know Much About the Bible* (New York: William Morrow & Company, 1998), 52.
15. Proverbs 1:7
16. Sylvia Charles, *Women in the Word* (South Plainfield, N. J.: Bridge Publishing, 1984), 21.
17. H. V. Morton, *Women of the Bible* (New York: Dodd, Mead & Company, 1941), 12.

18. John Milton, *Paradise Lost,* Book IX, lines 781-782.
19. Morton, *Women of the Bible,* 7.
20. 1 John 4:4
21. George C. Baldwin, *Representative Women* (New York: Sheldon, Blakeman & Company, 1856), 24-5.

Chapter Two: Potiphar's Wife

1. Gien Karssen, *Her Name Is Woman,* book 1 (Colorado Springs: NavPress, 1975), 60.
2. Herbert Lockyer, *All the Women of the Bible* (Grand Rapids: Zondervan, 1967), 170.
3. Genesis 43:32.
4. Gerhard von Rad, *Genesis* (Philadelphia: The Westminster Press, 1972), 364.
5. H. V. Morton, *Women of the Bible* (New York: Dodd, Mead, 1941), 55.
6. von Rad, *Genesis,* 365.
7. Morton, *Women of the Bible,* 55.
8. von Rad, *Genesis,* 365.
9. von Rad, *Genesis,* 366.
10. 2 Timothy 2:22
11. Virginia Stem Owens, *Daughters of Eve* (Colorado Springs: NavPress, 1995), 134.
12. Proverbs 5:3-4
13. Genesis 3:12
14. Colleen Reece, *Women of the Bible* (Uhlrichsville, Ohio: Barbour and Company, 1996), 28.
15. Edith Deen, *All the Women of the Bible* (New York: Harper & Row, 1955), 48.

Chapter Three: Lot's Wife

1. E. T. Endo, S. D. Malone, L.L. Noson, and C.S. Weaver, "Locations, Magnitudes, and Statistics of the March 20–May 18 Earthquake

Sequence" as quoted in P. W. Lipman and D. R. Mullineaux (eds.), *The 1980 Eruptions of Mount St. Helens, Washington: U.S. Geological Survey Professional Paper 1250,* (Vancouver, Wash.: USGS, 1981).

2. H. V. Morton, *Women of the Bible* (New York: Dodd, Mead & Company, 1941), 33.
3. Genesis 18:24
4. Genesis 18:32
5. Proverbs 5:6
6. Matthew 6:15
7. *Contemporary English Version*
8. E. A. Speiser, *Genesis,* vol. 1 of *The Anchor Bible:* (New York: Doubleday, 1964), 139.
9. LaJoyce Martin, *Mother Eve's Garden Club* (Sisters, Ore.: Multnomah Publishing, 1993), 83.
10. Jonathan Kirsch, *The Harlot by the Side of the Road* (New York: Ballantine Books, 1997), 25.
11. Morton, *Women of the Bible,* 32.
12. *New American Standard Bible*
13. Rose Salberg Kam, *Their Stories, Our Stories* (New York: Continuum Publishing Company, 1995), 49.
14. Kirsch, *The Harlot by the Side of the Road,* 27.
15. William Mackintosh Mackay, *Bible Types of Modern Women* (New York: George H. Doran Company, 1922), 214.
16. Martin, *Mother Eve's Garden Club,* 87.
17. Romans 2:8
18. Colossians 4:6
19. Morton, *Women of the Bible,* 29.
20. 1 Timothy 5:6

Chapter Four: Woman at the Well

1. Rose Salberg Kam, *Their Stories, Our Stories* (New York: Continuum Publishing Company, 1995), 215.
2. Exodus 32:24.
3. Kam, *Their Stories, Our Stories,* 216.
4. Janice Nunnally-Cox, *Foremothers* (New York: Seabury Press, 1981), 111.

Chapter Five: Delilah

1. H. V. Morton, *Women of the Bible* (New York: Dodd, Mead & Company, 1941), 95.
2. Henry Thorne Sell, *Studies of Famous Bible Women* (New York: Revell, 1925), 38.
3. Herbert Lockyer, *All the Women of the Bible* (Grand Rapids: Zondervan, 1967), 43.
4. Judges 17:10
5. William Mackintosh Mackay, *Bible Types of Modern Women* (New York: George H. Doran Company, 1922), 65.
6. J. Cheryl Exum, *Plotted, Shot, and Painted* (Sheffield, England: Sheffield Academic Press, Ltd., 1996), 176.
7. Judges 16:30
8. Morton Bryan Wharton, *Famous Women of the Old Testament* (Chicago: W. P. Blessing Company, 1889), 169.

Chapter Six: Sapphira

1. Sylvia Charles, *Women in the Word* (South Plainfield, N. J.: Bridge Publishing, 1984), 210.
2. Herbert Lockyer, *All the Women of the Bible* (Grand Rapids: Zondervan, 1967), 154.
3. Lockyer, *All the Women of the Bible,* 152.
4. Psalm 51:4
5. Acts 5:11, *The Message*
6. Francis Augustus Cox, *Female Scripture Biography,* vol. 2 (New York: James Eastburn & Company, 1817), 220.

7. Carolyn Nabors Baker, *Caught in a Higher Love* (Nashville: Broadman & Holman, 1998), 165.
8. Romans 6:23
9. Galatians 6:7
10. Proverbs 24:20
11. Virginia Stem Owens, *Daughters of Eve* (Colorado Springs: NavPress, 1995), 209.
12. Proverbs 1:7
13. James 4:17

Chapter Seven: Rahab
1. Leigh Norval, *Women of the Bible* (Nashville: The Methodist Episcopal Church, South, Sunday School Department, 1889), 74.
2. Edith Deen, *All the Women of the Bible* (New York: Harper & Row, 1955), 65.
3. Sylvia Charles, *Women in the Word* (South Plainfield, N. J.: Bridge Publishing, 1984), 55.
4. Isaiah 1:18
5. Proverbs 31:21
6. Matthew 25:13
7. Frances Vander Velde, *Women of the Bible* (Grand Rapids: Kregel Publications, 1985), 91.
8. William Mackintosh Mackay, *Bible Types of Modern Women* (New York: George H. Doran Company, 1922), 61.

Chapter Eight: Jezebel
1. Morton Bryan Wharton, *Famous Women of the Old Testament* (Chicago: W. P. Blessing Company, 1889), 260.
2. Leigh Norval, *Women of the Bible* (Nashville: The Methodist Episcopal Church, South, Sunday School Department, 1889), 159.

3. Virginia Stem Owens, *Daughters of Eve* (Colorado Springs: NavPress, 1995), 182.
4. Norval, *Women of the Bible,* 184.
5. Wharton, *Famous Women of the Old Testament,* 269.
6. Wharton, *Famous Women of the Old Testament,* 269.

Chapter Nine: Michal
1. 1 Samuel 18:7
2. 1 Samuel 18:9
3. 1 Samuel 16:12
4. 1 Samuel 16:7
5. 1 Samuel 13:14
6. Virginia Stem Owens, *Daughters of Eve* (Colorado Springs: NavPress, 1995), 58-9.
7. Rose Salberg Kam, *Their Stories, Our Stories* (New York: Continuum Publishing Company, 1995), 125.
8. H. V. Morton, *Women of the Bible* (New York: Dodd, Mead & Company, 1941), 117.
9. 2 Samuel 21:8-9
10. Gien Karrsen, *Her Name Is Woman,* book 2 (Colorado Springs: NavPress, 1977), 141.
11. Herbert Lockyer, *All the Women of the Bible* (Grand Rapids: Zondervan, 1967), 110.

Chapter Ten: The Sinful Woman
1. Luke 7:46
2. Don Francisco, "Beautiful to Me." Copyright © 1981 New Spring Publishing, Inc. (ASCAP) (a div. of Brentwood-Benson Music Publishing, Inc.) All rights reserved. used by permission.
3. Psalm 34:14

Conclusion: From Bad to Verse
1. Proverbs 3:34

ABOUT THE AUTHOR

An award-winning speaker, Liz Curtis Higgs has addressed audiences from more than 1,500 platforms in all fifty states and six foreign countries. She is the author of twenty-one books, with more than two million copies in print, including her best-selling nonfiction books, *Bad Girls of the Bible* and *Really Bad Girls of the Bible,* and her best-selling historical fiction, *Thorn in My Heart* and *Fair Is the Rose.*

Liz is delighted to hear from readers and enjoys keeping in touch once a year through her free printed newsletter, *The Graceful Heart.* For the latest issue, please write directly to her:

Liz Curtis Higgs
P.O. Box 43577
Louisville, KY 40253-0577

Or visit her Web site:
www.LizCurtisHiggs.com